THE MAKING OF AN
INSURRECTION

THE MAKING OF AN
INSURRECTION

Parisian Sections and the Gironde

—————◆◆◆—————

Morris Slavin

Harvard University Press
Cambridge, Massachusetts
and London, England
1986

Library of Congress Cataloging-in-Publication Data

Slavin, Morris, 1913–
The making of an insurrection.

Bibliography: p.
Includes index.
1. Paris (France)—History—Revolution, 1789–1799.
2. Girondists—History. 3. Montagnards—History.
4. France—History—Revolution, 1789–1799. I. Title.
DC184.S55 1986   944.04   86–4847
ISBN 0-674-54328-9 (alk. paper)

To the memory of my mother,
Vera Hansburg Slavin, and of
my father, Lazar Slavin

Preface

THE WAR with Austria and Prussia, which France had declared against the former on 20 April 1792, was going badly. Brissot de Warville and his supporters in the Gironde had miscalculated the strength of French arms and were now forced to defend generals who were unlucky, incompetent, or commanding poorly trained troops. Some, like Dumouriez, were traitors to the Revolution as well. At the same time the Girondins had armed the French people and had stirred them up against the king—a dangerous game, as they learned too late, for the sans-culottes had interests and aspirations of their own.

The overthrow of the monarchy on 10 August 1792 had strengthened the Paris Commune and its sections. Despite this force, the municipal authorities could not prevent the September massacres that followed. The split between the Montagnards and the Girondins deepened further when the Gironde began to agitate for an "appeal to the people" *(appel nominal)* on Louis's fate. Robespierre was convinced that such a policy, if adopted, would have led to civil war. The Jacobins began to understand that whatever the intentions of the Girondins, their policies were undermining the Revolution. Furthermore, they were aware that the war could not be won without harnessing the energies of the sans-culottes. But in order to tap this mass energy, the Mountain realized, it had to make certain economic concessions and even to embrace, or to give the impression of embracing, the sans-culottes' egalitarian, democratic principles. This the Girondins were unwilling to do. The result was that by the spring of 1793 the gulf between the Girondins and the Montagnards had become unbridgeable.

Like the historians who came after them, contemporaries differed on the meaning of the *journée* that overthrew the Gironde. To some it was an "insurrection morale," to others an "insurrection brutale." Although it is true that not one drop of blood was spilled during the uprising—and this despite the passions unleashed and the vast numbers involved—the expulsion of some two dozen Girondins from the Convention was something more than a moral act. The insurrection of 31 May–2 June 1793 struck at the prestige of the Convention as a body, a fact that Montagnards recognized as well as did their adversaries. The memoirs of participants who survived the Revolution are critical of the revolt because it lowered the prestige of the Convention even as it elevated that of the Paris Commune.

Superficial observers of this event tend to see the movement against the Girondins simply as a struggle between them and their Jacobin opponents. A closer examination, however, makes clear the important role the Parisian sections played in these *journées*. The aspirations and goals of the sectionnaires were quite different from the mere removal of some two dozen Girondin deputies and ministers. The intervention of the sans-culottes in the struggle had an important influence on its outcome. In examining the contest in the sections between them and their moderate opponents, it is clear that there are conflicting elements present. Not all sectionnaires were willing to settle for the purging of the Girondins from the Convention.

In addition to the division within the sections, there was a sharp split in the General Council of the Commune. Some members were willing to subordinate their own aspirations to the politics of the Mountain, but others wished to substitute for the whole parliamentary system a form of direct democracy. Perhaps because of this division, the Commune was unable or unwilling to stage the uprising. This decisive action was taken by an extra-legal body, the Evêché assembly, and its Comité des Neuf. During the three days of the insurrection, the assembly became the virtual government of France.

An exploration of the reasons why the revolutionary organ created by the Evêché assembly, the Comité central révolutionnaire, was unable to go beyond the limited ends proposed by the Montagnards-Jacobins is one of the main themes of this study. The mechanics of the insurrection help explain how the Comité des Neuf was subordinated and tamed by the Jacobins. In order to understand this decisive event, the insurrection must be viewed from below. This study attempts to explain the forces involved and to analyze the differences among the contending institutions.

Finally, I have examined the works of the great historians of the French Revolution who have written on the insurrection of 31 May–2 June 1793: Aulard, Blanc, Carlyle, Jaurès, Lamartine, Lefebvre, Mathiez, Michelet, Mignet, Quinet, Soboul, von Sybel, Taine, and Thiers. Needless to say I have benefited from their insight, but it must be admitted that, with the exception of Jaurès, none has dealt with the insurrection in detail. I hope, therefore, that this study fills a lacuna in the historiography of the French Revolution.

It is a pleasure to acknowledge the help of colleagues in preparing this book. The manuscript was read in its early stages by Eric A. Arnold, James Friglietti, and Edward T. Gargan. All three made valuable suggestions that I have tried to incorporate into the book, but of course none is responsible for whatever errors in judgment I may have made. Hildegard Schnuttgen, reference librarian of Youngstown State University, has been zealous in supplying me with books and brochures from several university libraries, including the Bibliothèque nationale in Paris. Renée Linkhorn has helped me translate a number of eighteenth-century French expressions that without her help would have led me astray. Agnes M. Smith, my colleague at Youngstown State University, read the first chapter and helped me correct a number of infelicitous expressions. Marc Bouloiseau and Walter Markov encouraged me to complete the manuscript, as did my former mentor, John Hall Stewart.

Susan Fogaras and Mary Belloto have spent many hours typing the manuscript, and the Media Center of Youngstown State University has reproduced a number of illustrations for me.

My wife, Sophie S. Slavin, made my work easier by taking on an extra burden of housekeeping.

Contents

THE MAKING OF AN
INSURRECTION

I

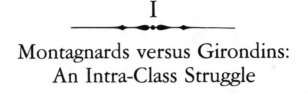

Montagnards versus Girondins:
An Intra-Class Struggle

Your properties are threatened, and you close your eyes to
this danger. They excite war between the haves and the
have-nots, and you do nothing to prevent it.

Lettre de Jérome Pétion aux Parisiens (Paris, 1793)

The worker who was content formerly with a piece of bread
and a glass of water also wants to live as comfortably
as his bourgeois.

Jacques-René Hébert, *Le Père Duchesne*

THE BREACH between the Mountain and the Gironde is proof yet again that an intra-class struggle can be as deadly as one between contending classes. Because no social class is homogeneous, differences over policy develop among various subgroups. Decades before Karl Marx wrote, James Madison concluded that different economic interests—landed, commercial, industrial, financial—tend to find their champions and to express themselves politically. If in addition to diverse economic interests differences of geography, of social background, of education, and of individual psychology obtain, the rift between parties or factions can become an abyss impossible to bridge. Few modern historians would agree with Edgar Quinet that Girondins and Montagnards "had the same goal, the same interest, the same enemies, the same dangers."[1]

The term *la Montagne* was first used by Lequinio in the Legislative Assembly on 27 October 1791, but it did not become popular until the autumn of the following year, when a group was formed in the Convention to defend the Commune and the insurrection of 10 August.[2] The name Girondins was used to designate the deputies from the Gironde department in 1793 and was interchangeable with Brissotins, Rolandins, and others.[3] The appellation Gironde or Girondins was in wide use during the

The insurrection of 31 May

Revolution to designate the right wing of the Convention.[4] Barère wrote that those who had been called Brissotins in the Legislative Assembly joined with those who were named Girondins during the early sessions of the Convention to form a coalition hostile to the deputies of Paris and its Commune of 10 August.[5]

Although the Girondins denied that they formed a party and believed that their coalition was based only on "friendship and regard for one another," in the words of Vergniaud,[6] they accepted certain broad principles. Yet unlike the Montagnards, they seldom acted as a coherent party, which may be why René Levasseur thought the Girondins were "without motivation and without a goal." If they enjoyed the support of the Convention's majority during its early days, this was due to a number of fortuitous circumstances; but when rigorous measures had to be taken for public safety, the Marais usually voted with the Mountain.[7] Garat thought that one reason why the Girondins enjoyed the support of the majority in the Convention was that the representatives-on-mission were mostly Montagnards, which deprived the Mountain of many deputies.[8] Alison Patrick agrees substantially with these characterizations, concluding that

Girondin "control" of the Convention was "artificial, resting not on the overwhelming strength of those opposing the Mountain, but on the dispersal of Montagnard resources in the service of the Republic."[9] George Rudé adds, "If the Montagnards were in fact a small minority, it is hard to explain why the expulsion of twenty odd of their opponents should have given them a working majority."[10]

What then was behind the split between the two parties?[11] Jacqueline Chaumié, who researched the backgrounds and beliefs of Girondins in fifty-three departments, concluded that like the Montagnards they were of quite modest origin, were of the generation elected in 1791, opposed slavery, and anguished over the conservative politics of the day. It would be wrong to confound the Girondins with the Thermidorians, she cautions, and under the Directory and the Restoration persecution united them with the former Montagnards once again. Moreover, it is well known that Robespierre saved some seventy-five Girondin deputies from the guillotine and that, even under the impact of the insurrection of 31 May–2 June 1793, as discussed below, he held the number of those accused to a minimum.[12]

Among the factors that made for differences between the antagonists was geography. The Girondins came from the maritime departments or those through which ran the main lines of communication (the Garonne, Loire, and Rhone rivers) and the roads that united the Mediterranean and the Rhone; the Montagnards were from Normandy and the East and from the poorer, mountainous, or more remote regions of the Dauphiné, the Massif Central, and the Pyrenees. Some, of course, were born in Paris or its environs. Thus the Girondins originated in the *pays* of written law, of fertile lands and temperate climate, of centers with a tradition of refinement.

They also were older than their Montagnard rivals by an average of ten years and had often been exposed to Jesuit education that emphasized literary studies. The Montagnards, in contrast, were products of the Oratorians, who stressed the natural sciences and the living languages; they were influenced, too, by Rousseau and his cult of sensibility. The Girondins had roots in the Erasmian tradition, in Montaigne, and in Arminianism. Furthermore, they were imbued with Stoic morality and the ideal of Seneca—the mastery of passions and emotions. They were thus the heirs of the Encyclopedists with their emphasis on reason and the *juste milieu*. The Montagnards, by contrast, recognized the tension between the ideal and reality, "entre la liberté et la force des choses."[13]

The Girondins never resolved the conflict between the power of the state and that of individual liberty. They favored the latter and extolled legality, but an insurrection quickly exposed this contradiction. When they attacked Robespierre for acting illegally, the Incorruptible gave a classic retort: "All these things were illegal—as illegal as the Revolution, as the overthrow of the throne and of the Bastille, as illegal as liberty itself. You cannot have a revolution without a revolution."[14] Moreover, for the Montagnards government was a necessary evil, a belief embodied in Saint-Just's famous maxim that one can never govern guiltlessly.

The two parties shared a respect for private property and recognized the value of work; both were suspicious of large fortunes and embraced the classical ideal that citizens should neither enjoy luxury nor suffer from poverty. They were sharply divided, however, over practical economic and financial policies. Although both opposed the *loi agraire* (redistribution of land), the Montagnards, unlike the Girondins, were ready to adopt measures limiting the rights of property. The latter continued to champion free market relations, but the former recognized the practical necessity of regulating prices and supplies. Without involving the sans-culottes in defense of the Republic, they saw, neither the foreign nor the civil war could be won, and so they did not hesitate to adopt the *maximum* (a price ceiling on the necessities of life) as a concession to the urban masses.[15]

Although he rejected the *loi agraire,* Robespierre posed the right of existence as superior to that of property.[16] In his address of 10 April 1793 he accused the Girondins of setting themselves against all partisans of equality, and after the insurrection of 2 June 1793 he wrote the well-known lines, "The internal dangers stem from the bourgeoisie. To vanquish the bourgeoisie, we must rally the people."[17] Thus, although rejecting the principle of redividing landed property inherent in the idea of the *loi agraire,* Robespierre attacked profiteers and monopolizers, whom he linked to the bourgeoisie. It was in some measure because of this that Brissot accused him of wanting to "level" everything. Robespierre in turn charged his opponent with wanting to govern in favor of the rich.[18]

There was also a marked difference between the two parties' attitudes not only on how best to utilize the popular zeal and energy for purposes of war but also toward the people as such. The Girondins expressed a distrust of the masses, for example in combatting the popular election of judges, and showed open contempt for the sans-culottes. Aulard was convinced that "contact with the people embarrassed and disgusted" the Girondins and that, although as democratic as the Montagnards in their ideas, "they were less so by their manners."[19] In addition, the Girondins lowered the wages of workers in *travaux du camp* around Paris before suppressing these works altogether, and they even demanded an end to paper money in small denominations, which would have injured small employers. In

September 1792, when consumers were feeling the effects of a declining *assignat* and a steep rise in the prices of necessities, Roland insisted on maintaining the price of bread at three sous per pound so as not to dip into the municipal treasury to subsidize bakers.[20]

Jaurès was convinced that the Girondins constituted "the party of the large bourgeoisie, the party of rich merchants, of speculators and engrossers."[21] He modifies this class analysis by writing that essentially the Montagnard-Gironde contest was a struggle of parties rather than of classes; no profound social antagonisms existed, and both factions wanted to guarantee respect for private property. Had the Gironde felt it could triumph by espousing a more radical social policy, it would have utilized the forced loan, the progressive tax, and the *maximum* against its opponents.[22]

In a section entitled "Conflit de parti ou conflit de classe" ["Party conflict or class conflict"] Jaurès is aware that his contention that the conflict between the Gironde and the Mountain was one of parties rather than of classes seems controversial, and he cites Marx's *Eighteenth Brumaire* in contrast. Nevertheless, he insists that the struggle was not solely one of classes. There was nothing in the conceptions of the Gironde that prevented it from reaching an accord with Danton and the Mountain, he argues. The Girondins had no clear political line nor party discipline. Against this background a group of brilliant individuals began to meet and to move about freely, "like ancient gods." Once war had been declared, however, the former *dispersion révolutionnaire* seemed irresponsible. The Girondins met resistance from a reconstituted Jacobin Club, the Parisian democracy, Robespierrist influence, and the groups around Danton and the Commune. These developments led to conflict, a conflict that "is not in social antagonisms; it is in the power of the most common human passions, ambition, pride, vanity, the egoism of power," writes Jaurès. It was on the basis of these feelings that the Girondins developed their theories and their arguments.[23]

This seems clear enough; yet once again Jaurès hedges when he writes that undoubtedly a muffled conflict of classes is involved. The Mountain could not help supporting the people who began to volunteer for the front and to second other vigorous steps to save the republic. Hence, the Montagnards embraced those economic measures that helped the people.[24] Jaurès cites Levasseur's statement that Girondin policy was alienating the people from the bourgeoisie although it was the people who possessed the active and energetic arms and whose numerous battalions marched to the front. The policy of the Gironde and "the ruling passion of our politicians pushed it [the republic] towards the abyss." It was the Girondins who "obstructed the progress of the revolutionary government" and who were compromising the fate of France in refusing to unite with the Mountain against Europe's aristocracy; it was they who were provoking a civil war.[25] But only the masses could repel the foreign invaders and crush the internal counter-revolution. "The bourgeoisie is passive by its very nature, and, moreover, is not numerous enough for such great measures." Thus the Mountain understood the importance of interesting the people in the success of the Revolution. Finally, in order to save the Revolution it was essential to save Paris. The policy of the Girondins would have destroyed both, concludes Jaurès.[26]

The rupture between the two antagonists had been provoked by the war as early as the winter of 1791–92. Brissot and Robespierre were at odds over the war and also diverged sharply on the wisdom of establishing a republic. The Girondins made no effort to investigate the royalists after opening the *armoire de fer* found in the king's chambers, and during Louis's trial the republicanism of many Girondin leaders became suspect. Michelet wrote, "This party [the Gironde] became little by little the asylum of royalism, the protective mask under which the counter-Revolution could maintain itself in Paris in the presence of the Revolution itself."[27]

Furthermore, the Girondins opposed the military reforms proposed by Dubois de Crancé in February 1793, and in May of that year they railed against attempts to recruit volunteers by supporting opponents of recruitment in the sections.[28] They also opposed—unsuccessfully—the unlimited powers given to representatives-on-mission. When the war broke out in the Vendée, Brissot in his *Patriote français* of 19 March 1793 blamed it on the emissaries of the Mountain, calling them the agents of Pitt. Nor were the Girondins such legalists as they claimed: from 23 September 1792 on, Kersaint advocated the gallows for his adversaries; and Pétion on 12 April 1793 boldly declared that the defeated party must perish. The same month the Girondins violated Marat's immunity; they clamored against the September massacres only later, when they saw the political gains that could be made from their opposition. Mme. Roland wrote after Varennes that liberty could not be installed until after "a sea of blood." The coup of the Girondins and their allies in Lyons preceded the insurrection of 31 May by two days.[29]

Thus Mathiez is convinced that whatever agreement existed between the Mountain and the Gironde in theory did not hold in practice. He cites Michelet's statement that the Girondins wanted "the Revolution without the Revolution, the war without the means of war."[30] Although the parties did not recognize it as such, theirs had become a genuine class struggle, he wrote. Pétion's *Lettre aux Parisiens* demonstrates this clearly enough. The former mayor of Paris warned, "Your property is menaced and you close your eyes to this danger. They excite the war between the haves and have-nots, and you do nothing to prevent it."[31] Brissot agreed: "The disorganizers are those who want to level all—property, riches, the price of goods, the various services rendered to society."[32] An appeal to merchants and wealthy businessmen was dangerous, of course, because many of them were royalists. "Are you sure," asked Danton, "that your illustrious *négociants* have become patriots?"[33]

Although about the same proportion (39 percent) of Montagnards bought national estates as did Girondins, the balance of property ownership began to tip markedly toward the latter. In the years 1791–1792 individual holdings in both groups averaged about fifteen thousand livres, but by 1793–1794 the gap between them had widened considerably: the Montagnards were worth on the average thirty-nine thousand livres, but the Girondins had risen to an average worth of ninety-one thousand livres. "The Girondin group reflected a bourgeois tonality; it rested upon a coalition which linked the former privileged with the *rentiers,* passing beyond the judicial profession and businessmen who were in positions of domination," wrote Soboul.[34]

It would be wrong to think that the Girondins were more merciful than the Montagnards. They had asked for the death penalty for political offenses, had sketched the law of suspects, and had even applauded the September massacres until they realized that indignation over them could be utilized as a weapon against their enemies.[35] Still, most had a horror of excess and rejected vengeance as a weapon because it undermined the ideal of liberty. The Montagnards, responsible for governing the country, felt they had to use terror in order to save France, but the Girondins could place liberty above efficiency because they had no power and thus no responsibility.[36]

Were the Girondins "federalists" who favored a policy that in essence undermined the unity and indivisibility of the Republic? Marat did not think so. The leaders of this "infernal faction" were too well informed to believe that a federated republic could produce a stable order among the French, he wrote.[37] Yet they did raise the departments. Aulard argues that the Girondins were no less centralizers than the Montagnards, but that unlike them they opposed the supremacy of Paris and wanted to limit the influence of the capital to no more than that of each department, one eighty-third of the whole. They had not always been so hostile to the city; only when Roland became unpopular (after proposing to move the government to the Loire or the Midi in light of Brunswick's invasion) did they try to federate the departments against Paris.[38]

Buzot particularly resented Barère's way of linking federalism with royalism. He denied that the Girondins were federalists but did not hesitate to point to the United States as a successful and happy example of a federated republic nor to emphasize that reliance on the departments did not constitute federalism. He did admit that the Gironde favored isolating Paris from the departments in a kind of "excommunication," to use Jaurès' term.[39] It should be added that if Marat did not think that the Girondins were federalists, it was because he was convinced they were royalists. They were bent on influencing the composition of various judicial tribunals and of removing the seat of the Convention from Paris, he wrote.[40]

Jaurès did not think that the Girondins were royalists, but he pointed out that by their opposition to the Paris Commune, the sections, and the Mountain they were reviving the hopes of royalists and encouraging attacks on the Republic. Had they succeeded in isolating Paris, they would have been forced to establish another capital in its place—at Bourges, perhaps. Yet even a temporary federalism would have led to chaos because it would have arraigned the departments against Paris, a conflict that easily could have led to the reestablishment of the monarchy.[41]

Thus strictly speaking the Girondins were not federalists; none desired to reconstitute the old provinces. What they did favor was the promotion of certain local powers that had been reserved for the departments, and in this sense they were decentralizers. They supported departmental autonomy and opposed further privileges and powers for Paris. The Jacobins, by contrast, were centralizers who stood for uniformity and the suppression of local differences in the line of Louis XIV, Napoleon, Clemenceau, and De Gaulle. Because they were from various provinces with individual customs, the Girondins felt that maintaining regional differences was another guarantee of liberty.[42]

Both Girondins and Montagnards were patriotic, but the former were universalists rather than nationalists, writes Chaumié. They were opposed to the military virtues, and it is doubtful that they would have sacrificed their lives to save the country from invasion. The Montagnards had a much more concrete and personal feeling for France. Moreover, they were from the invaded provinces; above all, they had the responsibility of governing the country while foreign troops were on her soil.[43] It is not certain that the Girondins would have comprehended Saint-Just's declaration that "a people that is unhappy has no country."[44]

The parties' differences on religion were even more profound. The Girondins were opposed to the revolutionary cults, the worship of Reason or of the Supreme Being. As followers of the Encyclopedists they saw these new creeds linked to the old, and they feared that Robespierre would become a kind of pope, with his own priesthood and ritual. Whether Christian or deist, none wished to eliminate the church; they favored a reformed institution in its stead and desired to unite science with faith, the Revolution with the Evangel. A number of Girondins took refuge with constitutional priests when they were hounded by the revolutionary government. Many Girondins felt that they were the spiritual descendants of Erasmus—they, too, favored a reformed church—and were tolerant in their beliefs. In their effort to establish a new religion, however, the Montagnards realized the popular need for a worship that would fill the void left by the suspension of Catholicism. As followers of Rousseau they knew the importance of emotion in the lives of the masses; hence their effort to create a new cult.[45]

The two parties also differed on the social and political role of women. The Montagnards were strongly antifeminist, none more so than Robespierre. One of the reasons why the Jacobins hated Mme. Roland was that she mixed in politics. Though she did not object to Rousseau's ideal of "la femme au foyer" for others, she refused it for herself. Of course, the Montagnards were only too well aware of women's intrigues in the court of Versailles. Their own wives were largely nonpolitical; Santerre must have spoken for many of them when he admonished Théroigne de Méricourt for her attempt to organize the women of Faubourg Saint-Antoine, "The men of this faubourg . . . arriving from work prefer to find their households in order rather than to see their women returning from assemblies where they do not always acquire a spirit of gentleness."[46] A striking example of this intolerance occurred when a delegation of men and women arrived during the session of a fraternal club affiliated to the Jacobins; its presiding officer, Chabrou, announced regretfully that he would receive only the male delegates.[47] And when the fraternal society of section Panthéon was charged with being "hermaphrodite," its spokesman replied that intriguers feared the observant eyes of women.[48] Early Jacobin support of the Revolutionary Women's Republican Club, led by Claire Lacombe and Pauline Léon, soon turned into bitter opposition that led to the eventual dissolution of all women's clubs.[49] The Girondins, in contrast, often promoted the interests of women. Condorcet, Fauchet, Brissot, and others were feminists, favored female suffrage, and strongly advocated education for both sexes. They desired to free women from their traditional bondage and surrounded themselves with intelligent women whom they met at various salons.[50]

Among the many charges leveled against the Mountain by the Girondins, none was repeated more widely or often than the accusation that they promoted a system of "anarchy." The *Patriote Français,* for example, was full of attacks on the "anarchistes" and their "système de diffamation."[51] These attacks seem to have been begun by Barbaroux on 25 September 1792 and were continued by Louvet on 29 October.[52] In a brochure entitled *A Maximilien Robespierre et à ses royalistes*, Louvet accused Robespierre of defending and excusing the Septembriseurs.[53]

What began as a skirmish between the parties soon turned into a struggle to the death.[54] The fear of anarchy led some Girondins to justify the Vendéens' defiance of the Convention. The revolts, wrote the *Chronique de Paris*, demonstrated the need for a republican constitution to succeed that of "the anarchy which is devouring us."[55] Lamartine, a liberal historian, linked the Paris Commune, its sections, and Marat, Danton, and Robespierre to "l'anarchie"; he expressed his sympathy with Vergniaud, who realized, he wrote, that it was impossible to stop "the anarchy."[56] This belief was shared by the conservative historian Heinrich von Sybel, who called the democratic mass movement a "communistic popular sovereignty" rather than anarchy.[57] Durand du Maillane, a future member of the Council of Ancients, described the General Council as being composed of "the most anarchistic sectionnaires" and could seriously hold that on the evening of 9–10 March (that is, during the so-called abortive insurrection instigated by Jean Varlet, Fournier l'Américain, and others), Jacobins and Cordeliers had united to "massacre the Girondins and *appelans au peuple*."[58] Of course there was not a word of truth in all this.

The Montagnards were no less ready to destroy the Girondins. The "bourgeois conservative" Carnot declared bluntly in an appeal to his colleagues, "We must pulverise [the Girondins] or be crushed by them."[59] The defection of Dumouriez, the troubles in the Vendée, and continuing economic distress all led to a sharpening of the crisis, to a kind of fear not unlike "la grande peur" of 1789.[60] Under the impact of this emotion it was becoming less and less possible to compromise. Garat warned Gensonné that the armed force in Paris was at the disposal of the Commune and would be used against him and his colleagues if they persisted in their appeals to combat, "which you can refuse, or, at least, delay."[61] Du Maillane admitted that the Girondins knew very well "that the multitude was for their adversaries,"[62] not for them.

If deputies and ministers in official positions could be so vindictive, the radical journalists were even more so. Hébert's *Père Duchesne* gave no quarter to the Girondins; issue after issue ridiculed, libeled, exposed, and threatened them in the colorful street language of which its author was such a master.[63] Hébert always referred to Roland ironically as "the virtuous Roland" or as "Coco" ("pet" or "darling," a child's word) Roland.[64] The Rolandiers and the Brissotiers wanted to place "the drunkard" Louis's "arlequin" on the throne by murdering the leaders of the sans-culottes, including the Père Duchesne, he wrote.[65] "Never had the infamous Capet done more harm to France than the Brissotins and the Girondins," he wrote. "Yes, f——, this infernal clique has decided to ruin the republic . . . It is left to the Sans-Culottes to save the republic, f——."[66] On the eve of his arrest Hébert warned of "a great plot hatched by the Brissotins and the Girondins to set fire to the four corners of Paris and to butcher in the tumult the patriots of the Mountain, the mayor of Paris, all the brave fellows of the Commune and the Jacobins in order to free the she-wolf Caper [*sic*], and the little Harlequin of the Temple, to return him in triumph to the Tuileries in order to crown him."[67] As for his enemies, the Girondins, they were "infamous deserters of the sans-culotterie, rogues fattened on the blood of the people, mostly men of law or *beaux esprits* of their profession, formerly businessmen or valets of nobles . . . Accustomed to live by rapine, they are fishing now in troubled waters."[68] If the tone of Girondin journalists, spokesmen, and pamphleteers was uncompromising, that of the *Père Duchesne* was equally adamant. Hébert's "grande colère" turned into a "grande joie" only with the overthrow of the Girondins.

Marat's language was no less vitriolic, if less colorful than that of Hébert. *L'Ami du peuple* described the Girondin leaders as follows: "Isnard the charlatan, Buzot the hypocrite, Lasource the maniac, and Vergniaud the stool pigeon."[69] Their relations with Dumouriez demonstrated their treachery and "their criminal activity" would reestablish royalty. Marat was especially sharp with de Bonneville, Fauchet, and Vergniaud, accusing them of wanting to light the torch of civil war, and he denounced Guadet's proposal to replace municipal authorities by presidents of the sectional assemblies as a move that would unleash anarchy in the capital.[70] He rejoiced after the Convention session of 27 May, when, like others, he thought the Commission des Douze had been suppressed.[71] During the insurrection Marat interrupted publication, resuming 4 June. In that issue he wrote that the Girondins ("Hommes d'état") wanted to unleash a civil war so that the following groups would triumph: "the capitalists, the large property holders, the wholesale merchants, the bankers, the engrossers, the speculators, the public blood-suckers, all supporters of despotism."[72] The hostility and bitterness against the Girondins reflected in Hébert's and Marat's journals and the Girondins' equal enmity and malice toward the "anarchistes" makes it difficult to see how Danton's attempt to compromise could have worked even if Vergniaud, Valazé, and Guadet had accepted his offer.

Levasseur testified, "I have already stated that if the Mountain was dear to the people who wanted to see equality finally established, vainly promised for the last four years, the Gironde continued to exert its influence upon the middle class frightened by popular fervour and easily attached to those who promised it emphatically the reestablishment of order and quiet, so necessary at all times for private transactions." Thus menaced by the forced loan and by recruitment for the Vendée, some of the middle class pronounced against the Mountain. The Girondins hoped to profit by this. Since volunteers were almost all from the poorer class, the Girondins began to undermine the municipal authorities who for a long time had opposed them. They attacked the "anarchistes" and the popular societies, but in doing so they rallied the patriots against them. Hardly five or six of the forty-eight sections belonged "to our enemies"; the others remained steadfastly attached to the republicans of the Mountain, Levasseur concluded.[73] The Jacobins heard proposals "to make a clean sweep" of the Girondins and avenge the people.[74] If they called for an insurrection, it was because they were convinced that they must strike first or be struck.[75] There was no choice now.

Although the opinions of leading Girondins are well known, estimates of the number who made up their party vary with the historian. Like the river of Heraclitus, into which one cannot step even once, any attempt to define their numbers precisely seems doomed because, like the river, they are in constant flux. Too many deputies changed their opinions on various questions. Those historians who have attempted to solve this problem have examined the vote of the Conventionnels on three questions: the *appel nominal* (roll call vote) of 15 January 1793 on what penalty to impose on Louis; the impeachment of Marat on 13–14 April 1793; and the reinstatement of the Commission des Douze on 28 May 1793.

Aulard arrived at the figure of 163 Girondins after examining the vote on impeaching Marat and the protests against the *journées* of 31 May and 2 June. Yet he admits that although 220 of 360 deputies voted against Marat, it would be wrong to conclude that these 220 were all Girondins "because the Center voted with the Gironde."[76] Mathiez is skeptical of arriving at an exact count, arguing that it is debatable whether the victims of the insurrection of 2 June 1793 or those who protested against it can be catalogued. "Such a criterion does not take into account the evolution and the life of parties," he warns.[77]

Alison Patrick analyzed the *appels nominaux* of the three events discussed above and concluded that there were between 175 and 178 Girondins.[78] She did not find them as divided between January and June 1793 as is usually claimed; moreover, after 2 June they were consistent in their opposition to Paris. But there is no evidence that they enjoyed the support of the Convention's majority in impeaching Marat or in reinstating the Commission des Douze. As to why individual deputies voted the way they did, she concludes that "the most important single concomitant of variations in political attitude seems to be not wealth, nor social status, nor local environment except in a restricted sense; it is experience of revolutionary public life and responsibility."[79] It must be said, however, that experience and responsibility do not occur in a vacuum but are themselves the products of profound social and psychological causes.

Sydenham differs with most historians, who divide the Convention into three distinct groups, arguing that the Plain was really made up of two parties—those who favored the Mountain and those who opposed it. Marat could not have been impeached nor the Commission des Douze reestablished, he writes, unless a considerable number of rank and file delegates belonging to the Center refused to support the Montagnards. "Certainly any serious effort to isolate a Girondin party from the body of the Convention breaks down through the impossibility of distinguishing between a Right and a Centre," he concludes.[80] This does not mean, however, that it is impossible to arrive at some acceptable number of Girondins: "Scholars of repute have agreed that between 160 and 200 members of the Convention may legitimately be called 'Girondins.' "[81] On the impeachment of Marat, for example, 131 of the 200 Girondins were present, of whom 110 voted for, 18 abstained, and 3 opposed (Patrick listed only one opposed). Thus although 61 percent of the assembly favored impeachment, of the Girondins present 83 percent cast their votes in favor of it. Nevertheless, a number of important Girondin leaders either were absent or abstained from voting, among them Buzot, Gensonné, Isnard, and Louvet.[82] This leads Sydenham to conclude that only the Montagnards acted as a coherent party. In contrast, "the supposed Girondin deputies consistently asserted their independence, speaking and acting as individuals even at the most critical moments of the conflict."[83]

Jacqueline Chaumié concluded that there were 137 Girondin deputies, whose social origins, geographical distribution, and ages she presents.[84] Soboul summarized the social origins of ninety-nine of these men, together with those of ninety-one Montagnards.[85] As might be expected, the largest group by far was composed of members of the legal profession: forty-five Girondins and forty-nine Montagnards were attorneys. Only two Montagnards were of modest extraction: one was a workman-carder, the other a *teneur d'écritures* (a keeper of records). Thus there is little difference between the two parties in their social composition, although Soboul adds that the Gironde tended to be closer to the high bourgeoisie and large wholesale merchants and manufacturers or former officers of the robe, whereas the Montagnards inclined toward the petty or middle bourgeoisie and toward the world of the artisan and the shop.[86]

Were the political opinions of the two groups fixed, or did they evolve under the impact of the dramatic events of the Revolution? As the difficulty of establishing precise numbers of adherents to each party indicates, few deputies remained unchanged in their politics. It is this change that Michel Pertué seeks to analyze, pointing out that both parties were ill defined, that they lacked discipline, and that a number of future leaders of the Mountain were Girondin in their earlier sympathies.[87] Since the *appels nominaux* were held some four months after the Convention met, they reveal little of the nature of the forces engaged in the elections. Moreover, as several contemporaries observed, too many deputies were away on mission.[88] The question in January 1793 was not, as Alison Patrick put it, "Voulez-vous la République?" but "Quelle République voulez-vous?"[89] Pertué concludes that it is better to abandon the list of alleged Girondins than to interpret it rigidly because most deputies "in their immense majority, were petty bourgeois intellectuals in whose ranks passed lightly a certain number of *négociants* and manufacturers, and Girondins, Montagnards, and centrists could hardly be distinguished from one another."[90]

Whether these differences were profound or superficial, the critical developments that marked the Revolution widened the gulf between the parties. On 3 April Robespierre attacked Brissot as news of Dumouriez's treason arrived. "I have no intention of sacrificing the country to Brissot," he proclaimed.[91] Five days later, section Bon-Conseil petitioned the Convention to remove the leading Girondins and to follow all leads in Dumouriez's conspiracy. Accusing Brissot and Gensonné of slandering Paris and of trying to arm the departments against the capital, Bon-Conseil's spokesman dared question whether some of Dumouriez's accomplices were not within the Convention itself.[92] On 10 April section Halle-au-Blé accused the deputies of making possible Dumouriez's treason by their indulgence and announced that if the Mountain could not save France they would do it themselves.[93] Pétion denounced the petition and demanded that the president and secretaries of the section be called to the bar and turned over to the revolutionary tribunal. Danton condemned the motion, and the proceeding had to be suspended because of the near riot that ensued.[94]

On 15 April Pache and Hébert appeared at the head of a delegation sent to the Convention by thirty-five of the forty-eight sections and joined the attack. The spokesman, Alexandre Rousselin of section Bon-Conseil, warmly defended Paris and denounced twenty-two Girondin leaders by name, demanding their expulsion from the Convention. The petition for expulsion had been adopted by the delegates sitting in the Evêché (or Archevêché, the archbishop's palace) situated on the Ile de la Cité in the heart of Paris, an assembly destined to play the role of an illegal Commune.[95] Marie-David Lasource and Jean-Baptiste Boyer-Fonfrède replied that if the departments had the right to exclude the twenty-two deputies, then all representatives ought to be judged by their constituents. They moved that the petition be submitted to the primary assemblies, a proposal that could have led to civil war. Deputies of both parties recognized the danger, however, and ignored the motion.[96]

Two days later Chaumette complained that the Commune's petition had been badly received by the Convention and demanded that it be sent to those sections that had not signed it. Furthermore, in order to foil those who would intimidate its supporters, he suggested that the Commune take the presidents and secretaries of the sections under its safeguard, thus guaranteeing freedom of opinion. This proposal was adopted unanimously by the General Council, and the resolution was sent out to the forty-four thousand communes of France.[97] At the same time the Council resolved to send a delegation to the Convention in order to explain "the spirit" of its petition.[98] On 18 April the Commune published some twelve thousand signatures against the twenty-two deputies, an action sharply condemned by spokesmen for the Gironde party. Vergniaud, Louvet, and especially Gensonné denounced the document, labeling it "une véritable conspiration contre la sauverainté du peuple." On 20 April the Jacobins urged citizens of the departments to report on their own "fédéralistes."[99] A few days later the Convention called the address calumnious.[100] While struggling against their enemies in the Convention, the Girondins did not neglect the sections of Paris. They saw how their confreres had won over a majority of the sections in Lyons,[101] and they hoped to repeat this experience in Paris. In his "Lettre aux Parisiens," Pétion sought to rouse his readers against "pillage and anarchy" and in defense of property. "Parisians," he exhorted in mixed metaphors, "rise up at last from your lethargy, and chase these venomous insects back to their haunts."[102]

When Claude Lazowski, a militant and commander of the battalion of Faubourg Saint-Marcel, died on 23 April,[103] rumors began to spread that he had been poisoned by the Brissotins.[104] These reports brought forth more petitions and addresses, and on 29 April the General Council resolved to ask the ministers for the dismissal of all employees who could not prove their patriotism.[105] The sections of Faubourg Saint-Antoine (Popincourt, Quinze-Vingts, and Montreuil) added their voices to those of the petitioners on 1 May.[106] On 13 May the Commune invited the sections to send three commissioners, one each from the general assembly, the revolutionary committee, and the civil committee, to meet in the Evêché for the purpose of discussing the forced loan and other matters.[107] The *Patriote Français,* reflecting contempt for its enemies, promised its readers that if their party were defeated the departments would avenge them.[108] Had the journal's editors read the report of Dutard, the police spy, they would not have been so sanguine. The latter wrote what should have been clear to any observer:

> the departments are not in Paris, that there would be time to kill, to massacre, to pillage, before the departments could move. Besides, it is not at all certain that they would come to Paris. As for me, I believe, on the contrary, it could be demonstrated that a great part would join the Parisians . . . As for the faubourg St. Antoine . . . in an insurrection, this faubourg contains hardly 600 members who are not members of the [insurrectionary] party; thus, you are relying on chimeras.[109]

The General Council sent a delegation to the Convention to protest the "slanders" of the *Patriote Français* and to ask it to suspend the journal. The Council argued that the articles of Girey tended to discourage recruitment for the war in the Vendée and that therefore their author ought to be turned over to the Revolutionary Tribunal.[110] On 10 May the *Patriote Français* reproduced a brochure composed by Louvet in which he repudiated the possibility of compromise "with brigandage and anarchy." It was impossible for "Cato to embrace Cataline, or for Brutus to embrace Caesar," he declared, adding: "Between virtue and crime, implacable war, eternal war!" Six days later he challenged the Jacobins, warning them that his party "was ready."[111]

Moderate sections like Fraternité denounced the effort of the Paris Commune and the more radical sections to establish an insurrectionary center by calling for delegates to meet in the Evêché. On 18 May the section condemned "the growing anarchy" in the capital, which it blamed on the Girondins.[112] The same day, on Barère's motion, the National Convention created its Commission des Douze, authorized to investigate rumors of an approaching insurrection, to examine the records and the *procès-verbaux* of the sections and the Commune, and to scrutinize the intentions of the extra-legal assembly gathered in the Evêché.[113] The struggle between the Gironde and the Mountain, pushed forward beyond the line at which the latter had hoped to stop by the growing agitation of the sections and the Commune, aggravated the crisis by establishing this commission. Jacobins, Montagnards, and militant sectionnaires now had a fresh issue on which to attack the Girondins and their supporters.

Were any efforts made to conciliate the two parties? Were there no deputies who saw the danger to the parliamentary system itself if the growing gulf between the parties widened? It is widely known that Danton had attempted to come to an understanding with the Girondins on numerous occasions but each time had been rebuffed.[114] The Committee of Public Safety tried to mediate the dispute as Barère called for mutual toleration. Cambon noted that the paragraph most applauded in Danton's speech was the one urging compromise.[115] The Girondins spurned these offers, however. It is difficult not to agree with Marc-Antoine Baudot, who wrote, "It was not the Mountain that initiated the war to the death against the Girondins; it was provoked by the Girondins themselves."[116] As for the Girondin propaganda that Robespierre, Danton, Marat, and Pache had held a secret conclave in Charenton for the purpose "of restoring the Bourbons" (no less!) and to launch another September massacre, this charge is hardly worth refuting.[117]

Robespierre, like Danton, realized the danger of a sans-culotte insurrection. At the same time he was shrewd enough to observe that the crisis could not be resolved without the active support of the sectionnaires. On the one hand, therefore, he favored arming the people, but on the other he continued to warn all against giving enemies and hostile journalists "a pretext" that might be misconstrued.[118] It should be added that "hostile journalists" hardly needed a pretext to "misconstrue" the intent of the militant sans-culottes or their supporters in the Mountain. Nevertheless, Robespierre understood that without the help of the sans-culottes it was impossible to vanquish the Girondins.[119] It is possible that he also knew of the growing mistrust that his moderate policies had aroused among the sectionnaires, who looked upon him as an *endormeur,* one who tended to soothe them rather than to rouse their revolutionary spirits.[120]

The Girondins knew, of course, that Paris had been lost to them. Too many of their early supporters from the departments who had come to the capital in order to rally around their representatives had been won over by the Jacobins, the Cordeliers, or the Enragés. When the Commune took "the revolutionary step" of appointing Boulanger as provisional commander of the National Guard, the Girondins attempted to undermine the local authorities.[121] On 16 May Guadet warned the Convention to beware of the Evêché assembly, citing the dissolution of England's Long Parliament by "the usurper" Cromwell.[122] Two days later he proposed replacing the current municipal officials with presidents of the sections and shifting the substitute deputies *(suppléants)* to Bourges, where they would be free from threats of dissolution.[123] This desperate measure was without prospect of success, even had it been enacted into law. There was no guarantee that presidents of the sections under continued pressure from militants in the general assemblies would have acted differently from their colleagues. The revolutionary committees probably would have taken over the tasks of local administration and become the new constituted authorities. Moreover, how much prestige would substitutes have enjoyed in a provincial town if the Convention had been dissolved in the capital? All that Guadet's proposal accomplished was to sharpen the division between the Girondin-led Convention and Paris.[124]

That Guadet's scheme was shared by others may be seen in Brissot's pamphlet, *Brissot à ses constituants,* in which he suggested the dissolution of the municipality and the closing of the Jacobin Club, proposals that destroyed whatever prospects of conciliation still existed.[125] Camille Desmoulins was so intemperate that in order to destroy the Girondins he was willing to slander the Revolution itself, writing in his brochure *L'Histoire des Brissotins* that a secret committee had been formed by England and Prussia to save them. Just as Richelieu had supported the republicans of England against Charles I in order to promote his own interests, so Pitt supported Brissot from the very beginning. Brissot's fight against slavery was proof that he wanted to undermine the commerce of France for the benefit of England. The revolution of 1789 was launched by agreement between England and members of the French nobility, wrote Desmoulins.[126] Aside from the absurdity of the charges, it is revealing that Desmoulins was willing to ignore his own role in the events of July 1789 so long as he could destroy Brissot and his party.

Barère's motion creating the Commission des Douze, designed to forestall the threat of insurrection, only deepened the opposition of those sectionnaires who saw their liberties menaced by the Commission. Talk of an "insurrection spontanée" was heard everywhere, and the reports of police spies on the public mood testify to the growing impatience with the status quo. An observer for the Commune wrote one week before the revolt, "We should not fool ourselves, for the uprising is *inevitable* and *very close,* if we do not adopt measures of relief for the people." Another admitted "that all citizens were discontented with deputies of the Convention" and were calling for another 10 August. A third observer spoke of "a dissatisfied people, which hates the Convention."[127] The police spy Dutard reported that crowds were showing their impatience with Robespierre when he admonished them to be prudent. "And Robespierre also begins to talk to us of prudence! . . . There goes Robespierre again!" Some raised their voices to demand that the "canon d'alarme" be sounded and action to purge the Convention commence.[128]

The Convention became an arena in which both sides hurled threats of civil war at their enemies. While the Girondins menaced the Jacobins with the departments, the latter encouraged the Commune and its sections to attack Vergniaud, Guadet, Brissot, and Isnard. A forced levy on the rich amounting to a "milliard" francs was passed, against the opposition of Vergniaud and others.[129]

It was reported that members of the revolutionary committee of section Temple and others had heard proposals by two police officials, Jean-Baptiste Marino of section Mont-Blanc and a member of the General Council and Etienne Michel of section Beaubourg and also a member of the General Council (arrested later with Hébert and Varlet by the Commission des Douze), to seize thirty-two members of the Convention (the Girondin deputies and ministers under attack), to conduct them to prison, and then to "make them disappear from the surface of the globe." The assembly at which this threat had been made was presided over by a police official. The following day (21 May), this scheme was revived, despite the presence of Mayor Pache. He threatened to adjourn the session if such a proposal were to be broached again[130] and assured the Convention a few days later that what had taken place in the Hôtel de Ville was no plot but merely "a simple deliberation on the composition of the list of suspects. A few *mauvaises têtes* had interrupted the discussion by some irrational proposals," but that was all.[131]

On 23 May Viger moved for the Commission des Douze to provide a reliable guard for the Convention and to force all sectional assemblies to adjourn by 10:00 P.M. Robespierre opposed placing an armed force in the hands of "scoundrels" who would betray the freedom that the existing citizens' militia was defending.[132] Danton spoke against the motion, and Marat denied that there was any threat to the Convention. A sharp exchange broke out between those who held that the greater threat was from the "hommes d'état" on the Commission and those who viewed the so-called anarchists as more dangerous. The motion was carried but failed to intimidate the radical sections or their Commune.[133]

The police spy Perrière wrote to Garat that the reason for closing the sessions at 10:00 P.M. was to exclude the workers whose labor did not permit their attendance at general assemblies before that hour. Dutard reported a revealing visit to an artisan, a bookbinder who owned his own shop and had several servants, though he was himself in modest circumstances. He complained that it was dangerous to have workers meet in assemblies after 10:00 P.M. as he did not want to be led by such people.[134] Of course the sans-culottes defied the law by simply adjourning at the prescribed hour and then resuming their sessions under the pretense of being a popular society.[135]

On 24 May the Commission des Douze issued a warrant for the arrests of Hébert, Varlet, and several others.[136] The following day delegates of the Commune demanded Hébert's release, and after the usual sharp outcries and accusations Isnard voiced the intemperate warning, "Before long one will search on the banks of the Seine to see if Paris ever existed."[137] This threat, as will be seen, only played into the hands of the insurgents. Parisians from all walks of life were referring now to the Commission des Douze as "the décemvirs."

The arrests of Hébert and of Claude-Emmanuel Dobsen, president of section la Cité, impelled militants of twenty-eight sections to demand their release and an end to the Commission des Douze. The spokesman of section Unité gave notice that "the time for complaints has passed. We warn you to save the Republic, or the necessity to save ourselves will force us to do so." The conflict came to a head on 27 May when Marat rose in the Convention to demand the suppression of the controversial Commission. Robespierre attempted to speak in favor of his petition but was refused the floor by Isnard, a denial that caused further disorder as Thuriot blamed Isnard for the troubles and Danton protested his "despotism." Feeling itself menaced by crowds occupying the exits, the Convention demanded a report on the state of the capital from Garat and Pache. The Minister of the Interior assured the deputies that things were under control, that the various meetings of sectional and municipal authorities were all legal, and that they were engaged in carrying out the Convention's decree against suspects.[138]

He was followed by the mayor, who reemphasized Garat's assurances to the effect that he had personally presided over assemblies where nothing of an inconsiderate or criminal nature was discussed. It was true, he admitted, that at one of the meetings some atrocious proposals were made (Marino and Michel's suggestion to arrest and do away with some thirty Girondins), but he had repulsed these suggestions "with horror" and had been supported by all present. The real reason for this agitation that was disturbing the capital was the arrest of Hébert, and nothing else.[139]

After giving Garat and Pache the honors of the session, the Convention replaced Isnard as president with Hérault de Sechelles. Delegations from various sections were then recognized, all demanding an end to "une commission odieuse." Hérault replied that "reason and the strength of the people are the same thing." If so, was this not an endorsement of the coming insurrection? When section Gravilliers's delegates offered the help of a hundred thousand armed men to end the reign of the Commission des Douze, Hérault replied, "When the Rights of Man are violated, it must be proclaimed: the Republic or death." Finally, amidst much confusion, it was decreed that the Commission des Douze was suppressed and that the prisoners (Hébert, Varlet, Dobsen, and others) should be freed.[140]

The next day, 28 May, the Girondins reopened the question of the

Commission des Douze, arguing that no clear vote had been taken, that petitioners had mixed with the deputies and had voted with them, and that because of the confusion and disorder many had had no opportunity to express their views. The Montagnards hotly denied these charges, but it was decided to put the question before the body once again by an *appel nominal*. Of a total of 517 delegates voting, the majority, 279, favored reestablishing the Commission, while 239 voted against it. "You have decreed the counter-revolution," shouted Collot d'Herbois. "I demand that the bust of liberty be veiled." Danton, too, voiced his strong objections,[141] but the Commission was reestablished, only to be suppressed for good on 31 May. Meanwhile, Hébert, Varlet, Dobsen, and the rest were free. The sections and the Commune had scored a partial victory, but the menace of the hated "décemvirs" impelled the insurrectionists to take the final step.

The following day, 29 May, Robespierre sanctioned the approaching insurrection. Speaking in the Jacobin Club, he called on the Commune to defend justice and the rights of patriots. He confessed that he was exhausted by four years of revolution and called for collective action. Why did he finally take this step? Sensing that the views of the Jacobins had shifted away from caution and moderation, he bent with the storm in order both to control it and to direct it. The great ferment in the Jacobins made plain the change in attitude. The radicals rejected Barère's report, on which Danton had collaborated. When Pierre-Louis Bentabole called Barère a moderate he was applauded enthusiastically.[142]

The term *insurrection morale* appears to have been used for the first time by the *procureur-général-syndic* of the Paris department when he reported that "the extraordinary movement which manifests itself in Paris ought to be considered as a moral insurrection."[143] Those Montagnards who, like Robespierre and Danton, were anxious that this movement remain an "insurrection morale" were aware that a purge of the Convention would be an attack on the parliamentary system itself. They realized, of course, that the Girondins had violated the system by ignoring Marat's parliamentary immunity, nevertheless, they saw the danger should the insurrection get out of hand. This was why Robespierre tried to limit the revolt against "the corrupt deputies." On 29 March 1793 he had stated his position quite openly: "When I propose firm and vigorous measures, I do not propose those convulsions which give the death blow to the body politic. I demand that all sections be vigilant . . . without attacking the inviolability of deputies. I do not want anyone to touch a portion of the national representation."[144] On 1 April Robespierre elaborated, "We must find the safety of the country within the genius of the people and the virtue of the Convention." "In the force of the people!" interrupted a member. "I do not speak through an interpreter," Robespierre continued. "I say only what I want to say. The Republic cannot be saved by a sudden outburst, by a thoughtless movement . . . the most fatal of all movements would be to violate the national representation."[145] Robespierre warned on 18 April, "To purge the Convention of all traitors? This would mean that we would be portrayed as men who want to dissolve the Convention."[146] On 26 May he reiterated his theme: "We republican deputies, we want to establish a government of the people by its mandatories . . . I invite the people to place themselves in insurrection within the Convention against the corrupt deputies."[147] It was only after it had become obvious to all that no "moral" uprising could succeed in purging the Convention that it turned into an "insurrection brutale," to use Michelet's term.[148]

Danton had evidently reconciled himself to the coming insurrection, for he told Garat that "it is necessary to let [the revolutionaries] break some presses, and to send them packing with that."[149] Naive though he may have been, the minister of the interior was shrewd enough to reply that he feared it would go beyond that. The events of 29 May in Lyons did not become known in Paris until 2 June, but the Parisians realized that what was being prepared against them in the departments could happen in the capital. Thus "it was in order not to be struck down themselves [that] the Parisian Montagnards rose up."[150]

On the last day before the insurrection, 30 May, the Convention witnessed a sharp confrontation between Léonard Bourdon and Lanjuinais. The latter had been defeated by Mallarmé for the Convention presidency, an indication that the Girondins could no longer rely on support of the Plain. While Bourdon urged the suppression of the Commission des Douze without delay, Lanjuinais insisted that this was no time to surrender to the insurrectionists. Before the debate was resolved, a delegation of twenty-seven sections with Alexandre-Charles-Omer Rousselin at its head arrived, demanding to be heard. Asked why the mayor was not with the delegates, Rousselin defiantly replied that they had a legal right to be there without him. He went on to demand that the Commission be dissolved and its members put on trial before a revolutionary tribunal, that its decrees—especially the one that closed sectional assemblies at 10:00 P.M.—be suppressed, and that its papers be sealed and turned over to the Committee of General Security.[151] This was to be the last petition before the insurrection. In less than twenty-four hours these demands of the sections were decreed by a submissive Convention and the Commission des Douze was finally suppressed.

II

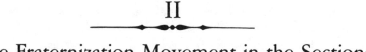

The Fraternization Movement in the Sections

> The real meaning of the word to *fraternise,* is unfolded here;
> it means to go in sufficient numbers or en masse wherever
> it's a question of rescuing from the opposition those so
> called good patriots, who quite probably should be termed
> intriguers, terrorists, etc., etc.
>
> BN, Lb⁴⁰ 530, *Rapport fait à l'assemblée générale de la section
> de l'Unité* (Paris, 1795)

THE DIVISION between Montagnards and Girondins in the Convention manifested itself among the sections as well. In a number of cases, sharp clashes of opinion and even physical confrontations took place as one party or the other sought to establish or retain control over either a section's general assembly or its revolutionary committee. The committees, with their power to interrogate and arrest suspects, were often at odds with temporary majorities of the assemblies, and a faction's control of them gave it an advantage.

The ultimate source of power, however, was the Paris Commune. Its General Council was overwhelmingly on the side of the Mountain, so its intervention in a local struggle often proved decisive. Nevertheless, a number of sections continued to defy the political trend favoring the Montagnards, and even after the insurrection other factions maintained some influence in their assemblies.

Since not all opponents of the Montagnards were necessarily supporters of the Gironde nor all who shared the Girondins' principles their partisans—there were, after all, divisions based on purely local problems, not to mention the usual personality clashes—it is best to use the terms accepted by most historians. Partisans of Robespierre, Danton, or Marat called themselves "patriots," while supporters of Brissot, Vergniaud, or Roland spoke of themselves as "moderates." In a sense the conflict reflected the differences between the social aspirations of the sans-culottes and those of their middle-class adversaries. Although the words "patriot," "sans-culotte," and "radical" may be no more accurate as descriptions of the one side than "moderate," "royalist," and "aristocrat" are of the other, for purposes of clarity and brevity they are nevertheless used to differentiate the local partisans of the Mountain from those of the Gironde.

It must also be acknowledged that it is difficult at times to define the exact political coloration of a section: was it Montagnard or was it Girondin? The answer may depend on the precise moment a section was surveyed. The sections, like the Convention, oscillated between the parties, so changes were quite frequent. Moreover, lack of documentation for some sections makes it impossible to determine the political beliefs of their assemblies. And under the guise of "fraternization," militant sansculottes would often impose their will on an obviously moderate sectional assembly, which they did by banding together supporters from several sections to take over a moderate section. Still, some conclusions may be reached for a majority of the sections (see Table 1).[1]

Shortly before the insurrection, the sections became agitated over two issues, the release of Hébert and Varlet and the condemnation of the Commission des Douze. Although it is impossible to determine with certainty whether a section was moderate or sans-culotte from its stand on these questions alone, they are of sufficient importance in themselves to be worth examining. On 25 May the general assembly of section Temple adopted its famous resolution inviting the other forty-seven sections to elect two commissioners each for the purpose of meeting in the Salle de l'Egalité of the Paris Commune to draft a petition asking the Convention why it had arrested Hébert and Varlet, "whose patriotism is generally recognized," and suggesting that until the Commission des Douze revealed the reasons for their arrest the two men should be provisionally freed on the responsibility of the sections.[2] Fifteen sections endorsed the resolution the following day.[3] How much is known about these sections, and can they be characterized as sans-culotte as the agreement with Temple implies?

On 25–26 May section Unité (Center), after hearing the address of delegates from section Temple, elected two commissioners to cooperate with the others for the release of Hébert and Varlet.[4] Two days later it adopted its own petition, entitled "Adresse à la Convention Nationale relative aux Enregistrements arbitraires," which began, "An unjust, arbitrary Commission oppresses the patriots and thrusts them into irons." Then followed a passionate attack on "traitors." Lafayette has triumphed instead of being confined in prison, the petition continued, and the blood shed by patriots cries out for *"resistance to oppression."* Save the Republic, it called on the deputies, and bring an act of accusation against the Com-

TABLE 1.   *Political affiliations of the Paris sections, 1793*

Moderate Sections (Soboul)

West	*Center*	*North*
1. Champs-Elysées	1. Muséum	1. Molière et la Fon-
2. République-	2. Tuileries	taine
Française	3. Gardes-Françaises	2. Mail
3. 1792	4. Fraternité	3. Poissonnière
4. Butte-des-Moulins		4. Amis-de-la-Patrie
5. Mont-Blanc		

East	*On Seine*	*Left Bank*
1. Fédérés	1. Pont-Neuf	1. Invalides
		2. Beaurepaire
		3. Croix-Rouge
		4. Luxembourg
		5. Finistère

Sans-Culottes Sections (Soboul)

East	*Center*	
1. Montreuil	1. Gravilliers	7. Arsenal
2. Popincourt	2. Marchés	8. Réunion
3. Quinze-Vingts	3. Contrat-Social	9. Marais
4. Temple	4. Lombards	10. Arcis
	5. Bon-Conseil	11. Cité
	6. Droits-de-l'Homme	12. Unité

Left Bank	*North*
1. Marseille	1. Faubourg-
2. Sans-Culottes	Montmartre
3. Panthéon-Français	2. Bondy

The following seven sections lack documentation (Soboul) and thus their adherences are unknown: Piques, Halle-au-Blé, Bonne-Nouvelle, Faubourg-du-Nord, Maison-Commune, Fontaine-de-Grenelle, Observatoire.

Moderate Sections (Pariset = P; Calvet = C)

West End	*Center*
1. Butte-des-Moulins (P; C says it was divided)	1. Fraternité (P; C says it was divided)
2. Gardes-Françaises (P)	

TABLE I *(cont.)*

3. 1792
4. Molière et la Fon-
   taine (P & C)
5. Mail (P)

Sans-Culottes Sections (Pariset = P; Calvet = C; Soboul = S)

Center	Left Bank
1. Contrat-Social (P)	1. Unité (P)
2. Gravilliers (P)	2. Panthéon-Français
3. Droits-de-l'Homme (P)	(P)
4. Pont-Neuf (P says it was "indecisive"; C agrees)	3. Beaurepaire (P says it was "immobile"; C says that a delegate of the General
5. Cité (P)	Council was badly
6. Marais (C says it was divided)	received by the section)
	4. Finistère (S puts the section in the moderate column)
	5. Marseille (P)

Faubourgs (lukewarm, according to P)
1. Observatoire (P; S puts it in the unknown column)
2. Invalides (P)
3. Champs-Elysées (P; S points out it abstained on 31 May)
4. Mont-Blanc (P; S puts it among the moderates)
5. Poissonnière (P)
6. Finistère (P; C says it favored the arrest of the Evêché committee)
7. Arsenal (P; S places it among the sans-culottes)

Thus Pariset comments on 6 moderate sections, 9 sans-culottes sections, and 7 "lukewarm" (tièdes) sections, a total of 22. Calvet comments on 7 sections.

mission des Douze; let it be judged by a jury composed of the departments. This address was submitted to the other sections for their endorsement and was to be presented to the Convention in their name, with the mayor at the head of the delegation.[5]

After the sans-culottes had been vanquished, a commission reported to its Thermidorian assembly that it was in April 1793 that the Commune, seconded by the Jacobins, had begun its "perfidious projects." The first act denounced was that of 19 April specifically accusing Lacroix, president of section Unité, of being "an agent of the Commune." On 24 May the section simply ignored the Convention's decree requiring that sessions of the general assembly end at 10:00 P.M.[6] "The reporter, Lucas, held Lacroix responsible for this defiance." The Convention removed the revolutionary committee of section Unité on 26 May for arbitrarily arresting five citizens who had spoken out in opposition to Robespierre and Marat.[7] During the next day's session, the commander of the armed forces called on all citizens to arm themselves and to report at the usual place of assembly; at the same session the assembly was made permanent.[8]

As early as 12 April the patriots of section Bon-Conseil (Center-North) had made a pact with their allies in section Lombards to act together whenever "aristocrats" threatened either section. During the night of 4 May the moderates took control of section Bon-Conseil for a brief time, but they were challenged by the sans-culottes the following evening in an assembly of some two hundred people. The stormy session led to a near riot, and an armed force headed by officials of the Commune had to be summoned to reestablish order. A fight broke out when the "factieux" tried to remove the newly elected officers. The "patriots" rallied, and "the fathers of families, the virtuous men, the true patriots" repelled the "agitators, the factious, the royalists."[9]

Shortly thereafter delegates from section Sans-Culottes, Marchés, Cité, and Amis-de-la-Patrie arrived to offer help and to read various resolutions adopted by their assemblies. The sans-culottes then repudiated the resolutions and motions the assembly had passed the night before and so informed the Convention.[10] The partisans of the Gironde were turned over to the revolutionary tribunal and imprisoned. Informing the Convention of their plight, Vergniaud rose in their defense and demanded that the mayor come to the bar and explain the arrests. Robespierre, on the other hand, defended the action against them and remarked that by pitying arrested individuals the Convention only promoted more Vendées. Pache released the prisoners, however, and thus avoided appearing before the Convention.[11] On 25 May section Bon-Conseil sent two commissioners to the Evêché assembly, and the following day it elected three others to help draft the petition proposed by Temple demanding Hébert's freedom.[12]

Faubourg Montmartre (North), like section Unité, adopted a strongly worded resolution (25 May) condemning the Commission des Douze (which it called "la Commission Despotique et Contre-révolutionnaire des Douze") for undermining the principle of the people's sovereignty by seizing the registers of the faubourg's meetings. The assembly resolved to go en masse to the Convention with its minute book but not to surrender it. Furthermore, it demanded the release of Hébert and the others.[13] After the insurrection, on 4 June, a delegation from the revolutionary committee of the section warned the General Council that there was trouble in the section. The latter sent two members to reestablish order,[14] which implies that the moderates had rallied and were still strong even after the insurrection.

Although section Droits-de-l'Homme (Center), like Faubourg Montmartre, had its share of moderates, news of Dumouriez's treachery had aroused a storm of indignation there and led to the adoption on 27 March of a strong resolution urging its sister sections to elect commissioners to deliberate on how to save the country from a "liberticide faction."[15] This action paved the way for the reestablishment of the Evêché committee, which had been dormant until twenty-seven sections responded to Droits-de-l'Homme's call at the end of March. Its political swings from right to left came to an end on 19–20 May, when the sans-culottes seized control of the general assembly and reorganized its revolutionary committee with the help of their fellow militants from Contrat-Social, Bon-Conseil, Unité, Lombards, Gravilliers, and Marchés. Amidst the highest enthusiasm and fraternal embraces, the assembly received the pledge of Guiraud, president of Contrat-Social, to assist the sans-culottes against "the aristocrats." Moderates were denounced as "monsters" far more to be feared than tyrants because "they mislead public opinion and chill patriotism in order to deliver a mortal blow to liberty." The assembly then adopted the principle that when several sections met together their joint sessions were to be considered as one and the same and their deliberations as common to all.[16]

On 25 May it adopted the Commune's address to the Convention demanding the release of Hébert and Varlet.[17] Four days later it declared itself to be in permanent session and elected Varlet and Gervais as commissioners to the Evêché assembly endowed with unlimited powers.[18]

Section Lombards (Center) had been won over by the sans-culottes on 18 May, a day before the political change in Droits-de-l'Homme, and had united with the militants of Gravilliers, Marchés, Contrat-Social, and Bon-Conseil "to defend the oppressed sans-culottes" and to purge itself of the "aristocrats." It agreed on 25 May to draft a petition for the release of Hébert and Varlet.[19] On 19 April 1794 its revolutionary committee arrested Nicolas Appert, a confectioner by occupation, for turning over the registers of the general assembly to the Commission des Douze although he held no official post entitling him to do so. Accusing him of wearing the mask of patriotism the better to mislead the assembly, it

charged specifically that he had disturbed the assembly, impeded the recruitment of volunteers for the Vendée, and favored the "honnêtes gens"
against the "canaille." In addition, he was blamed for calling a meeting for
2:00 P.M. when the sans-culottes were at work and thus could not attend.
This accusation led to his incarceration in the Madelonnettes prison.[20]

Although he was a Jacobin, the revolutionary committee considered
Appert wealthy and held him responsible for the grain troubles in the
summer of 1793. He was accused of intriguing to become president of
the section, using food shortages as a campaign weapon. Appert denied
that he had ever speculated in foodstuffs and pointed out that all his
workers had gone to the front. Moreover, he had faithfully reported all
merchandise he held, had personally served in the armed forces, and had
been elected to various posts in the section. Like other suspects he recalled
his financial contributions, especially those for the Vendée, and swore that
he had never signed any "liberticide" petition. Finally, he pointed out that
the revolutionary committee had found nothing of a suspicious nature
among his papers or effects.[21]

Another opponent of the *journée* of 31 May was Leroux, a hardware
merchant accused of applauding the assassination of Marat, of holding the
revolutionary authorities in contempt, of calling Jacobins scoundrels, and
of refusing to sell his merchandise at the *maximum*. Calling him a royalist,
the revolutionary committee charged that he was always on the side of
the "aristocrats" in the general assembly and had provoked trouble. It sent
him to the Luxembourg prison on 13 November 1793,[22] and probably
did not release him until after the 9th of Thermidor.

Section Fédérés (East) signed Temple's resolution on 26 May[23] and two
days later gave its adherence to Unité's petition, appointing eight commissioners to join the others but failing to sign the address.[24] Pressure
from the moderates undoubtedly reversed the assembly's earlier position.
On 9 October 1793 its revolutionary committee arrested Jean-Louis Caudel because on the previous 2 July he had allegedly struck a member of
the assembly while attempting to restore order in a fracas that followed
the entry of a delegation from section Arsenal. Caudel was thirty-two
years old and had been in the service of an elderly widow. He had inherited
a bit of property in the department of Oise from his parents worth about
two hundred livres a year.[25] Whatever the reason for his arrest (his position
as a domestic could have made him favor the moderate faction), it makes
clear that a month after the insurrection the sans-culottes still faced opposition in the section and had to rely on help from the outside "to restore
calm" in the general assembly. Although he was a domestic, Caudel had
been elected sergeant of his company. He had never signed any unpatriotic

petition, he frequented people of his own class, and "he burned with zeal for the public good," he wrote.[26] As late as 21 August 1794 Caudel was still petitioning the Committee of General Security to release him from prison.[27]

Although a lack of documentation makes it difficult to define, the political position of Bonne-Nouvelle[28] may be gleaned from the strong stand it took on freeing Hébert: it pledged its entire membership to act as surety.[29] On 25 April its delegates proposed that steps be taken to form battalions and to dispatch them to the Vendée against the counter-revolutionaries. The following day this proposal met with the approval of the Commune, which resolved to write the ministry of war on the matter.[30] Recruitment of an armed force for the Vendée was one of the demands raised by both moderates and sans-culottes in many sections, though the charge of sabotage of this measure was often leveled against the former by "patriots," as in Appert's case.

It is difficult to say what section Muséum's (Center) status was. Like others, it had signed both petitions. Its resolution of 25 May appointed four commissioners to carry to the Convention its first resolve, that it would be vigilant "so that public tranquility will not suffer any attack."[31] A week earlier the section had informed the General Council that it had denounced Champs-Elysées's resolution attacking the Commune for what it called "arbitrary acts." The general assembly of section Muséum viewed the action of its sister section as tending to sow anarchy in the capital, a statement received with applause by the General Council.[32]

Before the seven sections that sent delegates to endorse Temple's resolution but failed to sign it are examined, the assemblies that supported the address of Unité on 29–30 May must be reviewed. Section Quinze-Vingts (East) of Faubourg Saint-Antoine elected three commissioners to attend the deliberations in the Salle de l'Egalité of the Paris Commune but failed to attend and to sign Temple's petition.[33] On 29 May, however, it adhered to the address of section Unité against the Commission des Douze.[34] Section Montreuil (East), also of Faubourg Saint-Antoine, acted similarly: it sent no representative to deliberate on the petition to free Hébert but reversed itself on Unité's resolution and elected two commissioners for this purpose.[35] The third section of Saint-Antoine, Popincourt, endorsed both resolutions.

Section République (West) appointed four commissioners on 25 May to draft an address on the release of Hébert but failed to sign the petition the following day.[36] Although the section joined the insurrectionists on 31 May, its sans-culottes were balanced by its moderates. On 20 June a citizen of the section was called to order for attempting to inculpate sections Champs-Elysées and Butte-des-Moulins for their moderate conduct during the insurrection.[37]

Section Poissonnière (North) had signed the petition of Unité,[38] but on 31 May the general assembly reflected the division of its citizens. A long and tumultuous discussion followed the report of the Comité central révolutionnaire of the Evêché sitting in the Commune. It was finally decided to execute the decrees of the Comité central—to disarm all suspects and to arm the sans-culottes. Reassembling, the section proceeded to purge its membership and to reelect its officers. It then drafted an address to the Convention demanding "justice for the people." That the so-called unanimous resolutions did not express the true state of affairs is further demonstrated by the long discussion that followed the proposal of an anonymous citizen who demanded that the section state clearly whether it accepted or rejected the proposals of the Evêché committee. The person who had made this motion finally withdrew it on the pretext that the assembly was not sufficiently informed about the work of the Evêché committee and thus could not rule on its proposals.[39]

When the assembly resumed its deliberations the following day, few members were present because of the large number under arms. The president read a complaint from the Commune criticizing Poissonnière for not adhering to the resolution adopted by the other sections. On 2 June the assembly was invaded by a great number of "intriguers" (supporters of moderates in the section); it ruled to expel them and to publicize their names.[40]

Among the leaders of these "intriguers" was Alexandre-Guillaume Ruffier, a young man of twenty-five who resided on rue de l'Egalité and enjoyed a life income of six hundred francs. He had been a clerk to the *procureur* of the Commune at the commencement of the Revolution, then a "défendeur officieux," and finally a *commis* in the "administration de l'habillement des troupes." Ruffier was arrested on 10 February 1794 and incarcerated in Saint-Lazare prison on the charge of having been expelled from the general assembly. He was accused further of being responsible for persuading the section to adhere to the "liberticide" resolution of section Beaurepaire, which had assured the Convention on 29 May that the section remained loyal to the constituted authorities and to the preservation of property.[41] In refuting the charges against him, he argued that he opposed the decree of the Comité central révolutionnaire allowing the arrest of any citizen denounced by two others because such a measure would promote injustice since it would encourage personal hatreds. Moreover, if expressing an opinion was a crime, where then was freedom? He had been elected secretary and commissioner by the general assembly, yet he was prevented from speaking when he tried to reply to two citizens who had denounced him for opposing the insurrection.

In pleading for his release he recited a familiar revolutionary biography—patrol duty on 12 July, the Bastille two days later, and Versailles on 5 October. Although sick in bed on 10 August, he was so moved that he rose and joined the battalion of Finistère in attacking the Tuileries. Because he had been too ill to volunteer for the front, he instead donated a saber and money for the army. On 31 May he had committed an *error* (underscored in the text) that he had retracted a half hour later but which cost him nine months in prison. Ruffier ended his appeal, "Great God! Do I deserve it? Fellow of the section and known *as a Good patriot,* should I not be treated more gently because of my retraction?"[42] He was released on 2 July 1794.

Section Gardes-Françaises (Center), despite its strong faction of moderates, was forced to join the insurrection at the last minute. On 24 May its assembly resolved to transmit its register and that of its civil committee to the Commission des Douze. When it heard the delegates of Fraternité recite "the odious motion to massacre 22 members of the Convention," it reacted with "horror." Upon learning that its sister section had resolved "to take vigorous measures against the brigands who menace it," it endorsed this address of Fraternité and named commissioners to inquire of the Commune what steps it was taking to protect the Convention.[43] The following day Gardes-Françaises read the address to be presented to the Convention in the general assembly. As could be expected, it defended the moderates and repudiated the sans-culottes of its assembly.[44]

Once the insurrection was launched, the tables were turned. The temporarily defeated sans-culottes now in turn repudiated the moderates and their address. Charging that the petition adopted by their adversaries had been the work of a small faction and that it was basically an attack on the principle of the people's sovereignty, they expelled the moderates' leader, Claude-François Chazot. For good measure they dubbed him "the vile, the crafty individual (this Chazot, one of the leaders of the club of Feuillants) who had led into error several Citizens."[45] Yet it is revealing that during the three days of the insurrection a mere fifty-six citizens of the section were under arms, in contrast to the 1,457 of section Gravilliers and the 1,333 of Croix-Rouge.[46]

That Chazot exercised a good bit of influence in Gardes-Françaises may be gathered from the charges against him. A member of the section's popular society accused him of being a dangerous person because of his oratorical talents and his "crafty discourses" *(discours astucieux)* intended to mislead citizens. Furthermore, he denounced Chazot as being "like a spy of the section for the aristocracy" and called him a "chameleon" to his face.[47]

Chazot was born in Lyons in 1751 and became a designer (*dessinateur de fabriques* or *dessinateur en fleurs*—both terms are used in his dossier). He was married to a widow with an eleven-year-old child and had a child of five, probably by a previous marriage. Finding it difficult to make a living, he turned to journalism and began to publish a paper, *Correspondance de Maine et Loire,* which continued to appear until the advent of the Legislative Assembly (1 October 1791). After the overthrow of the king, on 17 August 1792, Chazot was elected *secrétaire-greffier* to his section's justice of the peace, a position he held for almost a year. He then left with the widow (whom he married shortly thereafter) for Arcueil, where he hoped to manufacture printed calico cloth (*d'indiennes*). The laws of the *maximum* forced him to suspend his business, however, and he was arrested in Arcueil on 24 December 1793.[48]

What had Chazot's address really said? It began by recognizing the unity of sections Tuileries, Fraternité, and Gardes-Françaises, opposed "the calumny and intrigue" of their adversaries, and demanded that the veil of patriotism be torn away. A "turbulent minority frightened by the return of order" was injecting fear into the inhabitants of the capital, it continued, and it called for an end to "cowardly plots" and "pillage." Then followed the sentences that were later to embarrass Chazot: "Legislators, you have left too long the revolutionary tools in the hands of the people. The evil that ought to be stopped grows ceaselessly, exhausting the Citizens."[49] Chazot demanded a free constitution capable of guaranteeing civil and political rights, and in a revealing phrase he spoke of fearing less an attack on the sovereignty of the people "than the anarchy in which we live." He ended the petition by pledging that the three sections would defend the Convention (that is, the Girondins) to the death.

"Le vil Chazot" was the sole support of his aged mother although his wife enjoyed an inheritance of twelve hundred livres from her first husband. When he was arrested Chazot had volunteered for the army and had outfitted himself at his own expense, as he hastened to inform the authorities. It is revealing, moreover, that the revolutionary committee of Gardes-Françaises noted that his dealings had always been marked by probity and that he had refused to sacrifice his independence to ambition. In his petitions for release Chazot wrote that as a bourgeois of Paris he had always supported the principle of the sovereignty of the people and that on 13 July he had been under arms in his district of Oratoire. Furthermore, he supported the idea favored by Lafayette of a citizen guard rather than that of a professional armed force, and had published his opinion to that effect.[50]

Like other leaders of the moderate party, Chazot had participated in all the decisive days of the Revolution and had opposed the appeal to the people during the trial of Louis. He admitted that he had not taken up arms during the late insurrection but insisted that he had always urged the people to "unite"—whatever that phrase meant. As to his "crafty discourses," he conceded that he had written and spoken out for the past four years and asked why then there was not a single piece of writing ever published against him. As for his phrase "Vous [the Convention] laissez trop longtemps aux mains du peuple les instruments révolutionnaires," it was perhaps "clumsy" *(maladroite)*, but all it meant was "You have allowed insurrections against the Constitution for too long a time; give us another." Moreover, he had voted for the Constitution of 1793 and still supported a republican form of government.[51] Although it is obvious that Chazot protests too much—his ingenious explanations lack conviction—none of this detracts from his revolutionary commitment nor denies his contribution to the Revolution before the insurrection of 31 May.

Despite the forceful repudiation of Chazot's address just a month later (2 July 1793), a member of the general assembly exhorted his hearers to recall all citizens who had been expelled from that body in late May and early June. That the moderates were back in control may be gathered from the fact that this motion won support and was adopted by a large majority.[52] Yet as late as 4 August 1794, the revolutionary committee of section Gardes-Françaises resolved that the public interest demanded the continued surveillance of Chazot, whom it held responsible for "the infamous petition" of the section. It argued that "intriguers" deserved punishment because they had misled their fellow citizens and that their release had already encouraged "the aristocrats" of the section to raise their heads. This is indeed surprising, coming as it did after the fall of Robespierre—and from a section that still had a sizable group of moderates.

Section Contrat-Social (Center) was also torn by factionalism. On 29 March, after the president of its general assembly had adjourned a meeting at 10:00 P.M. as required by law, the hundred or so members who remained in the hall made the assembly permanent and sent two commissioners to the Evêché.[53] On 4 April the assembly protested to the Committee of General Security the "illegal election" of the provisional revolutionary committee in its section. Two weeks later a riot almost broke out after a commissioner reported on his visit to the Commune to urge the establishment of "definitive" (permanent) surveillance committees in all the sections. This proposal led to such a tumult that the president had to suspend the proceedings. Shortly thereafter another heated debate occurred when complaints were lodged against several arrests by the revolutionary committee, once again leading to suspension of the session.[54]

On 21 April, following a discussion on how to keep undesirables ("malvaillants") from disturbing the assembly, a large delegation from section Lombards appeared and attacked "the royalist party of Dumouriez" in Contrat-Social. Less than a week later, on 27 April, the sans-culottes in the assembly resolved to fraternize with their brothers in section Gardes-Françaises. On 19 May a delegation from section Droits-de-l'Homme arrived to support its fellow militants, followed by delegates from Bon-Conseil; shortly thereafter a delegation from section Gravilliers was received "with transports of joy to fraternize with them in the name of the section." The assembly in its turn resolved to visit other sections where it was believed "the aristocrats were dominant."[55] On 28 May the section adhered to the resolution of Unité.[56] Despite this apparent victory of the sans-culottes, Contrat-Social continued to vacillate between the moderates and the patriots until well after the insurrection.[57]

The revolutionary committee arrested Clement, a clockmaker residing on rue Montmartre, and charged him with being a partisan of Lafayette. Two witnesses attested that he had boasted of having fired on and killed four persons at the Champs de Mars demonstration, among them a woman. In 1792 he had provoked women who were attending mass in the church of Saint-Eustache to demonstrate against patriots. Moreover, he never went to the general assembly except to ridicule it.[58] The committee also arrested Desmestiers, a dealer in old clothes residing on rue Tonnellerie, as a partisan of Lafayette who had allegedly formed a patrol to prevent women from marching on Versailles on 5 and 6 October 1789. He was accused in addition of having circulated the petition of eight thousand and of having troubled the general assembly.[59]

On 8 October 1794, numerous citizens of the section testified concerning the civic conduct of Clement. They agreed that from the first moment of the Revolution he had been a model citizen, that he had always upheld the law in his section, and that he was a good and honest man. A statement written in the margin of this document added that on 3 October Clement was called up to join his company, evidently for an attack on the Convention. Under the pretext that he had to relieve himself, he hid his rifle at a patissier's and went home, thus refusing to march against the Convention.[60]

Among the more active Girondins arrested by the revolutionary committee of Contrat-Social was Laurent Grapin, a forty-one-year-old merchant tailor who was married and had two young children. During a tumultuous session on 8 June 1793, the president of the section's general assembly was forced to resign and Grapin was elected to take his place, a development that prolonged the disorder. Shortly thereafter militants from sections Marchés and Bon-Conseil arrived, and together with their sansculotte brothers of Contrat-Social they regained control of the assembly.[61]

Two days later the assembly ruled that Grapin had lost its confidence and stripped him of his presidential powers. The following day he was suspended from the general assembly for six months, and on 22 July 1793 the assembly disarmed him as a suspect. The revolutionary committee of the section arrested him on 19 September, charging him with responsibility for the trouble in the section and for oppressing "patriots."[62]

Several months later, in an appeal for his release, Grapin's wife summarized his revolutionary career. He had been at the Tuileries on 12 July 1789, and the following day he had won over several Swiss Guards to the popular cause. He was at the Invalides when arms were seized and distributed, and on 14 July he was at the Bastille. Shortly thereafter he was appointed to help supply Paris with food. Upon the organization of the National Guard, Grapin was elected corporal, then sergeant, and finally bearer of the regimental colors. He volunteered for the army after Louis's flight to Varennes. When the king's palace was stormed on 10 August 1792, he was able to save the crown jewels and to deposit them with the Legislative Assembly. The following year he served successively on his section's civil committee, on the committee of subsistence, and as commissioner for supplying troops with uniforms. During the insurrection of 31 May–2 June 1793 he was under arms, and on 3 June he was elected vice-president of section Contrat-Social. He became its president on 8 June and resigned only in the wake of the disorder that followed. Because of this incident he was arrested and imprisoned in the Madelonettes. In requesting his release, Mme. Grapin termed her husband "a true sansculotte."[63]

After the fall of Robespierre, Grapin charged that his persecutors were ardent supporters of Hébert and Chaumette, and he called the Paris Commune "la Commune usurpatrice." In a letter to the Committee of General Security requesting his release, Grapin pointed to his patriotic conduct, recalled that he had rescued more than thirty possible victims of the "Septembriseurs," and called himself a "friend of Morality and Humanity."[64] The Committee ordered his release on 8 August 1794, and his section restored him to full citizenship on 9 June 1795.[65]

Section Gravilliers (Center) had taken no stand on Temple's resolution but had endorsed Unité's.[66] Its petition to the Convention warned that "the French Republic is on the point of being annihilated" but "the courage of the sans-culottes increases in the midst of storms." Hypocrites and scoundrels were forcing the people of Paris to make a third effort to show its power while "a horde of slaves" called the Parisians "anarchists, agitators, and bloodsuckers," it proclaimed.[67]

Section Finistère (formerly Gobelins) had denounced to the Convention the creation of the insurrectionary committee, the future Comité central révolutionnaire, and demanded the arrest of its members. It boldly informed the General Council of this resolution, an act of defiance unusual for the time.[68] Pauline Léon, president of the women's society Républicaines révolutionnaires, described the situation in Finistère at the society's session of 19 May 1793. She accused the rich in the section of oppressing the others and called for "an enormous tax" on them in order to assure food for the women who were to be recruited into an armed force. All female sans-culottes between the ages of eighteen and fifty were to be eligible. In order for this to succeed, Léon called on the Jacobins to proceed to section Finistère and to reorganize it.[69] By 30 May the sans-culottes had taken over the section as its assembly turned its back on the moderates.

Section Marais (Center) signed Temple's resolution and the same day (26 May) demanded the dissolution of the Commission des Douze.[70] In its petition to the Convention the section urged the arming of Paris and suggested that funds be appropriated for the purchase of twenty thousand rifles and the creation of ateliers to employ men to manufacture pikes and guns.[71] Although section 1792 (West) signed Temple's petition, all that is known of its internal politics is that it was regarded as moderate.[72] This was true of most of the western sections.

Section Marchés (Center) signed both Temple's and Unité's petitions.[73] On 8 June its militants together with those of Bon-Conseil forced open the doors of Contrat-Social's assembly and succeeded in purging its officers.[74] Popincourt (East), of Faubourg Saint Antoine, had also endorsed the two addresses and elected commissioners to draft the petition to free Hébert and Varlet.[75] The same action was taken by section Marseille (Left Bank), which housed the Cordeliers,[76] as well as by section Bondy (North).[77] Halle-au-Blé (Center) had endorsed the resolution of Unité in a joint session with section Marchés, as both elected eight commissioners to the Salle de l'Egalité on 28 May.[78] A delegate reported to the General Council on 26 May that section Panthéon-Français (Left Bank) had successfully repelled an attempt by its moderates to adopt the resolution of Fraternité condemning the revolutionary committees for wanting to purge the Girondin deputies.[79] Four days later it endorsed Unité's address,[80] as did Fontaine-de-Grenelle (East—Left Bank);[81] Finistère (Left Bank), which sent commissioners to the Evêché assembly;[82] and Sans-Culottes (Left Bank).[83]

Thus a total of twenty-five sections had approved either the petition of section Temple or that of Unité (see Table 2). Of the sixteen sections on Temple's list seven do not appear on that of Unité; nine are on both lists. There are seven additional sections on Unité's list (minus Unité) which do not appear on Temple's. As important as the two petitions are to understanding the course of the struggle between moderates and sans-culottes, it is obvious that a section's endorsement of either of them does not in itself tell us the relative positions the parties held there. Even those sections that can be characterized as moderate or sans-culotte vacillate often. For example, section 1792 is considered to be moderate (Pariset and Soboul), yet it endorsed Temple's resolution. Mail is notoriously moderate, as will be shown below, yet although it failed to endorse Temple's petition, it sent representatives to discuss it. Section Cité is sans-culottes (Pariset and Soboul) but it failed to endorse either resolution. Section Marais endorsed Temple's stand but was "divided," according to Calvet. Again, other factors must be taken into account in determining the political positions of the sections.

In addition to the twenty-five sections discussed above, seven had sent delegates to deliberate on Temple's address but had failed to endorse it. What can we learn about them? Section Arcis (Center) is a classic example of an aborted militancy. On 25 May, if the records can be believed, it unanimously supported the proposal of section Marais to elect two commissioners for the purpose of protesting Hébert's arrest. Three days later it denounced Isnard's remarks threatening to destroy Paris and accused the Commission des Douze of adding to his threat. "The People, your sovereign, want no compromise," the militants wrote; ". . . they demand that the members of the committee of Inquisition be punished with all their partisans."[84] This address was read by delegates to the General Council before being presented to the Convention.[85] Despite endorsing the resolutions of Temple and Unité "unanimously" in general assembly, however, section Arcis failed to do so at the gathering of delegates summoned for this purpose.

Section Réunion (Center) witnessed a class struggle in addition to the usual division between patriots and moderates. While the revolutionary committee was in the hands of the first, the second took over its general assembly. This conflict burst into the open during the session of 5–6 May. After the insurrection the police listed the names of twelve men deemed to have been in opposition to the sans-culottes of the assembly, among them ten who clearly reflected the interests of the propertied in the section:

TABLE 2. *Parisian sections endorsing Temple's and Unité's resolutions*

Sections that endorsed Temple's resolution of 25 May 1793

1. Temple	9. Lombards
2. Unité	10. Fédérés
3. Marais	11. Gravilliers
4. 1792	12. Popincourt
5. Bon-Conseil	13. Bonne-Nouvelle
6. Faubourg-Montmartre	14. Marseille
7. Droits-de-l'Homme	15. Muséum
8. Marchés	16. Bondy

Sections that endorsed Unité's resolution of 29 May 1793

1. Quinze-Vingts	5. Gardes-Françaises
2. Montreuil	6. Contrat-Social
3. République	7. Gravilliers
4. Poissonnière	8. Unité

Sections that sent representatives but failed to endorse Temple's resolution

1. Arcis	5. Faubourg-du-Nord
2. Réunion	6. Mail
3. Arsenal	7. Maison-Commune
4. République	

Additional sections that endorsed Unité's resolution, 30 May 1793

1. Fontaine-de-Grenelle	4. Panthéon-Français
2. Finistère	5. Marseille
3. Temple	6. Sans-Culottes

five *négociants,* an *avoué,* an *agent d'échange,* a merchant of lace, a commercial broker, and a wholesale grocer.[86] Interrogation of suspects and participants yielded the following picture of events.

During the night and early morning hours of 5–6 May, the general assembly, numbering some two hundred participants, openly expressed its suspicion and opposition to the section's revolutionary committee. The reason seems to have been the number of arms stored at the committee's premises on rue Bar-du-Bec. Some of these had been distributed to persons "constantly arriving in Paris"—that is, to sympathizers of the Mountain and the Commune from the departments—for the purpose of celebrating the Revolution's anniversary. At about midnight it was decided to close the doors of the hall so that no one could either leave nor enter, evidently in order to prevent interruptions and to discuss measures to disarm the revolutionary committee. The assembly proceeded to elect nine or ten commissioners from its midst to retrieve the official records of the committee from the hands of its secretary, Aristarque Didot. More important, the commissioners were to proceed to the premises of the revolutionary committee in order to count the guns stored there (estimated at between four and five hundred) and to seal its doors. In order to carry out the inventory "legally," however, the assembly authorized its commissioners to visit the home of Melchior Humbert Péligot, the section's justice of the peace, and have him accompany them.[87]

Among those interrogated by the departmental police was Bousquet, a member of the section's civil committee and a *négociant* by occupation. He claimed that when the motion had been made to shut the doors he had been asleep; upon awaking he was told that the reason for this unusual action was the approaching denunciation of the revolutionary committee. Although he objected to serving on the commission, he was informed that he could not refuse and reluctantly agreed to join it. A corporal and three armed men accompanied the commissioners as they started on their mission.[88] Other commissioners interviewed told much the same story.[89]

Péligot, the *juge de paix,* testified that six to eight commissioners had come to his home on rue Beaubourg at about 1:30 A.M. for the purpose of having him affix seals on the premises of the revolutionary committee. An armed force was also present as his clerk, Bourgoin, was drafting the order. The judge expressed his surprise at what he termed the assembly's extreme measures and tried to dissuade the commissioners. He urged them to postpone action until the following day when the assembly could see that its motion was the result of poor advice offered by bad citizens. The commissioners replied that they had no choice but to execute the measure. They then proceeded to the home of Didot, secretary of the committee, on rue Avoye. A domestic opened the door to them and they walked in. Shortly thereafter a commotion was heard, probably the result of an argument between Didot and the commissioners. The judge calmed all parties, and the commissioners withdrew.

Didot drafted a complaint in the judge's presence at 2:00 A.M. on 7 May in which he reported the arrival of the commissioners and the violation of his privacy.[90] The commissioners drafted their own *procès-verbal* at 2:30 A.M. In it they reported picking up the judge and his clerk and proceeding to Didot's home, where the secretary threatened them with a gun and called them "brigands." When he expressed surprise to find the judge with them, Péligot replied that he had been forced to accompany them. Since the law forbade them to use force the commissioners withdrew, they testified—not the most revolutionary behavior on their part. Before doing so, however, they did seal the doors of the revolutionary committee;[91] two administrators of the municipal police lifted the seals the following day.[92] The temporary victory of the moderate assembly was thus overturned. Without the support of the General Council, the section's moderates could do little against their own revolutionary committee. The fact that Réunion took Hébert and Varlet under its safeguard on 26 May signified, as the police spy Dutard realized when he wrote to Garat, that "the workers of this section have scored a victory today over the aristocrats."[93]

Section Arsenal (Center) was the scene of a riot on 24–25 May after a delegation from Fraternité appeared to read its address to the general assembly. As the president of Arsenal began to congratulate the delegates, he was interrupted by shouts from the sans-culottes present; the minutes report that "un grand tumulte s'élève." Some thirty to forty members of the patriotic party then walked out of the hall. Finally calm seemed to have been restored and the session resumed, but a new secretary had to be elected since the former one had walked out with his partisans. After a count had been taken to see if a quorum were present it was revealed that there were seventy-five persons on the moderate side and sixty on the other. Presumably, the moderates had succeeded in expelling the thirty or forty who had left the hall. Before verifying the membership cards of those present, however, the assembly decided to call in six armed men to maintain order. Demands were made that the names of those who had walked out be turned over to the Commission des Douze and to the Commune (quite a contradiction!), but no formal motion was adopted.[94]

The expelled sans-culottes took their complaint to the General Council, where they reported that they had been called to order for demanding proof of the plot denounced by section Fraternité. Destournelles, vice-president of the General Council, responded by declaring that "the Democratic revolution must not retreat a single step: it must not even come to a halt." The Council then asked the delegates to retire to an adjoining room while their mandates were being verified "so that no one would dare say that they were individuals without an occupation or a fixed residence *(sans aveu et sans domicile)*." Shortly thereafter the Council appointed two commissioners to accompany them and to explain to the sectional assembly that the charge of section Fraternité was false.[95]

The following night, 25–26 May, help arrived for the sans-culottes of Arsenal from their comrades of Droits-de-l'Homme, Quinze-Vingts, and Arcis.[96] The revolutionary committee of section Arsenal then prepared a list of thirty-nine names, among them Ledru, captain of its armed force, a nineteen-year-old by the name of Beudot, and an ex-monk named Villeneuve—evidently the active oppositionists to the sans-culottes of the section.[97] Among the charges against them was that they had sabotaged or attempted to impede recruitment of volunteers for the Vendée force. One of the witnesses, Jean Bertin, declared that for a long time various citizens had opposed the "patriots" of the assembly. This evidently was the gist of the dispute between the two factions. The Girondins naturally had their supporters in the section, who now were under suspicion and attack.

That the purge was no easy matter may be seen in the early failure of the Commune to reestablish order in the section. The General Council dispatched four commissioners to the general assembly on 25 May, but they failed to reconcile the parties or to impose a dictated peace. Only when the Commune added another twelve officials and mobilized the mass of sans-culottes from other sections did the patriots finally triumph.[98] This was confirmed in the address adopted by the assembly and read to the delegates of the Commune and of sections Fédérés, Droits-de-l'Homme, Quinze-Vingts, Montreuil, and Arcis.[99]

Among those arrested was Pierre Alexandre Grillot, a *procureur* and an *avoué* by profession, residing on rue Antoine, who was thirty-one years old at the time of the 31 May insurrection. He was arrested on 11 May 1794 for having caused trouble in recruiting for the Vendée and for writing the petition against dethroning Louis. In addition, the revolutionary committee of section Arsenal charged him with the usual depredations—he was a "cabaleur," a "royaliste outré," a "méchant"—and of having wormed his way into the confidence of the section's merchants and notaries in order to cause trouble.[100] Ultimately, the moderates were to have their revenge when they denounced the former "patriots" and functionaries of the section "sous le régime tyrannique de Robespierre." On 10 March 1795, the assembly resolved that it owed "justice" to the victims of June 1793 who had perhaps been slandered. It therefore decreed the creation of a commission, composed of seven people who had never been either officials or prisoners of the former regime, to examine the conduct of all former officers of the section from April 1793 to the 9th of Thermidor, Year II.[101] Needless to say, the "civic conduct" of those officials was now under suspicion.

After hearing two delegates from Bondy, Faubourg-du-Nord (North) also resolved to demand freedom for Hébert and Varlet,[102] but like République it failed to endorse the petition of section Temple. Maison-Commune (Center), which housed the Hôtel de Ville, similarly sent delegates to discuss the resolution of Temple but did not sign the petition.[103]

Section Mail (North) had sent representatives to deliberate on Temple's resolution but had failed to endorse it;[104] nor had it signed the petition of Unité. Yet on 23 April it had approved the resolution of Bondy that it had lost confidence in the twenty-two (Girondin) deputies of the Convention and resolved to so inform the General Council and its sister sections.[105] Furthermore, when a delegation from section Faubourg-Montmartre revealed that it had drafted a petition against the Commission des Douze, the president of Mail, Tranchelahausse, replied that his section had taken the same measures and had already elected commissioners to draft such an address to the Convention.[106] Nothing further came of these moves, however, because the moderates were too well entrenched to allow this attack on the Girondins to continue.

Despite the section's strong bent toward moderation, the history of its proceedings during the five weeks for which a record exists shows that its patriotic conduct leaves little to be desired. Mail endorsed the principle of equal sacrifice and called on those who possessed a "surplus" to share a portion of it with the less fortunate. On 18 April it lauded the role of Marat. The following day it condemned the commander of its armed battalion, who sought to punish officers failing to report the number of men above their muster list—a reflection of the struggle for control of the sectional armed force. This position of the assembly was accepted by the General Council when it demanded that the general in command explain his order.[107] On 29 April the section wrote to the minister of war that it had sent twenty-one fully equipped men to the front. The following day it agreed to create a *comité de bienfaisance* and collected money for this purpose, and by 7 May it had raised thirteen thousand livres for the families of volunteers. Nor was it averse to decreeing the arrest of suspects. It also demanded that a census be taken of those who had recently moved into the section. It immediately endorsed the resolution of section Cité to pillory the "counter-revolutionaries" in the Convention (the Girondins and their allies) who were sabotaging measures of public safety proposed by the Mountain. In sum, it seems that the radicals dominated the section for a time.

Early in May a political change occurred in section Mail. It adopted a sharp address to the Convention on 7 May denouncing the Paris Commune for what it held to be its usurpation of powers in levying a forced loan on the wealthy. The assembly hastened to add that it was not opposed in principle to levying a contribution on the rich; their wealth, it held, was a deposit to the advantage of all, like the "greniers d'abondance" a security against shortages. It was this contribution that had enabled the section to outfit the volunteers for the Vendée and to provide for their families. If the Commune had merely limited itself to convoking the sections in order to carry out this emergency measure Mail would have applauded it, but instead it had dared to usurp the authority of the Convention. The Commune, Mail stressed, is nothing but the bearer of powers residing in the sections ("car la Commune n'étant qu'une porteur déléguée des Sections"); the latter owe it obedience only when it carries out the law.

On 16 May delegates of section Champs-Elysées offered Mail not only fraternity but the aid of all its forces in order to "resist oppression," that is, pressure from the radicals. It reported, moreover, that the Commune was planning another gathering in the Evêché to draft a new petition to the Convention against the Girondin deputies. The following day a delegation from Fraternité read its support of Mail's stand against the resolution of the General Council attacking the Girondins. On 18 May Mail rejected the Commune's resolution regarding the interim appointment of a commanding general (Boulanger) in Santerre's absence and urged instead that the forty-eight sections be convoked to make the decision.[108]

Mail's general assembly showed its moderate bias again when it repudiated the suggestion of the Commune to elect delegates to consider means for imposing the forced loan on the wealthy. It then renewed its (bureau) officers by reelecting Tranchelahausse, who received 176 votes out of 298. This meant that 122 members of the assembly were in opposition to him, a substantial minority but a minority nevertheless. When the results of the vote were announced, Tranchelahausse declared that prolonging the term of the president beyond the conventional two weeks could result in abuses of the rights of sovereignty, and since he had already served a month, he asked to be permitted to resign. The whole assembly ("toute entière"), the procès-verbal reported, refused to hear of his resignation. As a result of this pressure Tranchelahausse accepted the position for another two weeks.[109]

On 21 May occurred one of the more dramatic confrontations between the moderates and the radicals. At 10:00 P.M., after most of the section's members had left, a delegation of fifty or sixty militants from sections Bon-Conseil, Contrat-Social, Arcis, and Lombards stormed into the hall where the Mail assembly was in session and took over the meeting. Dressed in a variety of uniforms and armed with sabers and clubs, they must have terrified the remnant of Mail's membership. Their spokesman, who identified himself as the vice-president of section Bon-Conseil, proclaimed that he had not come to address the "aristocrats" of the section but rather its "sans-culottes."[110] Tranchelahausse replied, "We are all brothers and all patriots: unity and peace reign among us . . . We want to fraternize with all sections of Paris and have declared war on tyranny and anarchy."[111]

One delegate immediately replied, "The aristocrats call the sans-culottes anarchists. They are mistaken." Another shouted, "There are other aristocrats . . . *these are all the rich, all the big merchants.*" They were for Lafayette and against recruitment of volunteers for the Vendée. "Les riches restent chez eux, ils voudraient une république aristocratique . . . telle est l'esprit de la faction Brissotine." We have come to fraternize with you, he added. Then he threatened, "No closed ballot or the cabal will triumph."[112]

Tranchelahausse suggested that the various proposals of the delegation be considered the next day, when they could be discussed properly, but the spokesman for Bon-Conseil insisted that they be put to the vote at once as on the morrow the "aristocrats" would appear in force to defeat them. Shouts were heard from the floor: "None are more cowardly than the rich"; "Nous les f—— de dans." Another delegate added, "We'll go to the rich with writs of arrest in our pockets, and in force. We'll seize their wallets; we'll count the *assignats* in them; we'll leave them what we want if they're reasonable." The rich and the Brissotins, they repeated, were opposed to recruiting volunteers for the Vendée.[113]

When a member of the section sought to defend Mail's record, he was attacked on the ground that his remarks were contrary to the interests of the sans-culottes. He replied that he would not yield to force but only to persuasion. A number of others came to his assistance, testifying to his patriotism and adding that all were impressed with his "fraternal cordiality and his republican pride." Another delegate then attacked Le Tellier, secretary of the assembly, as an "aristocrat." The president came to his secretary's defense, referring to his well-known patriotism. If his opinions were erroneous, Tranchelahausse argued, his sentiments were virtuous. This seems to have brought the proceedings to an end (at midnight), as no other objections were recorded. Ironically, the session ended with all joining to sing a hymn to liberty as they retired.[114]

The next day the resolutions forced through the previous evening were repudiated by the general assembly reinforced by its normal contingent of moderates. The assembly expressly stipulated that henceforth all business was to be transacted between 7:00 and 10:00 P.M., with any unfinished items to be left for the following meeting. Furthermore, it was decreed that no citizen would be permitted to take the floor unless he could prove by possession of a civil card that he was domiciled in the section. Delegations were to be limited to twenty unarmed individuals who had announced in advance their desire to visit the sectional assembly.[115]

When delegates from section Fraternité appeared, they were greeted with applause; it was evident that members of both sections were moderate and found support in each other's company. A member proposed that the section's armed force guarantee freedom from arbitrary arrest by the section's revolutionary committee. Another suggested that the civil committee together with the section's police inform the section daily if any arrests had taken place. The proposals were adopted unanimously by the four hundred members attending the session, which was adjourned at 12:30 A.M.

The address accompanying Mail's record when it was turned over to the Commission des Douze was directed to the Convention and sought to justify the section's political behavior and patriotic conduct. The appeal noted that Mail had raised proportionately more than its quota of volunteers for the Vendée and that the contributions of the rich were merged with those of the poor. Moreover, the section emphasized its strong stand against the "liberticides" decrees of the Paris Commune and its oath to protect persons and property against all arbitrary acts. "You will note," the petitioners urged, "the degree of error committed by several citizens in supporting disorganizers and anarchists." Finally, the address stated that Mail would enlighten the Conventionnels on the plots of the "ill-intentioned" and on the means to strike at their authors.[116] Thus, a week before the insurrection against the Girondins, section Mail stood strongly against the coming uprising of the radical sections, the General Council, and the assembly of the commissioners from the sections meeting in the Evêché.

III

The Struggle for the Sections

A still more infamous device is employed by the anarchists.
They assemble the brigands of several sections, parade
them from section to section and crush there
the republican majority.

Patriote Français, 20 May 1793

THE DISPUTE between the two parties was not limited to their positions on the resolutions of sections Temple and Unité, of course. Long before the creation of the Commission des Douze or the arrest of Hébert and Varlet, a split between the sans-culottes and the moderates was already clearly in evidence; the approaching insurrection merely sharpened the conflict. Nor had the overthrow of the Girondins in the Convention encouraged their partisans in the sections to surrender. The battle continued in a number of sections into the summer of 1793.

Events in section Amis-de-la-Patrie (North), where numerous arrests of Gironde supporters occurred, give an insight into the history of this struggle. Like other sections it fluctuated for a time between the moderates and the patriots. On 25 May it appointed two commissioners to inquire why Hébert and Varlet had been imprisoned, and the following day (probably after learning the circumstances of their arrest), it adopted the resolution of section Halles to go en masse to the Convention and demand the release of the two révolutionnaires.[1] Yet as late as June the moderates were powerful enough to be able to examine the registers of the section's revolutionary committee under pretext that they contained a list of proscribed citizens.[2] Their opposition to the radicals brought about the arrests of several leaders of the moderate party, among them Louis Nicolas Duval, a twenty-eight-year-old *négociant* residing on rue Martin. He had married in May 1791 and was the father of an infant son. Before the Revolution he had been a *commis marchand* without capital, according to his testimony, and since 1790 a hardware merchant.[3]

Upon his arrest on 19 November 1793, Duval was accused of speaking out against the Revolution as a royalist, of impairing recruitment of volunteers for the Vendée, and of troubling the general assembly. More specifically, he was charged with being "one of the principal authors of the troubles at the time of section Mail's address which opposed the arrest of suspects, and which invited the hon[n]êtes gens to meet together."[4]

Yet his political biography leaves little room to doubt his acceptance of the Revolution. He had taken up arms on 13 and 14 July, served in an armed detachment to obtain provisions for Paris, and marched with his district to Versailles on 5 October. He was again under arms on 10 August 1792, and he participated (perhaps reluctantly) in the insurrection of 31 May–2 June 1793. As captain of the Nineteenth Company, he had the confidence of his men from the very beginning of the Revolution, according to the testimony of those who had served under him, and he had volunteered to fight in the Vendée. Duval added that he had never signed any "anti-civic petitions" but had contributed funds and gifts regularly to various patriotic causes.[5]

In replying to his accusers, he dared them to cite one proof of his unpatriotic behavior and pointed out that he had been elected president of his section, a post he had refused. As secretary of the assembly he had read the correspondence from section Mail, an act that had precipitated the riot, but since his function was to read all correspondence without comment he could hardly be held responsible for the events that followed. As for his being demissioned as captain of the company, this was done by some thirty or thirty-five individuals present in the assembly shortly before midnight when most sectionnaires had gone home. Moreover, the general assembly had reversed this action a few days later.[6] Thus Duval's patriotism was hardly less warm than that of his opponents. Despite this, he was condemned by the revolutionary tribunal.[7]

Another oppositionist to the sans-culottes of the section was Jean-Baptiste-Firmin Flicourt, arrested on 15 November 1793 by the section's revolutionary committee. A baker by occupation, he was fifty-two years old and was married with no children. He was charged with having opposed the removal of "the last tyrant" (Louis), spreading alarm over shortages, slandering the Revolution, and advocating the destruction of the Jacobins. As for the events of 31 May–2 June, he was accused of making the motion to elect four commissioners to examine the alleged proscription list in the records of the surveillance committee of the section. In addition, the revolutionary committee denounced him as being "a leader of the aristocracy in our section linked to all aristocrats of his quartier."[8]

Flicourt replied that he had always attended meetings of the general assembly in order to "instruct himself," that he had participated in all the *journées* of the Revolution under arms, that he had made patriotic contributions, and that he had never signed any suspicious petitions—the denials made by all the moderates accused. There was no question that he had served in person in the National Guard. As commissioner of subsistences, a post to which he had been duly elected, he had reported that there were shortages. This resulted in the outrageous accusation that he had spread rumors that provisions were lacking. Flicourt replied that he could hardly have admitted that there was plenty to eat when it simply was not true. As for other charges—that he had slandered the local authorities and had moved in the general assembly on 1 June to examine the registers of the revolutionary committee—Flicourt simply called them false.[9] He was released from Luxembourg prison on 29 September 1794 by the Committee of General Security, and the seals were lifted from his effects.

In addition to Duval and Flicourt, the revolutionary committee arrested a number of others whose histories hardly differed from those of their opponents. Among them were Louis Taveau, an ironmonger *(quincaillier)* by occupation;[10] Eustache-François Rossignol, a *commis marchand;*[11] Hardoin-Thomas-Clement Ravette, a merchant hosier;[12] and François-Marie Paris, an *homme de loi*.[13]

Section Bon-Conseil was also torn by factionalism. Its revolutionary committee reported that from April until 6 May 1793, the general assembly of the section had been troubled by a faction composed of Raymond Pagès, *fils,* Langlois, Saguier (all three connected with the law as *procureurs* or *avoués*), and a wine merchant by the name of Gurnot. When the section prepared to send a battalion to the Vendée, the four did all in their power to prevent it, it was charged.[14] In addition to this group, the revolutionary committee arrested François Maillet, a cultivator of plants from which paper was manufactured.[15] Isidore Langlois was singled out as not only holding counter-revolutionary principles (a vague charge often added to more specific accusations) but as being a spy for the English. Langlois was studying surgery at the time of his arrest, and in his appeal to the Committee of General Security he asked that he be freed so that his talent could be used in the army, where he could help "assuage suffering humanity."[16]

Perhaps the political biography of Nicolas Gurnot, the wine merchant, makes clear the nature of the "faction" in the section. He was thirty-four at the time of his arrest and imprisonment in the Luxembourg on 14 October 1793. During the clash of 4–5 May, he had been president of the general assembly. The revolutionary committee accused him of always having been at loggerheads with the sans-culottes and of having opposed a gift of five hundred livres to the volunteers of the Vendée.[17]

In his appeal to the Committee of General Security, Gurnot reviewed his political career. It began when he accompanied a crowd that freed the Gardes-Françaises who had been imprisoned in the Abbaye. On 12 July 1789 he had gathered with the patriots at the Palais Royal, and the following day he mounted guard as one of the first members of the garde bourgeoise. On 14 July he was in the crowd that seized arms in the Invalides, and he did not rest for three days. Gurnot was among the first to enroll in the National Guard, where he had always performed personal service. When the country was proclaimed in danger, his brother enrolled in the section's battalion, armed and equipped at their joint expense. He had held a number of responsible posts in the section: president of the assembly, civil commissioner, member of the military committee, and officer of his company. Gurnot had written three previous letters asking the reasons for his incarceration;[18] it can be assumed that he was freed shortly after this fourth appeal.

Among the other oppositionists was Gérard-Jean Arfelière, who deserves more than a footnote. He was thirty-six, married with six children (the youngest a year old), and resided on rue de Tracy. A cabinetmaker *(menuisier)* by profession, he also worked as a mason and a carpenter. He was arrested on 19 November 1793 and charged with counter-revolutionary conduct for having opposed the departure of volunteers for the department of Eure and for being "the abbé Maury" of the section. The surveillance committee also accused him of fighting the patriots and of being "one of the leaders of the coalition organized in the general assembly to destroy the democracy." It held, too, that "his wealth is a bit questionable before the Revolution" and that he owned houses in the former Passage Honoré.[19]

Arfelière replied in a letter to the Committee of General Security that he was born to working-class parents without property who could not afford to give him an education. He had married a woman of the same class, a linen worker. On 13 July 1789 he had lent his shop for the purpose of organizing the citizens' militia *(corps de garde)* in which he served. Although lacking education, he had been reading "with great avidity" the works of Voltaire and Rousseau. At the time of the king's flight to Varennes he had purchased a national estate belonging to a former clergyman (thus demonstrating his patriotism and confidence in the Revolution, obviously). Although lame and thus unable to volunteer with his brothers for the army, he offered to go at his own expense to a battalion nearby in order to bring it news and financial help from parents of the volunteers. Furthermore, he denied that he had opposed the volunteers going to the Eure, listed his donations, and declared that as sergeant-major of his company he had carried out the orders of his captain on 31 May. As proof, he submitted a certificate signed by his captain and twenty-eight of his comrades in the company.[20] Arfelière must have been freed shortly thereafter.

Unlike Bon-Conseil, section Beaurepaire (Left Bank) remained moderate on the very eve of the insurrection. On 29 May its general assembly adopted a resolution that it read to the Convention pledging its continued loyalty to the constituted authorities and to the preservation of private property.[21] A member of the General Council reported on 31 May that he had been received with hostility by the section's general assembly.[22] When the insurrection broke out, it was reported in the General Council that Roland and Mme. Roland had been arrested but that Beaurepaire had taken them under its protection.[23] The Council sent six commissioners to place them under its own jurisdiction.

Butte-des-Moulins (West), which harbored the Jacobin Club, was also moderate. On 24 May it protested to the Convention the conduct of the Paris Commune and declared its own hatred of the "anarchistes," for which it earned the commendation of the national representation.[24] The following day a riot broke out in the assembly when the removal of the departmental authorities was proposed. A citizen of the section described to the General Council "the scandalous scene" that had taken place when the address of the Commune was rejected.[25] On 29 May delegates of the section's popular society read a denunciation of Collin (or Colin), president of the section's assembly. The General Council sent the evidence against him to the administration of police in order to have him arrested.[26] The following day, the popular society resolved to bypass the sectional assembly whose majority, in the words of a member, was guilty of "uncivic and counter-revolutionary spirit." Since the assembly had obstinately refused to send delegates to the Evêché, the society elected its own delegates, Jean-Baptiste Loys (who played a leading role in the insurrection) and Michel Boissière, endowing them with unlimited powers.[27]

After Thermidor Collin wrote to the Committee of General Security that following "les funestes journées" of 31 May–2 June he had fled the section, leaving the capital on 4 June. The same day the revolutionary committee sealed his papers and effects; it arrested him as a "fédéraliste" on 29 June in the department of Puy-de-Dôme, to which he had fled. Among the charges against him was that he had wanted to save Brissot.[28]

On 4 June a number of the section's moderates were arrested. This action prompted a large delegation of their partisans to demand an appearance before the General Council in their friends' behalf. They were told to furnish proof in writing that those arrested were indeed patriots and to turn this evidence over to the police.[29] Before the end of the month the moderates took over the revolutionary committee, and they continued to dominate the assembly as well.[30]

Champs-Elysées (West) remained a staunch opponent of the municipal authorities, launching a sharp attack against the Commune on 20 May for its alleged arbitrary acts against the interests of the sections. It proclaimed that "the municipal despotism is the worst of all" and called on the Convention to annul the various decrees of the General Council, which it found obnoxious. Moreover, it protested what it held was the illegal appointment of the provisional commander for Paris.[31] On 2 June the assembly elected a new president who admitted that some differences of opinion had manifested themselves and urged unity and fraternity among all[32]—a meaningless phrase under the circumstances. During the insurrection, the reconstituted general assembly—now dominated by the sansculottes—approved all measures taken by the Comité central révolutionnaire, including the arrest of its enemies.[33]

Unlike several of the sections discussed above, Cité (Center) was politically important, as many followed her lead.[34] Her president, Claude-Emmanuel Dobsen, had refused to deliver the records of the revolutionary committee to the Commission des Douze. On 26 May he was arrested,[35] only to be liberated in time to play an important part in the insurrection. His incarceration in the Abbaye unleashed a powerful agitation that reached into the streets of section Cité and her neighbors. The Société des Citoyennes révolutionnaires mobilized its followers and sympathizers and marched to the Abbaye. As the *Patriote Français* described it, "Yesterday, *these dames* rose altogether. They displayed a striking banner and a nice bonnet rouge. They sang the *litanies* of Marat, in awaiting the *requiem* of the Brissotins. They wanted to produce a general insurrection of men; but no one rose; and these dames have gone to sleep. The party has been put off for today."[36] The following day Cité's general assembly attacked the Commission des Douze in a sharply worded resolution comparing its action (Dobsen had refused to deliver the records of the revolutionary committee to the Commission), to the *lettres de cachet* of the Ancien Régime. "Representatives, the time for complaints has passed," it exhorted. "We warn you to save the Republic or the necessity to save it ourselves will force us to do it."[37] On 29 May thirty-three sections responded to this call and sent their commissioners to the Evêché.[38]

In contrast to Cité was Croix-Rouge (Left Bank), which was lukewarm to the insurrection.[39] On 27 May it adopted a resolution demanding the release of Hébert and the dissolution of the Commission des Douze,[40] yet it failed to sign either. Its revolutionary committee arrested Jean-

Pierre-Marie Cattin-Dubois, age twenty-three, a married man with one child who resided on rue Grenelle and was employed in the Imprimerie nationale. He was apprehended on 1 September 1793 for attempting to impede recruitment for the Vendée and for being the author of a "fédéralistique" resolution adopted by the Fifth Company of the section to which he belonged. The committee accused him of being a leader of "the counter-revolutionary cabal" in the section in June 1793 and wrote that he was "lié avec tous les aristocrates, et les royalistes les plus prononcés de la Section."[41]

In requesting his release, Cattin-Dubois testified that he had served in the regiment of Port-au-Prince in Saint-Dominigue and had returned to France when he was wounded and discharged as a result. Despite the obstacles to obtaining citizenship, he enrolled in the National Guard and also made financial sacrifices in favor of the women and children of volunteers. In August 1792 he swore to fight for liberty against royalty. Cattin-Dubois ended his letter by pointing to his detention of seven months, calling himself "a poor sans-culotte," and asking to return to his family.[42]

Section Fraternité (Center) remained a strong opponent of the sans-culottes until the insurrection brought about a change in its general assembly. It read its address on 18 May through its spokesman, Royer-Collard, who had been its chief composer and one of the leaders in repudiating the Commune's decree of 13 May levying a special tax on the wealthy. As could be expected, he defended the Girondins and denounced the attacks of the "agitators." Sections 1792 and Butte-des-Moulins gave their adherence to the oration, and the Convention applauded it and inserted it in its *Bulletin*.[43] On 24 May Fraternité followed with another petition, probably a slight variation on the first, adopted the day before, which strongly condemned the "journée" being prepared against the twenty-two members of the Convention.[44] This address aroused a commotion in the more radical sections as well as in the Commune. Section Arsenal demanded to know its origin and those responsible for it, and the General Council drafted a reply and appointed commissioners to present it the next day to the Convention.[45]

Like Fraternité, section Molière et la Fontaine (North) was one of the more moderate sections that repudiated the insurrection of 31 May.[46] It sent six commissioners to the Convention with a resolution declaring that "prudence commands that we unite with the constituted authorities."[47] Four days before the insurrection, Molière et la Fontaine's general assembly had resolved to march to the aid of the Convention and sent four commissioners to so inform that body.[48] Its *procès-verbal* of 31 May reported that the resolution of section Cité inviting the sections to send commissioners to the Evêché was read and passed over without comment. It responded to the invitation of the departmental authorities on 29 May to send commissioners to the Jacobins by electing only two observers. As an armed force gathered before the Convention, the section sent delegates to inquire of the Commune if this act had been sanctioned by the authorities. Furthermore, the sectional assembly unanimously replied to the decree adopted by the Comité central that it arrest all known suspects by denying the existence of such persons within its boundaries. It also adopted a resolution demanding that the General Council take steps against "enemies of public good" and questioned the legality of Hanriot's appointment as commander of the National Guard. When a member of the assembly moved on 1 June that the section ask Hanriot for orders, it simply passed to the order of business, assuring Hassenfratz, who spoke in the name of the Comité des Neuf, that the section continued to support the constituted authorities. It played a passive role the next day, merely hearing reports of what transpired in the Convention and reading decrees of the Comité central révolutionnaire.[49]

Among the leaders of its moderates was Augustin-Pierre Roland, who was arrested on 21 September 1793 for his role in the events of 31 May. He was forty years old, worked as a *commis* in the Bureaux de la Marine, and had young children. His father was a "marchand mercier" who had given his son a good education. Roland bore an unfortunate name, "un nom proscrit" as his wife admitted in a petition for his release. He was charged with declaring his doubts on the possibility of establishing a republic, of denigrating the constituted authorities, and of questioning the legality of Hanriot's election. Moreover, he was linked to the "solderatistes" of the section, those who received the forty-sous subsidy to attend sectional meetings. His character was described as "turbulent en tête fougeaux," and he was accused of always being opposed to the patriots of the section.[50]

Roland replied that from the very beginning of the Revolution he had defended the interests of the Third Estate and that he had enrolled in the battalion of district Petits Augustins and borne arms in all the decisive days of the Revolution—14 July 1789, 20 June 1792, and 10 August 1792. Furthermore, he had never signed any "anti-civic petitions," had been present at the installation of the busts of Marat and Lepeletier, and, he claimed, had accepted the Constitution of 1793 enthusiastically. In refuting the charge that he had expressed doubts about establishing the republic, he replied quite sensibly that it was difficult to destroy such an accusation because it was so absurd. But even if the imputation were true, he hastened to add, he had the right to express his opinion. As for the election whose legality he questioned, Roland attested that he did not know Hanriot or his rival, Ruffer (who, incidentally, had gained 600 votes to Hanriot's 133). This only demonstrated that the success of the insurrection was due not to any general but rather to the people themselves, he concluded.[51] Whatever denials and special pleading may be expected from a man anxious to leave prison, much of his testimony bears the ring of truth. He was released from Carmes prison on 4 August 1794 after testimony from his section that he had always been an excellent citizen.[52]

Section Mont-Blanc (West) also had its share of moderates. A leading member was Pierre-Rémi Fielval, captain of its battalion, who had presided over its assembly on 5 June 1793, three days after the insurrection. Fielval was thirty-three years old at the time of his arrest and had been employed in the Bureau des domaines. He was accused of opposing a motion presented on 5 June to make the assembly permanent on the grounds that it had been made at 10:15 P.M., a quarter of an hour past the time legally allowed for assembly meetings. Because he had adjourned the session, his enemies held him responsible for the tumult that followed. Supporters of the motion insisted that "the people" had not sanctioned such a curfew and attacked Fielval physically. In the melee that followed he defended himself with a swordstick *(canne d'epée)* and wounded one of his attackers. He was also denounced for allegedly having attacked the revolutionary committee when it prepared its proscription list against moderates. All this led to his interrogation and arrest on 5–6 June.[53] Fielval had participated in all the *journées* of the Revolution, had never signed an anti-civic petition, and consorted only with fellow employees of the Bureau des domaines, he wrote.[54] It seems that despite his exemplary conduct during the Revolution, at least up to 31 May, he was condemned by the revolutionary tribunal on 12 July 1794.[55]

As early as 6 May delegates of section Pont-Neuf (Center—on the Seine) reported to the General Council that trouble had broken out in their general assembly, that citizens with red cards (issued to foreigners) had been permitted to deliberate in the meetings, and that they had helped thwart the revolutionary committee's attempt to affix seals to the effects of suspects. Hébert had moved to send an armed force to arrest those responsible, and six commissioners were dispatched. The moderates had evidently taken control and had dismissed the former members of the revolutionary committee. On their return, the commissioners reported to the General Council that they had removed the seals placed on the effects of the revolutionary committee and had reinstalled its members in their former positions.[56]

The moderates returned to power sometime later, however, for on 27

May the general assembly resolved to support "the security of the Convention" as well as the right of individuals "to express their opinion."[57] This opposition to the sans-culottes became more evident when on 31 May the commander of Pont-Neuf's armed forces refused to honor Hanriot's order to sound the alarm under the pretext that the document lacked a date. When the president of the assembly and two others took their grievance to the departmental authorities the latter refused to act on their complaint, holding that they were under orders of the Convention.[58]

A number of other sections remained moderate until the insurrection brought the patriotic party into power. Invalides (Left Bank), for example, heard Unité's address on 29 May but refused to sign it. Instead it adopted a noncommital resolution to the effect that it opposed arbitrary arrests by any authority whatsoever,[59] an obvious repudiation of the sans-culottes and the Commune. Section Luxembourg (Left Bank) was moderate,[60] as was Tuileries (Center), which submitted its registers to the Commission des Douze for examination on 24 May.[61] Section Observatoire (Center-South) was characterized by Pariset as "lukewarm,"[62] though once "regenerated" after the insurrection it joined Finistère, Sans-Culottes, and Panthéon-Français in an attempt to make the Rights of Man something more than lofty principles untouched by reality.[63] Too little is known of section Piques,[64] but its revolutionary committee took an active part in the insurrection without losing its sense of balance,[65] as described in Chapter VII.

Several interesting individuals furnish good examples of what Girondin partisans in the capital were like, and they deserve more than a cursory glance. The first, a strong adversary of the sans-culottes in section Unité, was a professor at the collège des Quatre-Nations, Antoine Le Tellier. He was born at Louviers, department of Eure, and became a republican in the course of the Revolution but despised the Jacobins and supported the Girondins. In a dispute with an adversary on 15 May 1793 he was arrested, and during a search of his premises he was compromised by verses he had written celebrating such well-known assassins as Ravaillac, Clement, and Damien. These were coupled with unflattering references to Robespierre, Danton, Marat, Jacobins, Cordeliers, and so forth. Le Tellier expressed contempt for the people whom he called "stupid and blind instruments of Pitt and de la Clos."[66]

On interrogation by the revolutionary committee of section Unité he stated that "he was an enemy of anarchists; [but] he was at all times a republican" and that the ideas expressed in his verses had never been communicated to anyone. This denial did not save him from being transferred to the Conciergerie prison. Among his friends was the Girondin deputy Depuis, but he was in no position to do anything for him, not even to visit him in prison. His students, however, petitioned the Convention to free him and were well received by the deputies. It is possible that Le Tellier was freed for several days (Depuis's last letter to him is dated 26 May), but the insurrection of 31 May doomed him ultimately.[67] A member of the Comité de législation revealed that five citizens of section Unité had been arrested by its revolutionary committee and observed that no charge existed against them except that they had spoken out against Robespierre and Marat. It was then that Marat intervened and stated that he opposed the release of Le Tellier because of his royalism.[68]

On 3 June Le Tellier was returned to prison. When his students requested his release for the second time, Collot d'Herbois, who presided, refused to hear them. Depuis wrote to Le Tellier, meanwhile, to be patient because the Convention was frightened by the Vendéens and Fédéralistes, hinting that this was no time to irritate the deputies with demands for his release. But another correspondent wrote in a more pessimistic mood that nothing could be done for Le Tellier because the Convention was no longer free.[69] Le Tellier appealed from the Abbaye prison to various colleagues (11 August 1793) to take advantage of an offer from the police administration to release him under the voucher of two citizens. He probably was freed again, but he was arrested for the third time at Neubourg on 16 May 1794. When asked who had written to him, Le Tellier is reported to have replied that "it's quite enough to have one victim if he had to be one, and that he would not say."[70] He was condemned on 24 June 1794 by the Tribunal criminel révolutionnaire and executed. He was fifty years old.[71]

Another victim of the revolutionary tribunal was Louis David Tassin of section Mail, a banker by profession. Like other Girondins in the section, he had an impressive political history. In April 1789 he was sent as an elector from the district Filles-Saint-Thomas and appointed first a commissioner to reduce the *cahiers* of the Third Estate of Paris and then a substitute to the National Assembly. On 13 July at the Hôtel de Ville he was the third person elected to the Comité permanente, on which he remained until 8 September. Shortly thereafter he was elected *notable adjoint* by his district and was one of 120 men who selected the eight members of the Tribunal municipal. He was the first man to be chosen for this court, on which he served until 7 March 1792. During 1791–1792 Tassin was one of the 144 representatives who sat in the Paris Commune, the Commune définitive; he was also elected as one of the forty-eight municipal officers. Tassin served as administrateur des domaines et finances until 7 March 1792 and remained on the General

Council until 10 August 1792. In 1792 he served on the section's civil committee, and the following year he became a member of the Comité central de bienfaisance, representing his section until his arrest. Tassin summarized his contributions by writing, "If it were possible to have done more for the Revolution it appeared difficult to him to have done more."[72]

Why was he arrested? A letter denouncing him, dated 13 November 1793 and written by one Cudier, gives a clue. "Naturally it is impossible," Cudier wrote, "that the class of Bankers, financiers, and others not become enemies to be feared when one possesses a Brilliant fortune and which earns Much. It is morally Certain that these gentlemen are not patriotic Sans-culottes." In addition to demonstrating a class bias, Cudier accused Tassin of disliking the Jacobins and damned him because his brother, a former commander-in-chief of district Filles-Saint-Thomas's armed force, had defended the Tuileries on 10 August. The revolutionary committee of Guillaume Tell (former Mail) charged Tassin with "provoking Federalism" and of being one of those who on 31 May demanded that "Vergniaute" (Vergniaud) be heard. Moreover, he had concerted with others to adopt a resolution in favor of "Brissotins, Girondins, et Rollandins." Then came the usual charge that he had hindered recruitment for the Vendée and was linked to its traitors "et avec tout les riches." The committee declared that he was opposed to the popular society, to the Montagnards, and to itself. Furthermore, men like Tassin had succeeded "in having expelled the patriots from the general assemblies whom they affected to call openly anarchists, Maratists, Septembriseurs in order to excite against them the fury of the people and to mislead public opinion." As a banker and with a brother who had defended the king, he was especially suspicious, the revolutionary committee concluded, and it arrested him on 4 February 1794.[73]

Brought before the revolutionary tribunal with thirteen others, officers, noncommissioned officers, and soldiers of the battalions of Filles-Saint-Thomas and of Petits-Pères, and accused of having defended Louis during the attack on the Tuileries, he was condemned to death on 3 May 1794.[74]

The president of section Mail, Jean-François Tranchelahausse, possessed an even more impressive political dossier than did his confrere Tassin. He was born at Verdun-sur-Meuse sometime in 1756 into the family of a vine-grower (vigneron) and came to Paris in January 1789, later bringing his wife, their two children, and her parents to live on rue des Vieux Augustins. Tranchelahausse was a "médicin empirique," a profession he had learned during a ten-year residency in Italy. When imprisoned on 27 March 1794, he had been on a mission to the Army of the Rhine, sent by his employers Saint-Just and Lebas from the Army of the North to treat the wounded and the sick. This practical physician boasted that he had invented a medicine, "Régénerateur Universel," which he had dispensed freely to cure the poor. Tranchelahausse emphasized that he lived off his labors, adding, "I never possessed and never saw any dividends from investments."[75]

Tranchelahausse had enrolled in the National Guard, Company Flamant, but practiced medicine every day until 2:00 P.M. at his home, where he treated rich and poor alike. In addition, he was busy serving on various sectional committees and regularly attended meetings of the general assembly. Among his contributions, Tranchelahausse listed the following duties he carried out as commissioner of the section: "commissaire à la saisie des chevaux de luxe, à la quit[t]e pour les pauvres, aux différentes enrolemens volontaires, aux enrolemens pour contingent, aux enrolemens pour la Vendée, comité de trente six commissaires près le fédérés des 83 départemens aux Jacobins, commissaire près les diverses sections, dans les crises de la République, commissaire à plusieurs assemblées à l'Evêché et ailleurs, commissaire aux accaparemens." He was also a member of the section's civil committee.[76]

Tranchelahausse added that he had opposed the adoption of the 1791 Constitution because he still lived in a "maison garni" and thus was deprived of suffrage as his family did not join him until the beginning of 1792. Since October 1792 he had been president of the section "during all the difficult days," working on 30 and 31 May and 1, 2, and 3 June "night and day." Furthermore, he had authored many of the section's proclamations against enemies of the Republic. When the Constitution was adopted (July 1793), it was he who presided over the proceedings in the primary assembly, and he headed several delegations to the Convention. Although he was elected to the surveillance committee and to the "Directoire de l'Administration du bien des pauvres," he was forced to refuse because of lack of time, but he did serve on the "Tribunal criminel du département."[77]

Why was such a "patriot" arrested? Aside from his moderate politics, he had incurred the opposition if not the personal hatred of Brichet, a "sous chef" to the Committee of General Security who denounced him to the revolutionary committee of section Guillaume Tell by writing that his conduct "is too notorious to necessitate tracing it for sans-culottes as revolutionary as you."[78] Shortly thereafter, three members of the surveillance committee arrived at Tranchelahausse's home, only to find that he was on mission. After interrogating his wife, the commissioners sealed his papers and gave the police orders to arrest him and conduct him to La Force prison. Among the reasons for his detention the committee wrote

that Tranchelahausse "has been constantly at the head of royalist conspirators" and that he had presented the "patriots" in a bad light.[79]

What had been Tranchelahausse's role during the insurrection of 31
May–2 June? On 1 June delegates of the forty-eight sections and the Paris
department objected to the two commissioners sent by section Mail and
demanded their replacement. This precipitated a discussion in the general
assembly as one member after another rose to defend the assembly's
choice. Tranchelahausse, presiding, stated that the visiting delegates were
free to select anyone they wished from their midst. One of the two men
they chose was Brichet, the "sous chef" who was to denounce Tranchelahausse to the section's revolutionary committee. Despite this decision,
the discussion of the section's past politics continued. A commissioner
from section Mail to the Evêché assembly rose and declared boldly that
the same spirit animated his sectional assembly as that which pervaded
the Evêché. Others asserted that the section had always defended the
principles of republicanism. Still others insisted that since 10 August
the section had been "l'amie des Sans Culottes" and had always defended
the freedom of opinion. The outcome of this exchange was that the spokesman of the delegation who had come to criticize section Mail congratulated
those present and retired amidst applause. Following the delegation's departure, the assembly promptly reversed the visitors' choice of commissioners and elected two others in their stead. It was obvious that the
moderates were still in control of the section.[80]

Following this exchange, the assembly was informed that section Butte-
des-Moulins had convinced the masses of Faubourg Saint-Antoine that it
was indeed republican and had been embraced by the latter's demonstrators in a show of fraternal unity. The assembly resolved to join the demonstrators with the president at its head. "The session is suspended during
this civic promenade," wrote the secretary. Joining the "immense crowd"
on rue Saint-Honoré, Tranchelahausse addressed the demonstrators, saying among other things, "Your brothers the Sans Culottes of the heart of
Paris, the whole section of Mail comes to give you the fraternal kiss." The
moderates of section Mail had been transformed into "sans-culottes" over-
night! Upon returning to the hall Tranchelahausse continued his address,
assuring all "que nous étions de vrais sans-culottes." The assembly then
moved to send a delegation of twenty to the General Council in order to
reiterate its oath to defend liberty.[81]

After the installation of the new president of the section, Peltan or
Pelletan, a citizen moved that the general assembly give honorable mention
to Tranchelahausse for his role in the events of 1 June. Although the
former president opposed the motion, insisting that he had only done his

duty, the assembly voted unanimously "that the Citizen Tranchelahausse has worthily represented the Section in difficult circumstances."[82] In appealing for freedom, Tranchelahausse held "l'intrigant Brichet" and his "cabale" responsible for his arrest, writing that Brichet had been expelled from the Jacobins on a motion of Robespierre.[83] After 9 Thermidor Tranchelahausse said nothing about this expulsion, naturally; instead, he trimmed his arguments to the new situation, writing that he had been opposed to "the usurpation" of power by the municipality and to the revolutionary committee dominated by Brichet. He had been called a Girondin, a Fédéraliste, and so on, and he denied responsibility for cashiering the first surveillance committee.[84]

In addition to submitting to the Committee of General Security summaries of the *procès-verbaux* that demonstrated his patriotic role, Tranchelahausse attached various other testimonials, including a letter from Saint-Just and Lebas stating that there was no suspicion of his emigration.[85] The Committee of General Security freed him "instantly" on 27 August 1794.[86] It is probable that despite his imprisonment Tranchelahausse continued to take an active part in politics, although the nature of his participation is lost to history.[87]

How did the moderates justify their role in the Revolution, and specifically, how did they defend themselves against the charges of the sansculottes? To begin with, it must be admitted that absurd and intolerant acts, coupled with exaggerated accusations and denunciations of political opponents, marked the sessions of various assemblies. A flagrant example of the former was reported to the general assembly of section Mail: section Pont-Neuf, it was alleged, had ruled that before a member of its assembly could take the floor he had to place the cap of liberty, the *bonnet rouge*, on his head. When a member by the name of Daubanton refused, he was excluded from the assembly for a year amidst general applause.[88]

Two equally striking cases of injustice occurred in section Unité. Drugnon, a notary, was denied a certificate of civic conduct because it was at his home that the Petition of Twenty Thousand had been signed.[89] When the captain of the section's armed company, Lahourde, sought to justify himself in an unspecified action, he was simply demoted and refused a hearing. The reporter, Lucas, observed that on the basis of one denunciation, without citing any proof or motive, the assembly had arbitrarily become a court and had refused Lahourde a trial. It went even further and prohibited him from ever again holding any office in the section. In addition, the assembly decreed that it would take under its safeguard all who had denounced "traitors" in the section, particularly the person who had brought charges against Lahourde.[90] And what can one say to the pathetic testimony of Roland's wife that one reason for her husband's continued imprisonment was that he bore "un nom proscrit"? Moreover, it is hardly necessary to deny that whatever politics the moderates embraced they were certainly not "aristocrats." Nor can it be denied that they had the constitutional right to express their opinions—opinions that the sans-culottes had an equal right to reject.

Perhaps the most glaring injustice in this whole confused mess of a struggle is that the sans-culottes appropriated the term "patriot" for themselves, implying that their opponents were unpatriotic, a damning indictment in time of war. If the political biographies of the moderates are examined, it is difficult to deny that their personal commitment to the Revolution was hardly less warm than that of their opponents, a fact that in no way undermines the position of the Mountain and its supporters that the politics of the Gironde was proving disastrous for the Revolution.

As has already been indicated, the moderates in the sections examined were often from the upper ranks of the middle class. There is little question, therefore, that the sans-culottes tended to view them with hostility and suspicion. When the general assembly of section Unité called on the General Council for help against its conservative opponents, for example, it specifically mentioned as "enemies of recruitment" (for the Vendée) "clerics, notaries, and bankers."[91] Class differences played a role in the division between the sans-culottes and the moderates, but they do not account entirely for the intolerance and name calling on both sides; the war and *la vie chère* undoubtedly encouraged this intransigence. But in addition to these factors there must have been many subtle, unconscious antagonisms of a purely individual nature: what began as a political difference gradually turned into a personal antipathy for one's adversary. In the zealous and heated atmosphere of the spring of 1793, matters could hardly have been otherwise. Conversely, what began as a personal dislike could eventually be given a political rationalization. No *procès-verbal* can tell us this, of course, but given the normal course of political conflicts it can safely be assumed that such was indeed the origin of many divisions.

Thus the hostility between the followers of the Mountain and those of the Gironde festered and grew until it exploded in the *journée* of 31 May. The sections were unable to resolve the conflict so long as the Paris Commune could not or would not take the initiative on their behalf. Fraternizations, moreover, were temporary affairs. And members of the General Council were closely linked politically to the Montagnards, who were reacting rather than initiating the revolutionary measures that were to remove the Girondin leaders. This meant that only an extra-legal body, a truly revolutionary organ willing to bypass both the municipal authorities and the various executive committees of the Convention, could take decisive action. This was to be the role of the Evêché assembly, created by the more militant sections, and its executive organ the Comité des Neuf, later to become the Comité central révolutionnaire. The insurrection of 31 May–2 June 1793 was to be their operation alone. The Montagnards, the Jacobins, and the representatives of the sections in the Commune merely followed their lead. It is time, therefore, to examine this extralegal body formed by the sections.

IV

The Paris Commune and the Evêché Assembly

The Paris Commune had pretentions of power and influence
incompatible with public tranquility and with the calm
necessary for the work of the Convention.

Bertrand Barère, *Mémoires*

THE LAW of 21 May 1790 had established the Paris Commune as the
municipal government of the capital. The forty-eight sections sent 144
delegates or representatives to the General Council, three from each section, for two-year terms. These representatives were elected by the active
citizens in their primary assemblies. Until 10 August 1792 voters had to
be twenty-one years of age or older and living off their labors or investments, but after the fall of the monarchy representatives were elected by
an almost universal male suffrage. Before taking their seats delegates had
to pass a *scrutin épuratoire,* the close scrutiny of their fellow representatives.
If twenty-five or more sections rejected a delegate, his section was requested to replace him. This permitted the parent body to establish control
over imperfect purges and scrutinies in individual sections. The process
took a long time because after the election the assemblies were reconvoked
to vote on the 144 names without discussion and then met for a third
time to choose the officials who constituted the municipal administration.
Since the votes were scattered among the 144 delegates, it took about
nine months to complete the process.[1]

The affairs of the municipality were divided among five departments:
subsistence, police, national estates and finances, public institutions, and
public works. The Corps municipal (municipal body) was composed of
forty-eight officials elected by the sections from among the 144 representatives. Sixteen administrators, presided over by the mayor, were elected
from this body to form the Bureau municipal and to direct the five de-

partments. The thirty-two officials who were not members of the Bureau made up the Conseil municipal of Paris. Finally, the General Council of the Commune (Conseil général de la Commune) was composed of the municipal council plus ninety-six representatives *(notables)* elected by the sections. The General Council of the Paris Commune discussed important matters and passed various ordinances and decrees.[2]

Theoretically, Paris as a municipality was under Paris as a department and had no legal right to execute the laws it passed unless they were approved by the department. Because the sections elected both groups of officials, however, when the Commune spoke the department was inclined to agree. Moreover, the mayor, the *procureur,* and the *procureur's* two substitutes were inviolable and could hardly be touched by the central authorities. The municipality was sole mistress of the only armed force, the National Guard, and controlled the police administration as well. And because each company of the Garde Parisienne elected its own officers, their political opinions tended to be of the same persuasion as those of the militiamen who had elected them.[3]

The *scrutin* for the Commune définitive began on 24 December 1792, an action which resulted in the return of many delegates who were to the left of those who had preceded them. Because it took many months for the vote, the examination of the delegates elected, and their final confirmation to be completed, the Commune persuaded the Convention to grant it the right to co-opt newly elected members without waiting for the purges and reelections. Hence the Paris Commune now contained three distinct elements: those who had sat in it prior to 10 August; those elected in November 1792; and finally, the new members who were authorized to take their places by the decree of 3 April 1793. Since the last element was preponderant in both numbers and influence, the Commune assumed a new audacity, reflected in a more rigorous supervision of the royal family in the Temple, in more frequent house visits, in arbitrary rulings on passports and civic cards, and in more frequent denunciations of suspects or those deemed to be suspect.[4]

Barère declared flatly that the Paris Commune was "incompatible with public tranquility and with the calm necessary for the work of the Convention."[5] The Commune, being closer to the grassroots, tended to reflect the needs of the sans-culottes, which were not necessarily compatible with those represented by the deputies, Right or Left. As an institution embodying popular sovereignty on a local scale, it encouraged the expression of public opinion, which at times troubled deputies like Barère because it upset the decorum of the Convention. More important than the ungentlemanly conduct of its members and spokesmen was the Commune's championing of measures like the *maximum* and the guarantee of provisions that were at variance with laissez-faire economics.

The Commune was especially resentful of the menaces indulged in by the Girondin deputies and their supporters in the departments, who threatened to discipline the Parisians by troops from Bordeaux, Marseilles, or Lyons. In its appeal of 29 April 1793, for example, it denounced to the forty-four thousand communes of France efforts of the Girondins to form "a praetorian guard, in order to dominate us by terror."[6] At the same time it sought to assure its opponents that it had no desire to harm Girondin deputies, wishing merely "to assassinate their ideas."[7]

In order to act in a revolutionary manner against the Girondin deputies it sought to purge, the Commune and its sections had to create an extralegal organ, for after all the municipal government was bound by certain legal norms and practices. This was done by creating a revolutionary assembly sitting in the Evêché, from which would come forth the Comité des Neuf, replaced in turn by the Comité central révolutionnaire that was destined to direct the insurrection of 31 May–2 June 1793. On 16 May the General Council decreed that each section elect three members—one each from its general assembly, its civil committee, and its revolutionary committee—to act as delegates of the section to form the revolutionary assembly sitting in the Evêché. The nominal purpose of this gathering was to discuss the forced loan, but this was merely a cover for the revolutionary steps about to be taken against the Girondins.[8]

François Bergoeing, a deputy from the Gironde and member of the Commission des Douze, wrote to his constituents citing a number of depositions made to the commission by individuals who had attended the meeting in the Hôtel de Ville where plans for the insurrection had allegedly been discussed. Several reported hearing speakers who advocated the arbitrary killing of accused representatives ("il faut les septembriser") and the drafting of a list of suspects. A member of the revolutionary committee of section Fontaine-de-Grenelle, listed simply as "D . . . ," testified that on 19 May the agenda included identifying members of the Convention to be proscribed and "the aristocrats" of sections against whom revolutionary measures were to be taken. "D . . ." recalled the motion of a certain Bisé that thirty-three of the suspect deputies be "Septembrisized," and this action be justified by reporting that they had been émigrés. "D . . ." did admit that the mayor denounced this proposal as a crime because Paris constituted a trust for all deputies and demanded that all such discussion cease. Bergoeing adds, however, that Pache opposed discussing the motion in the town hall, not because he was against proscription as such. The assembly later gathered in the Evêché.[9] Whatever truth is in these reports, there is little question that some of the depositions cited by Bergoeing were based on wild exaggerations. Tom Paine's letter alleging that Marat told an Irish general by the name of Ward that foreigners as well as more than three hundred "brigands" of the Convention ought to be beheaded must not be accepted at face value.[10]

Meillan also cites the report of a member of section Panthéon-Français, referred to as "L . . . ," who at the same meeting heard proposals to do away with the suspected deputies. The mayor refused to allow such talk and held that such a motion had not been put before the assembly.[11] Meillan cites the testimony of "Louis P . . ." of section Tuileries that two police administrators, Marino and Michel, had proposed the measure to lynch the deputies.[12]

Others continued to discuss the need to arrest the suspects in the Convention; but when someone mentioned that Robespierre and Marat were concerting their efforts on the coming insurrection, voices cried out, "We must not name anyone!" Meanwhile, a member of section Fraternité was expelled for taking notes. The mayor warned, however, that molesting the deputies would unleash a civil war.[13]

What precedent was there for creating an illegal committee that would remove deputies from the Convention? The Commune of 10 August, which had engineered the coup against the monarchy, was one such prototype.[14] Although it was unsuccessful, the abortive insurrection of 10 March 1793 also taught militants how to organize an uprising and what measures must be taken to avoid failure.[15] Two weeks later the general assembly of section Droits-de-l'Homme adopted a resolution declaring "that after deliberating on the dangers facing France" it had unanimously "risen to save the country and liberty." It urged therefore that the sections send elected commissioners to a central point where they would discuss means of saving the country from a "liberticide faction."[16] The following day twenty-seven sections responded by sending commissioners to the Evêché. On 1 April they assumed the name "Assemblée central du salut public et de correspondance avec les départements."[17]

On the day section des Droits-de-l'Homme adopted its resolution, the General Council decreed the formation of a Comité de correspondance with the forty-four thousand municipalities of France. Among the five members appointed, two were to serve on the revolutionary committee of the Evêché assembly that would direct the uprising of 31 May: Duroure and Seguy.[18] A third member, Bodson, was an Hébertist and is mentioned by Babeuf. The fourth was Dorat-Cubière of section Unité; nothing is known of the fifth.

The Comité de correspondance had first been proposed after the over-throw of the king as a kind of universal commune of all the departments, not a scheme to federalize them as the Girondins held. When the Hébertists went on trial in March 1794, Louis Roux, a former municipal official, testified, "Hébert and Chaumette tried to usurp the national authority in order to concentrate it within the Commune which they hoped to dominate."[19] Whatever independence Hébert and Chaumette tried to develop from the Convention and its Great Committees, there is no evidence that they wanted to supplant those bodies with the Commune. Once the Convention adopted the revolutionary decrees of 4 December 1793 that created National Agents under its control, Chaumette's brief attempt to bind the revolutionary committees to the Commune collapsed without a blow.[20]

The roots of the Evêché assembly may in turn be traced to a meeting of ninety-six commissioners from several sections charged with discussing the problem of provisions.[21] Section la Cité suggested to others the creation of a federation of all sections to defend the republic. By January 1793 a sort of central committee had been formed in Paris, supported by the Jacobins, the Fédérés, and the popular societies.[22]

On 13 May the sections began to prepare the insurrection through their commissioners in the Evêché.[23] The following day Dutard informed Garat that a central committee of the sections had been organized and outlined the stages of the coming insurrection, to be led by the Evêché committee. Half of Paris was to be disarmed as "suspect" and anyone who refused to cry "Vive Marat!" was to be imprisoned.[24] Whether this report was true or not, the Girondins and their allies began to denounce the assembly, and Barère launched an attack against it on 16 May.[25]

In addition to the Commission des Douze, deputies in the Convention sought to learn what was afoot and called on the mayor to give them the latest news. On 19 May a letter from Pache informed the Conventionnels that when an improper motion was made in the Evêché assembly to arrest the chief suspects (the Girondins), it was unanimously repudiated. The mayor assured the representatives that there was no need to be disquieted, that all was peaceful and under control. Bourdon de l'Oise demanded that this report be published in order to expose the "calumny" of Guadet. Marat, too, demanded its publication. After a tumult had broken out over the motion, the Convention finally voted to insert it into its *Bulletin*.[26]

The reports of the municipal police indicated warm sympathy for the coming revolution. Dutard revealed how, sitting in the galleries of the Convention on 17 May, he heard talk of the need to take matters into the people's own hands: "Il faut que le peuple se lève encore," spectators declared, expressing enmity toward the "noirs" of the Convention.[27] The contrast between their expectations and the bitter reality was especially striking, he wrote. They had hoped to be happier and even better off; instead, "I eat less than I ever have," as he quoted an imaginary protester. Dutard concluded, "It appears that 'le peuple anarchiste' always attach themselves, without any regard for their old patrons, to him who appears to follow them further in their dissoluteness; that they love Marat, Robespierre only in as much as the latter say to them: 'let us kill, let us pillage, let us assassinate.' "[28] Whatever the prejudices of this police spy, there is little question that he reported the growing agitation of the sans-culottes with a fair degree of accuracy. Information reaching the ministry of the interior advised that the principal cause of the ferment was the growing disunion in the Convention and the high prices of the necessities of life.[29]

Levasseur cites Garat's report that the Evêché assembly was perfectly legitimate, that it was an open assembly rather than a secret conclave *(conciliabule),* and that it had been called forth by action of the Commune to discuss certain decrees passed by the Convention. Recalling that the administrative corps had been authorized by the Convention to take measures against suspects, to levy a contribution on the wealthy, and to make requisitions, Levasseur wrote, "It was to carry out these measures that the mayor had convoked the commissioners of the sections; thus this committee was legally assembled."[30] Technically speaking, Levasseur may have been right, but the purpose of and the actions taken by this body, "legally assembled" though it may have been, were certainly not legal.

The Commune could not associate itself overtly with a revolutionary assembly sitting in the Evêché, but it could and did take advantage of its legal position. It was, after all, in direct communication with all the active revolutionary forces of the capital. Ultimately, it was to harmonize its actions with those of the extra-legal body, and it soon recognized that the center of power had shifted to the Evêché. The General Council of the Commune served as an intermediary among the sections and between them and itself as the municipal government of Paris. The police administration of the capital, which kept counter-revolutionaries under surveillance, also acted as an intermediary between the Commune and the "effervescent sections." It was the police who, on 15 May, first proposed forming a revolutionary army and arresting suspects. The previous day the police administration suggested that an assembly be convoked in the Hôtel de Ville in order to adopt measures of public safety and to draft a list of suspects. Everyone knew that among the latter were the leaders of the Gironde.[31] On 17 May the General Council appointed Boulanger

commander of the troops in Paris because Santerre, the well-known militant and "Bastille conqueror," was about to depart for the Vendée.[32]

One of the first acts of the Commission des Douze was to arrest Hébert,
Varlet, Dobsen, and others on 24–25 May in an effort to frustrate the
plans of the Commune and its sections. Garat pleaded with the Commission not to imprison Hébert, pointing to the repercussions that had followed the detention of Marat and his ultimate triumph some weeks before.
Moreover, he was convinced that Hébert's libels were no worse than those
of other journalists, and that his imprisonment would merely arouse the
"hommes violents" against the "gens raisonables et sages, bons amis de la
liberté," in the sections. He admitted "that power rests on the law, but
for power to rest on the law, it is essential that the law begin by having
power." And that power was obviously in the Paris Commune.[33]

Hébert was arrested for an article that appeared in the *Père Duchesne*
in which he denounced the Girondins as plotters of the counter-revolution
in the pay of Pitt and as responsible for the Vendée outbreak. For good
measure he added that they were royalists, and he called on the sans-
culottes to rise up and crush them.[34] Appearing before the Commission,
Hébert justified his use of intemperate language as necessary for the sale
of the *Père Duchesne*; without it, it "would lack punch." In reply the Commission noted ironically, "What language for a magistrate of the people
to use."[35]

During the night of 24–25 May, the Commune received a communication from the Commission des Douze demanding to see its registers, as
provided by decree of the Convention. The General Council decided to
comply as it was not ready to challenge the law. Immediately thereafter
Hébert reported that a warrant for his arrest had been issued by the
Commission des Douze. Chaumette embraced him, saying, "Go, my friend,
I hope to join you soon." The General Council then resolved to be in
permanent session and to appoint commissioners from its midst to give
periodic reports on the detention of its magistrate. Shortly thereafter it
learned that Hébert had been incarcerated in Abbaye prison. The Council
resolved to protest his arrest before the Convention as a violation of the
freedom of the press.[36]

Of course Hébert's fulminations were no different from those of a dozen
journalists of his day, and certainly similar to the slanders of the *Patriote
Français*. As an official of the municipality, however, he was open to the
charge of the Commission des Douze to which ordinary journalists may
not have been subjected. The day after the arrest, Chaumette reported
to the General Council that he had visited Hébert in prison but had not
spoken to him as he was resting. The Council then decreed that all sections

be directly informed of the arrest and of the previous day's events by their representatives in the Commune at their general assemblies that evening.[37]

In its address to the Convention the General Council denied the accusation of sections Fraternité and Champs-Elysées that it was preparing a "journée" against the twenty-two deputies of the Convention. Section Fraternité had adopted its resolution to that effect on 23 May and had presented it to the Convention on the following day. Needless to say, it had aroused much opposition in the more radical sections as well as in the Commune itself.[38] The General Council demanded in its reply that "the plotters" be punished by being turned over to the public accuser. Furthermore, it sought to reassure the deputies by reminding them that the delegates of the Commune were magistrates of Paris and friends of the Conventionnels and by denying that they were plotting against them, citing the statement of "the virtuous mayor." Pache had confirmed the declaration of Garat that the plots referred to by the Commission des Douze were imaginary: that there was nothing to fear since the armed force around the Convention was quite strong.[39]

After reports from several sections, the Commune heard Unité's resolution to detain its volunteers for the Vendée until the present troubles had been resolved. Destournelles, one of the vice-presidents of the General Council, assured Unité's delegates that there was sufficient support among the patriots in Paris to contain the counter-revolution and that the section's volunteers were needed in the Vendée. On the morning of the twenty-fifth Chaumette reported that when he visited the Abbaye to see Hébert, the prisoner had been asleep—proof of his innocence, he hastened to add. Meanwhile, the Commune continued to inform the sections on what was taking place, and in order not to launch a premature action and to control them it posted armed men under Hanriot to guard the cannons.[40]

A number of sections reported on troubles in their assemblies the following day, and others read resolutions demanding Hébert's release. Several had taken him under their safeguard, and in the course of struggle against local Girondin supporters they had repulsed efforts to bring help to the enemies of the Montagnards.[41] During the Commune's session it was reported that sixteen sections had adopted Unité's resolution to free Hébert and that the Council had learned from Cité that its president, Dobsen, had been arrested by the Commission des Douze.[42]

On 27 May section Unité communicated the address on freeing Hébert that it was to present to the Convention, which the General Council suggested it share with the other sections. When it was reported shortly thereafter that the Commission des Douze had been suppressed, there was an outburst of applause and shouts of joy.[43] The following day Hébert appeared and was greeted warmly. After being presented with a crown of laurels, which he placed on the bust of Rousseau, he acknowledged the applause as being not for him but for the "principes eternels de la justice." He then attacked the Commission des Douze for having exercised "a dictatorial power."[44]

Although the Commission was reestablished temporarily, the prisoners had been freed and the movement against it, far from being intimidated, rose in sharp confrontation with the Gironde. For example section Arcis, in an address to the Convention that it first read to the General Council, asked the legislators to explain the threat of Isnard to annihilate Paris. Yet Chaumette still spoke in broad principles, and just before Hébert's release declared that even if he were not freed the people would avenge him, "but above all, no arms, no blood. (Vifs applaudissements.)" The only force he would entertain was "the union" of the people; no force must be used nor steps taken against "les sections égarés." Hébert, on the other hand, favored chasing "the intriguers" out of the sectional assemblies, arming the sans-culottes, and arresting suspects, but the General Council took no action.[45] When it was reported that several sections had been disturbed in their assemblies by "intriguers and Rolandists," the Council did appoint commissioners to reestablish order in these general assemblies,[46] but the decisive steps would have to be taken by the Evêché assembly.

Section Cité had taken the initiative on 28 May to convoke delegates from the sections to meet in the hall of the Evêché assembly, which was within its boundaries.[47] A secret Comité des Six acted as the assembly's executive organ, to be followed by the better-known Comité des Neuf. There seem to have been two plans under deliberation when the assembly met the following day. The first was public and was discussed openly by the delegates of the sections and electors of 10 August who were present; on the whole, the proposals they heard were moderate in tone and were noncommittal about the insurrection. The second plan, in contrast, was formulated by commissioners who were tacitly invested with a sort of executive mandate to determine the course of action. This plan was meant to launch the insurrection. Therefore, when the Girondin deputy, Bergoeing, reported on the meeting of the Evêché assembly, he was unaware of this second group acting for the assembly as a whole;[48] it would hardly have revealed its intentions in public.

Entry to the Evêché assembly was upon presentation of the card of a patriotic society. In addition to the five hundred or so persons present in the hall, another hundred sat in the galleries. Louis-Pierre Dufourny,[49] in the name of the Commission des Six formed on 27 or 28 May, proposed to send six commissioners to the Commune to agree on the election of a provisional commander of the National Guard. Without this first step, there was hardly any point proceeding further. On 27 or 28 May an unnamed woman spoke up on the corruption in the Convention (a remark obviously aimed at the Girondin leaders) and on the need to take measures to reform the state of things. She was the first, therefore, to be appointed to the Commission des Six, the delegates who were to visit the General Council.[50]

Dufourny imposed silence on the gathering and criticized several members for speaking and thereby revealing the measures that ought to be taken. He proposed that an address be drafted by the sections to the Convention demanding that Isnard be punished for his threat against Paris. This address was to serve the purpose of developing a common impulse for the movement. After a number of speeches the assembly was adjourned until the next morning, 30 May. Thus it appears that the insurrection was planned on the 29th. Dufourny was successful in silencing those who were about to reveal the secret plans of the sectional commissioners, and he made clear that they had no time to lose in long discussions. The Evêché's executive organ during this early stage was the Commission des Six, which immediately took steps to enlarge the movement and to rally all Paris to its support. Isnard's threats served as a focus for the movement, and once united against him it could easily be turned against the whole Gironde. Jaurès cites Auguste Blanqui, who studied the insurrection of 1793: "One does not create a movement; one derives it." In order to reassure property holders, section Cité took property under the safeguard of the sans-culottes, a move common to all sections and later to the Comité central révolutionnaire as well. Hassenfratz stated, "The first deliberation had for its object to calm the uneasiness of the property holders."[51] The stage was now set for the events that were to follow.

The assembly of delegates that had met on the afternoon of 29 May in the Club central of the Evêché was turned into a revolutionary organ the next day. Its sixty-six commissioners, representing thirty-three sections, had determined to resort to extraordinary measures in order to bring the political crisis to an end.[52] During the night and early morning of 30–31 May this revolutionary assembly declared Paris to be in insurrection against "the aristocratic and liberty-oppressive faction," the Girondins, and announced its own permanence.[53] Its first act was to elect a committee of nine members, the Comité des Neuf, which became the Comité des Dix when the president of section Cité, Claude-Emmanuel Dobsen, joined it upon his release from prison in the early morning hours of 31 May.[54]

On 29 May the General Council of the department of Paris had convoked an assembly of commissioners to meet two days later in the hall of the Jacobins. These commissioners represented, in addition to the authorities of the Paris department, the general councils of the districts of Saint-Denis and Bourg-de-l'Egalité, the General Council of the Paris Commune, and the Evêché assembly of the Paris sections.[55] This assembly of the department appointed eleven members to the Evêché's Comité des Neuf, and at about the same time the General Council of the Paris Commune added another four members.[56] Thus the original insurrectionary Committee of Nine had become enlarged to one with twenty-five members—ten from the Evêché assembly of the sections (including Dobsen), four from the Paris Commune, and eleven from the department of Paris. It was to have far-reaching consequences on the course of the insurrection. The name used by this enlarged committee as it took over control of the insurrection from the Comité des Neuf in the early hours of 31 May was the Comité central révolutionnaire.[57]

It should be noted that the commissioners who met in the hall of the Jacobins were sitting at the same time as the delegates of the sections meeting in the Evêché assembly. Once the fifteen members of the Jacobin assembly fused with the ten from the original Evêché, the formal name used by the insurrectionary committee was Comité central révolutionnaire, although variations of this title are frequently found.[58]

What makes for confusion is that the General Council of the Paris Commune continued to sit side by side with the Comité central révolutionnaire despite having been cashiered by that body. Although it had been removed from office by the Evêché assembly through its Comité central, it had been immediately reinstated. It now assumed the name Conseil général révolutionnaire for the duration of the insurrection.[59] Thus as the insurrection began two assemblies sat side by side. In the chamber called la Grande Salle, the voices of Hassenfratz, Varlet, Chabot, and Marat could be heard. In a neighboring hall the Comité des Neuf was about to declare itself in a state of permanence and of insurrection.[60] The Evêché committee organized itself into ten different departments: correspondence with the Convention's Committees of Public Safety and of General Security; interior police; public works; émigrés; legislation; armed forces; finance; ministerial correspondence; procès-verbaux; and correspondence with the interior. Exercising the powers embodied in these departments made the Evêché committee the real government of France. For a few days, it was just that.

The committee made clear, however, that it was subject to recall by the sections despite the fact that it had usurped the powers of the legally constituted authorities.[61] This admission that the sections were the ultimate source of its power did not prevent the Comité des Neuf from taking the initiative so necessary during the confusing first moments of the insurrection. Theoretically, even its members could be recalled by their individual sections, but in practice once the uprising was launched the enlarged committee of twenty-five members took control of the insurrection. Its personnel included a variety of militants ranging from sans-culottes to ex-noblemen. Despite their different social origins, all were united in the practical and immediate task before them. Only after the forced resignation or removal of the leading Girondins would the differences between the original Comité des Neuf and the enlarged Comité central révolutionnaire manifest themselves.

V

The Comité Central Révolutionnaire

> Nay a "Central Committee" of all the Forty-eight Sections
> looms huge and dubious: sitting dim in the Archévêché,
> sending Resolutions, receiving them: a Centre of the Sec-
> tions; in dread deliberation as to a New Tenth of August!
>
> Thomas Carlyle, *The French Revolution: A History*

WHO WERE the twenty-five members of the Comité central révolutionnaire that directed the insurrection?[1] At its head was Claude-Emmanuel
Dobsen, "l'homme du 31 mai," born on 23 December 1743 not far from
Soissons, the son of an iron merchant of Noyon. After studying law he
became an *avocat,* then moved from one judicial post to another. Although
he enjoyed good relations with many bourgeois and even noblemen, he
warmly defended the demands and interests of the rural proletariat as well
as those of the petty *vignerons.* In 1789 he was defeated in election for
deputy of his baillage, but the following year he was elected an officer in
the National Guard. Shortly thereafter he was appointed to the tribunal
of Epernay; he then became first judge in the court of the sixth arrondissement of Paris and was appointed its president on 2 March 1791. He
was active in the political life of his section, Cité, presiding over many of
its assemblies, and helped in overthrowing the monarchy. He seems to
have carried out his duties with moderation and calm. In December 1792
he ran against Chaumette but lost; he subsequently became a *commissaire
nationale* on 13 March 1793. His biographer calls him "le véritable directeur, le chef de cette insurrection du 31 mai."[2]

   Although he played a key role in the insurrection, was a witness in the
trial of the Girondins and defended Robespierre on 9 Thermidor, he not
only managed to survive but took the place of Dumas as president of the
court when the latter was guillotined. He managed to save many of those
compromised by the events of 9 Thermidor but after Carrier's execution
was dismissed from the court. Arrested on 2 April 1795, he remained in
prison until the amnesty of October 1795. Dobsen conspired with Babeuf

but escaped the latter's fate, and he helped found the republican Club du Manège. Under the consulate he was made *procureur-général* before the new court of Trèves. Together with Jean-Bon Saint-André, Dobsen founded a masonic lodge, Les Amis de l'Humanité, of which he became the *orateur*. In 1811 he was forced to retire at sixty-eight years of age.[3]

Jacques Marquet was born in 1764 at Montfort l'Amaury, the son of an *entrepreneur de batiments* of Montfort-le-Brutus. He was active in the political life of his section, Bonne-Nouvelle, and seems to have used the alias Charles for a time. Before the end of the monarchy Marquet installed himself in the home of Hébert, where he remained until 1 July 1793. A police record noted that he was tipsy ("en ribote") with a valet of Dumouriez's and was accused of striking a soldier on guard duty. Brought before a justice of the peace, Marquet pleaded that as commissioner of his section he should be freed. He was rescued by the intervention of Hébert and a municipal officer. On 31 May he was elected president of the Evêché committee, and although he played a lesser role than did Loys, Hassenfratz, or Marchand, he signed some of the important documents of the Comité central.[4]

He was arrested by the Committee of General Security shortly after the leading Hébertists had been seized but was released upon demonstrating that he had merely printed the *Père Duchesne* but had had nothing to do with its composition. On 7 September 1795 he requested the Committee of General Security to annul its original order of arrest, which it did a few days later.[5] Upon the execution of Hébert and his wife, Marquet adopted their daughter, then five years old.[6]

Jean-Michel Wendling, or Vendeling, of section Halle-au-Blé, was of Alsatian origin, a boot- and shoemaker by occupation, and a resident of France since 1772. He lodged on rue de Grenelle in 1778 and married Elisabeth Benoit-Weiland on 7 February 1786 in the parish of Saint-Germain-l'Auxerrois. A son, Charles, was born to the couple on 18 July 1790. Wendling was described as being five feet, one inch tall, with chestnut hair and eyebrows, a large countenance, an average brow, grey eyes, a long nose, an average mouth, and a round chin. He joined the National Guard and was made sergeant of his company on 5 July 1789 and then sergeant of battalion Saint-Honoré. He rose through all the grades until he became a captain in May 1791; at the same time he was elected to Halle-au-Blé's civil committee. From 3 April 1793 he served on its surveillance committee until his election by the Evêché assembly to the Comité des Neuf.[7]

Jean Varlet, whose name appears third on the list of committee members, was the well-known Enragé;[8] a fuller discussion of him appears in

Chapter VIII. Louis François Bonhommet was born in Etampes, the son of a merchant of children's toys. He was thirty-seven years old in 1793 and was an elector of his section, Bon-Conseil. Bonhommet had been a member of the Commune of 10 August and had been sent by the Committee of Public Safety on a mission to the Armée du Nord. He was arrested by the Committee of General Security and interrogated because of his relations with François Desfieux, the wine merchant from Bordeaux, and the foreigners Proly and Pereyra who perished with the Dantonists. Nothing suspicious was found in his papers, however, and he was released. He was interrogated again because of his relations with another member of the Comité central révolutionnaire, Loys of section Butte-des-Moulins.[9] Nothing further is known about him.

Jean-François Génois was twenty-five years old at the time of the insurrection and lived on Bourg-l'Abbé in section Amis-de-la-Patrie. Little information is available about him except that he signed the order to beat the general alarm and activate the armed force, probably on 1 June. The *procès-verbal* of the department's Comité de salut public speaks of him as being a "directeur de manufacture." He moved from the Evêché committee after its resignation to the committee of the Paris department and was expelled from his sectional assembly by virtue of a *mandat d'arrêt* issued against him after the Prairial insurrection in May 1795. Génois was released on 9 September 1795.[10]

Jean-Baptiste Loys, called Loys *cadet* to distinguish him from his two brothers, was born in Arles on 3 January 1757 and resided in section Butte-des-Moulins. He was first a gendarme, then became an *avocat* or an *homme de loi* and finally a merchant at the Palais Royal and at Fontainebleau. In 1790 he was a member of the departmental administration of Bouche-de-Rhône, becoming a *procureur-syndic* of the Marseilles district the following year. On 6 December 1791 Loys was elected to the General Council and became a municipal officer of Marseilles. On 5 October 1791 he had married Aimée-Nicole Jacquemin, the widow of an older man, whose business interests were being managed by the Girondin deputy Charles-Jean-Marie Barbaroux. It was with Barbaroux that Loys arrived in Paris on 31 January 1792 to denounce the counter-revolutionaries of his native town. Loys read the denunciation at the bar of the Convention on 20 February 1792 in an address prepared by the Commune of Marseilles.[11]

He allegedly joined in the denunciation of his two brothers: Pierre, mayor of Arles in 1792 and "chef des Chiffonistes" (royalists of Arles), who was expelled by the representative-on-mission, François-Trophime Rebecqui; and Henri, a former royal gendarme who fled Arles for Lyons, where he hid until he was caught and guillotined on 13 March 1794.[12]

Soon afterward he became ill and returned to the Midi; later his enemies accused him of having helped his brother Henri to flee. Loys was denounced in the patriotic club of rue Thubaneau (the local Jacobin club) on 23 March 1792 by a member, Ricord. He was excluded as a result but managed to justify his conduct and was readmitted on 24 October 1792.[13]

Returning to Paris in July 1792, he joined the Jacobin Club and took up residence on rue Française in section Bon-Conseil. On 18 July he became deputy of the Jacobins from Nîmes to the *société mère* of Paris, where he championed the views of his constituents: protection for the department of Gard; conservation of popular societies; and congratulations to Pétion for the events of 20 June 1792. He also denounced the directory of the department of Gard to its deputies, spoke frequently in the Jacobin Club, and became known gradually as a principled revolutionary. On 1 August 1792 he wrote to the popular society of Nîmes that in case Louis should flee again they must seize the local aristocrats and hold them as hostages.[14]

On 10 August 1792 Loys was wounded in the attack on the Tuileries. Five days later he moved in the Jacobins to have a court martial installed to judge supporters of Louis. In April 1793 he returned to the Midi and the following month was appointed to the Evêché committee, where he spoke primarily as a Jacobin and worked closely with his friends Clémence and Marchand. As president of the Comité central révolutionnaire, he signed its first petition to the Convention. He also drafted the second address to the Convention. On 1 June he was sent by the Comité central together with Dobsen, Laugier, and Dunouy to the Convention's Committee of Public Safety in order to deliberate on steps to save the country. On 2 June Loys offered himself, Laugier, and Dunouy as hostages. After the crisis had been resolved it was he who reported to the General Council and to the Jacobins on the work accomplished by the Comité central and on its relations with the Committee of Public Safety.[15]

Barbaroux described him after they had become enemies as an "exalté," a "fou," and "un ambitieux" who seriously had proposed a dictatorship, a protectorate, or a triumvirate. He allegedly told Barbaroux that the Roman system of senate and plebs "deliberating in the street and on the housetops . . . was the most philosophical of constitutions." Barbaroux also noted his warlike spirit and saw him above all as a zealous *clubiste* never repelled by violent measures and a determined partisan of popular intervention in the game of politics.[16]

The old accusation of aiding his brother's flight was launched against him in Paris during the Thermidorian reaction, but it proved unsuccessful as he possessed testimonials of patriotism signed by deputies of Bouche-de-Rhône—M. Bayle, F. Granet, B. Laurens, Pelissier, and Leblanc.[17]

On 23 September 1794 he was denounced by several deputies, among them Fréron, for allegedly proposing the massacre of prisoners in Marseilles. Jean-Bon Saint-André also reproached him for having betrayed his brother Pierre as an aristocrat. Loys denied that he had had anything to do with the troubles in Marseilles, pleading that he had already denounced Robespierre on 8 Thermidor and the next day had come to the Convention to pledge the support of his section. While in prison he had become gravely ill. Both his section and the Jacobins, of which he had become secretary, asked for his release, which was granted on 25 October 1794.[18]

Simon of Halle-au-Blé was a painter-gilder by occupation. He was arrested twice by the Thermidorians for having been a partisan of Robespierre and for having helped to organize the insurrection of 31 May. Boissy d'Anglas intervened on his behalf, however, and obtained his provisional freedom on 27 June 1795.[19] Mitois (or Mithois) of section Unité had edited the *Télégraphe politique ou Journal des fondateurs de la République,* which appeared from 4 March to 8 November 1794.[20] Jean Henri Hassenfratz (1757–1827) of section Faubourg-Montmartre, a mining engineer by profession and head of the Bureau à la Guerre, was widely known for his active role on 10 August. As a member of the General Council he did not play the important part assigned to him by the Comité central révolutionnaire, but during the *journée* of Prairial he was at the head of Faubourg Saint-Marceau. After the fall of Robespierre he was denounced for having arrested citizens of his section during the Terror, but he defended himself vigorously and insisted that he had arrested only counter-revolutionaries and other "scoundrels." On 24 May 1795 he was sent up before the revolutionary tribunal of Eure-et-Loir, then had to hide in Sédan until the amnesty of Brumaire, after which he became a professor at the School of Mines. He held this chair until the return of the Bourbons.[21]

Next on the list is Jean-Baptiste-Henri Tell Clémence of Bon-Conseil, a law student who came from a large family. His father, Louis-Joseph, was a beadle of Notre-Dame de Bonne-Nouvelle and boasted that he had prepared all eight of his children for life by educating them despite his modest fortune. When the Revolution broke out young Clémence seems to have retained the rebellious instincts of youth: he was picked up by the police of district Petit-Saint-Antoine, pretended that he was a gendarme, and cursed the guards on his release. On 14 July and 10 August he joined the insurgents. He was appointed a member of the Provisional Executive Council on 29 August 1792 on the recommendation of Merlin de Thionville and Roland. Together with Marchand, he arrived in the departments of l'Oise and Seine "to stifle the fanaticism and to propagate the spirit of republicanism." Destournelles, Ministre des contributions publiques, had amicable relations with him and offered him a position in his *bureau*, later nominating him for the Executive Council. Shortly thereafter Clémence became adjutant-major of the revolutionary army.[22]

Upon returning to Paris he took up residence on quai Pelletier as a *commis à la fabrication des assignats*. On 29 May 1793 his section elected him a kind of envoy extraordinary, giving him the authority to go anywhere and render aid to any citizen who needed it. A member of the Comité des Neuf, he signed many of its documents as secretary, and he was part of the delegation that congratulated the Convention on 3 June. He was denounced, arrested, and imprisoned on 2 August 1794. The Convention freed him after receiving many testimonials to his republicanism but had him rearrested after new denunciations. He was brought before the revolutionary tribunal of the department of Eure-et-Loir together with Marchand, Pache, Audoin, and Bouchotte and released by the Tribunal de la police correctionnelle on 25 May 1795.[23]

Jean-Honoré Dunouy of section Sans-Culottes was an engineer and a municipal officer. Nothing more is known about him.[24] Jean-Baptiste-Benoit Auvray of section Mont-Blanc was forty-four years old at the time of the insurrection. Before the Revolution he was a *huissier audiencier* of the bailliage de Montmartre and later of its commune, and after 10 August he served the revolutionary committee of section Mont-Blanc in the same capacity and commanded its armed force. He was arrested with Marchand as a terrorist and sent to Plessis prison after the events of 12 Germinal, remaining there as late as 13 September 1795.[25]

Jean-Michel Seguy of section Butte-des-Moulins was a physician by profession. As a member of the General Council of the Paris Commune he helped investigate the cause of Lazowski's death, thought widely to have been poisoned by counter-revolutionaries. After the insurrection of Prairial, a *mandat d'arrêt* was issued against him. Seguy surrendered to the authorities of Bourbe prison but protested vigorously that he had never been a partisan of tyranny. He pointed out that he had been opposed to conducting two prisoners past the crowds in the Tuileries during the insurrection against the king for fear of their being lynched. He resigned from the Commune on 28 August. Letters in his dossier attest to his humanity.[26]

Balthazar-Marie Loyer (Laugier) of section Fontaine-de-Grenelle was thirty years old and a justice of the peace. He had been a private secretary, a *secrétaire-greffier* of the commission of police, a member of the Commission des subsistances, and an agent of the Commission d'agriculture and des arts. His section displayed his name prominently as one of its leaders, and he was widely known for his Jacobinism. After the Prairial insurrection he was arrested, but representative Hugues-Guillaume-Bernard-Joseph Monmayou testified that Loyer had come to the help of the Convention of 9 Thermidor. The Commission d'agriculture and des arts also testified in his favor.[27] It can be assumed that he must have been freed shortly thereafter.

Pierre-Joseph Bezot, of canton d'Ivry, was forty-two years old, an entrepreneur by occupation, and an elector of Issy. He had been elected to the administration of the Paris department on 8 January 1793.[28] It is possible that he was appointed to the committee in order to give the cantons around Paris some representation.

Guillaume-Simon Marchand was born in Paris on 16 April 1768 and resided on rue du Faubourg-Montmartre in section Mont-Blanc. From October 1785 to January 1790 he served in the sixth Regiment of dragoons. Shortly thereafter he married Anne-Nicole Henry, then eighteen. Two days after the fall of the Bastille, Marchand organized a general assembly of soldiers in his regiment to take an oath of support for the laws of the nation. Soon he had an opportunity to defend the right to speak for the sergeant-major of his squadron. He composed a drama while stationed in Reims and played the role of Coligny in *Charles IX*. He was in Givet (Ardennes) at the time of Louis's flight to Varennes. Marchand called together the soldiers of the Régiment d'Alsace to counteract the maneuvers of the royalist officers and swore them to recognize only the authority of the National Assembly.[29]

Because he remained on close terms with the patriots of various regiments, Marchand presented the address of his town to remove the "tyrant-king." From September 1791 to September 1792 he was employed as a director in the Bureau des voitures. He was ill in a Paris hospital as the encounter with the king's soldiers began on 10 August but took part in the assault on the Tuileries with a crutch under one arm and a saber in the other hand, then returned to his bed. Before the attack on the palace he had covered the wall of his chamber with anti-royalist graffiti. He composed another play, *L'Homme vertueux*, which was performed in 1793. He possessed little property; the certificate of his section lists less than six hundred livres *rente*. For his patriotism and disinterested behavior a Thermidorean pamphleteer awarded him the title "the petit Robespierre" of his section. Marchand played one of the primary roles in the Evêché committee: it was he who arrested Mme. Roland on 1 June, and the following day he was spokesman for the delegation in the Convention that demanded the arrest of the Girondins. After that was done, Marchand was among those who felicitated the Convention on its action.[30]

Marchand became judge of the tribunal of the first arrondissement and was arrested together with Clémence for having organized the insurrection of 31 May. The Committee of Public Safety charged both men with supplying Paris and with other missions. On 2 August Marchand justified himself by saying that during the events of 9–10 Thermidor he had defended the Convention. He added that the person who had brought charges against him (a Sieur Gourreau) had attempted to seduce his wife and that of his colleague, Clémence, by offering a sum of six thousand livres to each. Having evidently failed, he induced the authorities to bring charges against the two before the revolutionary tribunal of Eure-et-Loir on 5 June 1796. Marchand was finally amnestied on 29 October 1795.[31]

Pierre-Joseph Crepin of Gravilliers, thirty years old, a carpenter or a carpenter-entrepreneur by trade, was an elector of his section and a substitute member of the directory of the Paris department. He was also president of his section and of its popular society, Vertbois. Crepin was arrested on 28 March 1795 but freed on 18 October. Shortly thereafter he became an administrator of municipality in the fourth arrondissement.[32]

Alexandre-Charles-Omer Rousselin, comte de Corbeau de Saint-Albin (1773–1847), of section Unité was only twenty years old in the spring of 1793. He had just completed his studies at the college of Harcourt when the Revolution burst upon him. Showing a rare perspicacity he allied himself with Danton, and at the young age of twenty he became first commissioner to Paré, minister of the interior. He was also employed by the Bureau des administrations civiles, polices, et tribunaux and was a national agent at the commune of Troyes, Danton's birthplace. Among his other duties was to edit the *Feuille du Salut public*, which was subsidized by the ministry of the interior. After the fall of Danton he was arrested in the Jacobin Club on a motion of Robespierre and Couthon as "executeur testamentaire de Danton" but was acquitted by the revolutionary tribunal on 20 July 1794, together with twenty-seven co-defendants. Two days later he was rearrested, and he remained in prison until after the fall of Robespierre. He was rearrested again on 11 December 1794 and remained in prison until 13 June 1795, when he went free for a few days, then was arrested yet again. He must have been released in the general amnesty of Brumaire, because by 1796 he was able to resume his career as a public functionary. During the Restoration he became a successful political journalist.[33] It seems that Rousselin's noble birth did not prevent him from earning the confidence of his fellow insurrectionists, and it could hardly have harmed his resumption of a normal career.

Louis-Henri-Scipion Grimoard-Beauvoir Duroure, known as Scipion of Marseilles, represented Faubourg-Montmartre at age thirty-two. A noble by birth, he repudiated his class and was active in the section. He had sired the infant of his English maid and enjoyed an income of twenty-five to thirty thousand livres a year. After Louis's overthrow, Duroure was elected to the Commune and then became a municipal officer. Because of his class background, he gave considerable sums as patriotic gifts in an attempt to show his devotion to the Revolution. In addition to his municipal role, he was active in the Société des Hommes révolutionnaires du 10 août. He was an intimate of Hébert, upon whose arrest he was sent to Saint-Lazare prison. Among the charges against him was that he rode in a carriage which he had often shared with Hébert and his wife. He protested that since he had to walk on crutches often (evidently he suffered from a disease or an injury that affected his legs), he was forced to use a carriage, which he was pleased to share with others. He then listed his patriotic gifts. Robert Lindet demanded his release on 28 September 1794, which was granted.[34]

Charles-Louis Perdry of section Butte-des-Moulins was an *homme de loi*, age thirty-five. He was secretary of the section's primary assembly, a Jacobin, and president since 13 February 1793 of the tribunal of the second arrondissement. From November 1792 until July 1793 he served in the General Council, and he was sent to Orléans as a commissioner for the Paris Commune. On 31 May 1793 he was co-opted by the departmental authorities to serve on the Comité central révolutionnaire. Exactly one year later he was arrested, probably because of opposition by his fellow judges. The civil committee of his section called him an "anarchist" because of his role in the insurrection of 31 May.[35] Although members of the tribunal and his section wrote on his behalf, he probably remained in prison until after the Vendémiaire coup.

Michel-François Caillieux of Amis-de-la-Patrie, thirty-two, had been a member of the Commune of 10 August and was sent as a commissioner to two battalions of the Eure department. He was then elected a municipal officer and to the administration of subsistences as well as to that of the police. Removed from his post by the Committee of Public Safety, he was arrested on 14 April 1794. On 19 May his sectional assembly and the revolutionary and civil committees gave strong testimony on his behalf and petitioned the Committees of Public Safety and of General Security to release him, but he still had not been freed as late as 11 August, two weeks after Robespierre's end.[36] It can be assumed, however, that he was released in the general amnesty of Brumaire.

Pierre Colonge of section Bonne-Nouvelle carried out many missions as an agent of the Committee of Public Safety in the department of Aisne and in the Palatinate. He was denounced as a terrorist by his section on

29 May 1795 but declared that he had been on the side of the Convention during the events of 9 Thermidor. Louis-Félix Roux, deputy from the department of Haute-Marne, testified to his patriotism, and he was released on 8 September 1795.[37]

Jean-Baptiste Baudrais of section 1792 was an *homme de lettres* forty-two years old. He was a member of the General Council, of the administration of police, and of the Jacobin Club, where he aroused the hostility of Robespierre. He was arrested on 29 March 1794 and imprisoned until the representative, François-Martin Poultier, wrote on his behalf. He was released on 24 August 1794, rearrested, released, and finally deported to Cayenne, Guiana, in 1802, where he remained until 1817. He died in Paris in 1832.[38]

The last name on the list of committee members is that of Denis-Etienne Laurent of section Marseille, age thirty-one, without a listed occupation. He was a member of the General Council and a municipal officer. Laurent was outlawed on 9 Thermidor and executed the following day.[39]

In addition to the twenty-five individuals on the Comité central révolutionnaire, a number of others had been proposed but for one reason or another rejected. Among these was André-Marie Gusman (or Guzman) (1753–1794), of section Piques. Born in Granada, Spain, he had established himself in Paris by 1773 and became a naturalized French citizen in 1781. He was given the soubriquet Don Tocsinos because it was he who had sounded the tocsin on 31 May. Gusman seems to have been an adventurer with plenty of money, either inherited or gained from operating gaming tables in the Palais Royal. Officially a banker, he passed himself off as a former colonel, a German baron, or the son of the Elector of Cologne. He was condemned with the Dantonists on 2 April 1794.[40]

François-Louis Fournerot, secretary of the Comité des Neuf in its early hours, was twenty-three years old and resided on rue Lenoir in section Quinze-Vingts. He was a worker-carpenter by occupation and a hunchback. Fournerot's physical description was as follows: he was four feet, six or seven inches in height, with chestnut hair and eyebrows, a high forehead, grey eyes, a large mouth, a short chin, and a pock-marked face. Despite his infirmity, Fournerot was a participant in all the *journées* of the Revolution: he fought at the Bastille; participated in the march on Versailles on 5–6 October; was present at the Champs de Mars in 1791; and was one of the petitioners on 20 June 1792. During the night of 9–10 August he presided over the assembly of his section, then became a member of the Paris Commune. When the "abortive insurrection" of 10 March 1793 broke out, Fournerot was one of the activists with Varlet. Among his early accomplishments was the founding of a popular society in Faubourg Saint-

Antoine. He was also in the delegation that congratulated the Convention on 3 June 1793.[41]

Arrested as an accomplice of Robespierre on 9 Thermidor, he remained in prison until released by the Committee of General Security on 9 January 1795. An attempt was made to rearrest him after 12 Germinal, but a great throng of people prevented the police from seizing him. Fournerot had a pregnant wife, a twelve-year-old girl in his care, a sick mother, and a grandfather who was seventy-five—which may account for the action of the crowd in his behalf. On 7 September 1795, the *mandat d'arrêt* issued against him was revoked.[42]

A third man proposed for the Comité was Pierre-Louis Moëssard of section Guillaume-Tell, residing on rue Montmartre, a wigmaker by profession and the father of three children. He was forty-seven years old at the time of the insurrection. Moëssard took up arms on 14 July 1789 and presided over the general assembly that day. Shortly thereafter he joined the National Guard. On 10 August he served on the insurrectionary commune. It is possible that he took part in the September massacres, though he denied this charge. On 4 September 1792 he was appointed as a commissioner to execute the decrees of the Commune and on 30 October served as vice president of the General Council. He was called to the Comité central révolutionnaire on 31 May but for an unknown reason failed to be appointed. Later he became a member of the Paris department's committee of surveillance. On 9 Thermidor he seems to have supported Hanriot. He was arrested three days later and sent to prison, where he remained until 10 December 1794. He was rearrested on 25 May 1795 and petitioned for release in Messidor and Fructidor.[43]

The fourth prospective member, mentioned by Clémence, was Bouin either of section Halles or of Marchés. He was an *ouvrier en bas* (a maker of stockings) and was known under the name of le Petit Père Gérard. Bouin was sent as an agent to the department of Aisne by the commission of subsistences and was a leading Jacobin of his section. He was the first to be nominated by the Jacobin Club to serve on the committee to prepare the insurrection of 31 May. Why he failed to serve on the Comité central révolutionnaire remains unknown. On 24 November 1794 he was deprived of his position as justice of the peace by the Comité de législation, and on 6 February 1795 he was arrested, to be freed when deputy Nicolas-Sylvestre Maure interceded on his behalf. Bouin proved that he had drafted an address urging all to rally around the Convention on 9 Thermidor. The section, still in the hands of reactionaries, demanded his arrest once again. It took the personal intervention of another deputy, Roux, to free him on 26 June 1795. Two weeks later he was arrested yet again and some

time later sent up before the officier de police de sûrêté of his arrondissement.[44] It can be assumed that he, too, was freed at the time of the
Vendémiaire coup.

A number of sectionnaires played important roles in the early hours of
the insurrection though they were not members of the Comité central
révolutionnaire or its predecessor, the Comité des Neuf. This could be
expected, of course, since the revolutionary atmosphere and the long
campaign against the Girondins encouraged committed revolutionaries to
come forward. One example of these unofficial participants is François
Richebraques of section Homme-Armé, a commissioner in the Bureau
des domaines, who signed the order at 2:00 A.M. to inspect the barriers
to see if they were guarded. What is known about him?

It seems that at midnight on 30–31 May he was sent by section Homme-
Armé to the Evêché assembly. The presiding officer, a man named Lavaux,
asked for nominations for president of the meeting. The men from Homme-
Armé already sitting in the Evêché nominated Richebraques because of
his fine (and stentorian?) voice, and he was elected. He remained in the
chair for two hours, and only then did he learn that the Evêché assembly
had been meeting for some days. Thus he sanctioned measures of which
he was completely ignorant. The only noteworthy thing about him seems
to be his proposal to ask section Cité if the Evêché assembly could use
its seal since it had none of its own. After his two hours of glory, he
returned to the shadows whence he had come.[45]

Garat was convinced that the real authors of the insurrection were the
men who met in secret in a café called Corazza. These were Gusman,
Desfieux, Proly, who was "a natural son of Kaunitz" and claimed to be a
friend of Robespierre's at this time, plus François Chabot and Collot
d'Herbois. The minister admitted that he had been ridiculed for this exposé and that when the tocsin was heard on 31 May, Lanjuinais said to
him in derision, "Well, Garat, it's the café Corazza!" What could he say
in reply, says Garat, since the revolutionaries were acting legally, and Lulier
never ceased protesting "piously" that this insurrection was "toute morale."[46] It is difficult to account for Garat's naiveté, despite his "caractère
doux," as attested by many of his contemporaries. A minister of interior
should be made of sterner stuff.

Of the eighteen members of the Comité whose ages are known, four
were in their twenties, ten in their thirties, three in their forties, and only
one, Dobsen, was as old as fifty. It can be assumed that were records of
birth available for the other seven they would be found not to have differed
from their colleagues. Clémence, for example, was a student of law, which
means that he was probably in his twenties. Wendling married in 1786,

so he must have been in his twenties in 1793. Tuetey remarks on the committee members' youth, which he thought accounted for their ardor.[47] Older men, after all, do not make revolutions.

More remarkable still is the social composition of the committee. Only three members can be termed sans-culottes: Marquet, a printer; Wendling, a shoemaker; and Simon, a painter-gilder. Crepin was a master carpenter who employed a minimum of two workers. It is important to note that two men were ex-nobles or strongly connected to the nobility: Rousselin and Scipion. Two, Loys and Bezot, were engaged in commerce; six were connected with the law: Dobsen, Clémence, Auvray, Loyer, Marchand, and Perdry. Five were in the liberal professions—Mitois, Hassenfratz, Dunouy, Seguy, and Baudrais—and public functionaries numbered six: Varlet, Bonhommet, Genois, Caillieux, Colonge, and Laurent. It is difficult to say what their original professions were. Varlet was a graduate of the college of Harcourt and had an independent income from his family. Laurent, who was executed with Robespierre, was a municipal officer, but his occupation before he assumed office is unknown. The same may be said of several others. Although Marchand is listed with men of law because he became a judge, this appointment occurred rather late in his career as a revolutionary.

It must be stressed that the vast majority of the committee was certainly not sans-culottiste. This fact may not be surprising, but what is curious is that so few master craftsmen appear among its members. The vast majority is middle class, using the term in its broad meaning. In light of the facts that the insurrection had the active support of the sans-culottes, that the exhortations of the Mountain and the Jacobin leaders were couched in terms to appeal to the sans-culottes, and furthermore that the sections took such an active role in launching the Evêché committee, it is strange indeed that the leaders did not come from among the artisans, craftsmen, journeymen, workers, or petty shopkeepers. One explanation may lie in the maneuver of the Jacobins and the departmental authorities to take control of the uprising by co-opting the eleven men to the original ten.

The members of the Comité central represented fifteen different sections and one canton. Of these, only Bon-Conseil had three commissioners; seven other sections each had two, and the remaining seven had one apiece. Thus thirty-three sections had no commissioners in the Committee, but many were of course represented in the Evêché assembly. One more characteristic of the committee is worthy of note. It might be assumed that in the contest between the Commune and the Convention of 9 Thermidor, the insurrectionists of 31 May would have supported the commune against the revolutionary government. But this was not the case. Only one, the young Laurent, had committed himself to Robespierre and the Commune (a tamed body, it should be added, after the execution of the Hébertists). Almost all the rest had rallied around the Convention. Was this mere prudence, a shrewd assessment of the strengths of the two forces, or were there supporters of Hébert among them who saw a chance of avenging the death of their leader? Whatever the reason, the members' allegiance did not prevent their arrest and imprisonment after the Germinal and Prairial uprisings. The Thermidorians in the sections made no distinction between the "terrorists" of Robespierre's day and the "terrorists" who supported the hunger revolts of 1795. It was the royalist putsch that finally released them from prison.

VI

The Insurrection Begun

That execrable 31 May, which degrades forever the national
representation.

Bertrand Barère, *Mémoires*

Legislators, The men of fourteenth July, of 10 August and
of 31 May are within your midst. Delegates of the people
who have never betrayed its cause, they have come to help
you against the conspirators. Liberty triumphs once again.

Orator of the delegation of the sections in the Convention

THE TOCSIN began to ring at about 3:30 on the morning of 31 May, the
first overt act of the insurrection.[1] The order to sound the alarm was given
by Jean Varlet, acting as provisional president of the Comité des Neuf.[2]
This meant that the bells of Notre Dame were rung on the order of the
insurrectionary committee of the Evêché *before* it had removed (and reinstated) the General Council of the Commune. This explains the confusion
that followed: it seems that the General Council had not been consulted
as to the precise moment when the insurrection was to begin. The Commune sent out couriers to urge citizens to remain calm; only at 5:00 A.M.
did it send commissioners to ask Hanriot by whose order the alarm was
being sounded. Because he could not be found the Council decided to
beat the *rappel* calling the men of the sections to report with arms in hand
to their respective posts. There must have been much confusion: while
the tocsin was summoning all to insurrection, the Commune was still
urging people to remain calm.[3]

Dobsen and his fellow commissioners left the Evêché for the Hôtel de
Ville at about 6:30 A.M. to annul the powers of the legal authorities and
to substitute those of the revolutionary organ created by the thirty-three
sections.[4] In a resolution also signed by Varlet as *président provisoire* and
by Fournerot as secretary, the Comité des Dix (the Comité des Neuf plus
Dobsen) appointed a commission to suspend the municipal authorities of

Suspension of the municipal authorities, signed by Varlet

Paris. The resolution read, "Resolved by the Revolutionary Committee of Ten, sitting in the Evêché, deliberating on measures of public safety, instructing citizens Sergent, Vernon, Vaillant, Violet and 2 others, to suspend the Mayor, the municipal officers and the General Council of the Commune of the city of Paris. 31 May 1793."[5] The resolution suspending the powers of the mayor and municipal authorities announced, "The year

2d of the French Republic, this 30 May./ In the name of the sovereign people, The mayor of Paris is provisionally suspended, the General Council of the Commune, the municipal body, the administrators equally and shall be reelected by the same sovereign people./ Done and decreed at the Comité des Neuf."[6] The reappointment of the suspended officials by the same revolutionary authority that had removed them was embodied not only in the above resolution but in another to this effect: "Paris, this 30 May, the year 2d of the Republic./ Maison Commune, In the name of the sovereign people, the Comité des Neuf reintegrates provisionally the General Council of the Commune in the plenitude of its functions. Done and decreed by the Comité des Neuf."[7]

The decision to remove the local authorities and to reinstate them after they took the oath of loyalty to "the sovereign people" as embodied in the commissioners of the Evêché assembly must have been made in the last hours of 30 May, before the eight or nine delegates had arrived in the Hôtel de Ville shortly after the sounding of the tocsin and before the co-option of Dobsen to the Comité des Neuf. The smoothness of the ceremony that cashiered and reappointed the municipal authorities leaves little doubt that the procedure was discussed in advance.[8]

Just what took place in the Hôtel de Ville as these proceedings went on? According to an observer, an officer of the National Guard by the name of Bachelard, Pache was resting ("stretched out" on the bench), waiting for things to happen. The tocsin was sounded from the Hôtel de Ville, and it seems that an officer was called to stop the ringing but then was informed that the new commander, Hanriot, had countermanded the previous order not to sound the tocsin. Shortly thereafter the sound of drums calling the general alarm was heard. Then a group of drummers entered the hall, causing a great tumult. At about 6:00 or 6:30 A.M. a crowd of excited onlookers invaded the corridors and stairs of the Mairie, led by eight or nine individuals. (These were the commissioners appointed by the Comité des Dix to remove and then reinstate the municipal authorities). The leader of the group was dressed in an odd and dirty outfit; Sainte-Claire Deville thinks it could have been Dobsen. Although Bachelard does not give the names of the commissioners there is little doubt that Varlet was in the delegation. Dobsen took the chair in the Grande Salle and went through the ceremony of suspending and restoring the powers of the municipal authorities.[9]

The same procedure and resolutions were adopted for dealing with the authorities of the department of Paris. The first resolution suspended the Directory and the General Council of the department; the second directed citizen Wendling, member of the Comité des Neuf, to proceed to the departmental authorities and carry out the first resolution. The third motion provisionally reestablished the suspended departmental officials in their duties. They were to take an oath to confine themselves to fulfilling exactly the functions assigned them and to communicate with the Comité des Neuf. All three documents were also signed by Varlet and Fournerot.[10]

The General Council of the Paris Commune issued a proclamation to the sections of the capital: "Open your eyes; great dangers surround you. Some citizens . . . want a new insurrection . . . The General Council has just declared itself in permanence; do the same, correspond with it, and let the greatest surveillance keep in check the enemies who are in your midst."[11] This warning was issued at 4:30 in the morning, that is, at least two hours before Dobsen and members of the Comité des Neuf left the Evêché assembly for the Hôtel de Ville. Who were these "enemies in your midst" to which the Council referred? It is not clear whether they were the moderates or the "citizens" demanding another insurrection, that is, members of the Evêché assembly and its Comité des Neuf. In either case, it appears that not only was there confusion in the early hours of the insurrection but also mistrust of, if not active opposition to, the leaders of the revolt. Only after the Comité des Neuf took decisive steps and it became evident to most leaders of the Paris Commune that the Evêché committee had overwhelming support did they drop their opposition to the insurrection.

Once this was done, however, the Commune took prompt steps to disarm suspects and arm "patriots," imposed a levy on the rich, and drafted a petition to the Convention to expel "the traitors" from its midst. It also launched domiciliary visits for suspected counter-revolutionaries, closed the barriers around Paris, and threatened deputies with the revolutionary tribunal if they excited the departments against the capital. In addition, the Commune voted the forty-sous subsidy for the poorer sectionnaires, ordered the arrest of Roland and his wife, and authorized the opening of all suspicious mail.[12] In order to follow what was taking place in the Convention, it ordered police commissioners to report every half hour to the Commune. It was relieved to learn shortly after taking these actions that the hated Commission des Douze had been cashiered and the papers of its individual members sealed.[13]

Did the General Council of the Paris Commune passively accept its demission? Were there no protests that the commissioners of the Evêché were acting illegally? Immediately after the resolution of the Comité des Neuf became known, the General Council began a discussion of its suspension. Destournelles, the vice-president, remarked that if the confidence of citizens in the Council ended its authority must also terminate. All power rested in the people, he asserted. They had the right to remove their authorities, but this must be done by a real majority, "legally obtained." He then asked to see the Committee's mandate, declaring that members of the Council were ready to die at their post if that mandate were of a minority only. Having verified the "unlimited powers" given to the commissioners of the thirty-three sections, the Council proceeded to surrender its powers to "the sovereign people." This action was followed immediately by "the reintegration of its functions."[14]

Was this a mere "comedy," as Mortimer-Ternaux wrote?[15] Jaurès was convinced that it was essential for the members of the General Council to maintain their dignity and just as important for the Evêché committee to insure the cooperation of the municipal authorities. Reinstalling them in their functions prevented a rupture and assured continuity of office; thus the rivalries and quarrels that had beset the Commune of 10 August 1792 were avoided. Moreover, this action prevented the dictatorship of a sect, something that would have led the Convention to distrust the Parisian authorities. The fusion of department and Commune also allowed public energies to evolve and the popularity of the reestablished officials to develop.[16] When the mayor and delegates of the General Council gave their report to the Convention they were received favorably, and their patriotism, like that of the city of Paris, was highly praised.[17] This rather optimistic view of the relationship between the Convention and the Commune, which Jaurès holds, must be modified in light of the events of 2 June, discussed below. The Convention could not help but feel itself threatened by the revolutionary power created by the sections and the Paris Commune.

The General Council refused to endorse the insurrection when it was first launched by the Comité des Neuf. Even when the delegates from the Evêché assembly informed the Commune of the uprising, the Commune hesitated because it could not be certain that these delegates really had the sections behind them. The General Council decided, therefore, "to resume the business of the meeting awaiting the wishes of the sections."[18] Equally revealing is the mayor's retort to section Luxembourg's report that it had closed the barriers and had risen in "a sacred insurrection": it could not be "sacred" since it was "partial," not having been approved by the General Council.[19]

How much active opposition there was it is difficult to say. The General Council's communication reflects this uncertainty to some degree, although the term "enemies in your midst" is vague enough so that it could cover its retreat. The Commune did accuse the Evêché committee of acting too hastily in sounding the alarm; it probably wanted to be certain that the committee indeed had the support of the sections as it claimed.[20] Moreover, Mayor Pache was concerned that the Comité des Neuf would clash with departmental authorities, thus endangering the insurrection. He reminded the General Council that the delegates of the sections must unite with the Jacobins. "Toute autre mesure est funeste," he proclaimed. More important, he admitted to the Council that he had been unable to persuade the Evêché assembly to rescind its order to launch the insurrection by firing the alarm cannon.[21] The tone of his remarks leaves little doubt that many if not a majority in the Council must have shared his sentiments on what appeared to be a precipitous decision to launch the uprising. At the same time, he must have seen the need for the insurrection and could hardly have endangered the action taken by the Comité des Neuf. Only the Girondins would have benefited by such a split.[22]

Pache ordered the guarding of prisoners not only because he wanted to avoid another September massacre but, equally important, because they were needed as hostages against the menace of the departments. When the General Council learned of Pache's order forbidding the alarm, Destournelles replied that when it was given the revolutionary authority had not yet been established, that is, the Evêché committee had not yet asserted its powers. Immediately thereafter the Comité central révolutionnaire gave a new order to sound the cannon of alarm.[23] Again, it must be pointed out that the order to fire was given not by the General Council but by the Comité des Neuf, although by this time the Commune had accepted the leadership of the Evêché assembly—not without some hesitation and doubt.

As might be expected, there was also uncertainty and opposition to the insurrection within the General Council. Chaumette was still warning his colleagues to "join prudence with the grandeur of measures." This evidently irritated some of the more impatient and determined councillors. One of them rose up and demanded that the Council stop wasting time listening to long-winded speeches and instead take prompt, practical measures to assure the success of the uprising. Then, throwing all caution aside, he accused the *procureur* of weakness and offered to lead the Commune in the necessary revolutionary operations. He was quickly silenced, but Hébert too cautioned delay.[24]

This was not the end of the affair, however. Another spokesman went further than his predecessor and offered to lead an armed force against the Convention itself. He was quickly called before the officers of the Commune and interrogated, but he was dismissed as being "too ignorant" for the Council to bother with. The mayor warned, meanwhile, that such proposals would unleash a civil war. When another member of the Council demanded the arrest of those (Girondin) deputies who had been censured by public opinion—the whole point of the insurrection, after all—Chaumette rose in indignation and with great vehemence denounced this proposal.[25] It seems that the *procureur* had few supporters in the General Council even though it was obviously divided.[26] Yet when someone of Chaumette's persuasion proposed that the Council resolve not to violate the Convention, the members refused to support this suggestion. It was clear that the Commune was still vacillating, awaiting decisive action from another body.[27]

Chaumette was a strong opponent of the insurrection. During the trial of the Hébertists in Germinal, Year II, Marchand, a member of the Comité des Neuf, made this observation to the public accuser before the revolutionary tribunal: "That as a member of the Comité central révolutionnaire on 31 May, I witnessed Chaumette bend all his efforts to shackle this glorious revolution, to denounce at every turn all measures that public safety demanded, shout, cry, tear his hair, and make the most violent efforts to convince [us] that the Comité central was effecting the counterrevolution. His conduct was such that one could have taken him for a madman."[28]

Thus the split within the General Council paralleled the differences between that body and the Comité des Neuf. Equally important was the opposition of the more conservative sections to the insurrection. Although the "patriots" were in control of many sections, the Girondins had supporters in several of them. The general confusion caused by the early lack of coordination between the Evêché committee and the Paris Commune undermined the willingness or ability of a number of these sections to take revolutionary measures. The commander of the forces in section Pont-Neuf, in which the alarm cannon was stationed, refused to honor Hanriot's early order to fire the cannon. The law provided the death penalty for firing the cannon without the express approval of the Convention. The commissioners of the Hôtel de Ville tried to persuade the commander and his soldiers that in time of revolution they ought not to expect strict formalities, but they were unsuccessful and had to return to the Mairie frustrated.[29]

The Mountain was in a quandary: if it disavowed Hanriot it would be playing into the hands of the Gironde. If it embraced him, however, it might encourage radicals such as Varlet and like thinkers in the Comité des Neuf. Furthermore, there was always the danger of precipitating a civil war with the departments. The General Council faced the same dilemma. Nevertheless, after hearing what had taken place it immediately ordered (or more likely assented to) the Evêché committee's executing the order to sound the cannon.[30]

Section Molière et la Fontaine dispatched three commissioners to the Commune to ask if the armed force at the Convention had been sent there by the General Council, and if so, why the section had not been notified. Furthermore, it demanded to know how Hanriot had been elected, why the alarm was being sounded, and by whose orders the barriers were closed.[31] The commissioners brought back the weak reply that "c'était le peuple." The sectional assembly resolved that only its own revolutionary committee had the right to arrest a resident of the section and that it would not honor any warrant of arrest obtained "illegally." Furthermore, when it was reported that section Butte-des-Moulins had fraternized with Faubourg Saint-Antoine and that Molière et la Fontaine ought to do the same, the assembly ruled to ignore the suggestion.[32]

The section was not alone in opposing the insurrection. Sections Marais, Butte-des-Moulins, Observatoire, Fraternité, 1792, Lombards, Invalides, and Finistère refused to join the insurgents, and a member of the General Council was badly received in section Beaurepaire. Section Marais (Homme-Armé) wanted to know the motives for the insurrection, for the election of the revolutionary committee of the Evêché, and for the appointment of the provisional commander, Hanriot. A member of the Homme-Armé delegation told the General Council that his section was divided, which was why the orders of the day contradicted each other. This had happened because they were the result of the vote taken by those who happened to be present. The same thing had occurred in section Contrat-Social.[33] Section Finistère even denounced to the Convention the formation of the Comité central révolutionnaire and demanded the arrest of its members. It also had the courage to inform the General Council of that resolution. As might be expected, the Commune reacted with indignation.[34] Finistère's spokesman then pointed out that his section was in complete ignorance of what was taking place and had received contradictory orders. He assured the Council that once the situation was clarified the section would join the others. The General Council then sent Jacques Roux and Dangé to brief the section. When the commissioners returned they reported that "the republican spirit" was still not dominant in the section and the "patriots" were not in control. Only later did Finistère send two delegates to the Council to report that the "aristocrats" of the section had been defeated.[35]

Section Montreuil also had an opposition party. Michelet claims that the section showed its antagonism to the insurrection by arguing that although the powers of the commissioners sitting in the Evêché were undefined, they were not unlimited. The same kind of clash seems to have occurred in section Popincourt. Both of these sections were in Faubourg Saint-Antoine, of course, and were influenced by a member of the revolutionary tribunal, Herman of Arras, who was an intimate of Robespierre. It seems that even in this radical *faubourg* there was chaos and indecision.[36] To add to the confusion, many sections hesitated between accepting the summonses of the Jacobin assembly, where the authorities of the department were gathered, and adopting those of the Evêché assembly, which had "only a furtive and indirect support" of the Paris Commune. The sections were therefore asked to send commissioners to each of the two assemblies.[37]

Even Unité experienced some trouble, as it refused to recognize the provisional commander. A spokesman claimed, however, that this was the result of opposition by a tiny number of merchants and shopkeepers in the section.[38] "Tiny number" or not, they were able for a time to exert enough influence to impede the section's majority. A conflict within the assembly of section Lombards is reflected in the fact that it had to ask the General Council if it should sound the general alarm and was told to do so without delay. Later the section's delegates announced the dismissal of their former revolutionary committee and the election of a new one, thus assuring the insurrectionists' control of the section.[39] Section Marais also demanded to know the reasons for sounding the alarm cannon. It was by this time 3:00 P.M., which "astounded" the Council. A member of the section revealed that its assembly had been divided for some time, which was chiefly the fault of the same citizens who had put the question to the General Council.[40] As the insurrection was launched, divisions persisted in the section. In section Droits-de-l'Homme, the revolutionary committee arrested several suspects, among them André Deon, who demanded to see the written orders from the man who was sounding the alarm. A domestic who had failed to report to his post when the tocsin sounded was also arrested.[41]

Rumors had convinced the militants of Faubourg Saint-Antoine that the armed force of section Butte-des-Moulins, which had occupied the gardens of the Palais Royal, was displaying the white cockade, symbol of reaction. Mobilizing their own armed forces, the *faubouriens* of Saint-Antoine began a march on the well-known conservative section. Just when a confrontation appeared to be inevitable, the officers of the *faubourg*'s militia were persuaded to see for themselves how false the rumors were. When they saw the national colors floating above the section's armed men, they embraced their antagonists, and the two groups fraternized in a spirit of reconciliation. The danger of a civil conflict was thus avoided.[42]

It is possible, of course, that the rumors of an "aristocratic" reaction in section Butte-des-Moulins were planted or encouraged by the Commune to rouse a revolutionary spirit among the sections.[43] Louvet accused the Jacobins of wanting to disarm the section's military force, whose existence had disquieted them for a long time because of the moderate position of Butte-des-Moulins.[44] In any case, as the *Chronique du Mois* wrote, "les aristocrates et les anarchistes" had embraced. This was the Girondin formula of the *juste milieu*, wrote Jaurès.[45]

Tensions were heightened still further when the sections' delegates to the Convention reported their cold reception. The spokesman was convinced, he said, that the majority of the Convention was incapable of saving the country and that the people had to rely on themselves. It was then that the dispute broke out between those in the Council who favored bolder measures and others, like Chaumette and Hébert, who condemned their "impetuosity." Vergniaud's motion that the sections of Paris had "merited well of the country" only confused matters; and although the Mountain sent its fraternal greetings, it warned that the right wing of the Convention was ready to call on the departments for help.[46]

Despite these conflicts and uncertainties, the Comité central révolutionnaire and the Conseil général révolutionnaire took immediate steps to guarantee the success of the insurrection. François Hanriot was appointed commander of the armed forces by the Comité des Neuf and was ordered to seize the Arsenal and the artillery park in the early morning of 31 May.[47] His role was to prove decisive in two areas: protecting the Convention from those who, like Jean Varlet, were ready to dissolve it and substitute direct democracy for the parliamentary system; and surrounding the legislative body with armed men in order to bring pressure upon it to surrender the proscribed deputies. At the same time, the revolutionary committees were urged to arrest suspects in their respective sections, to be vigilant against plots, to sound the general alarm, and to place their armed forces in a state of readiness for combat.[48]

The first order of business was apparently to draft a list of thirty deputies to be arrested.[49] The insurrectionary committee also decreed that the workingmen under arms would be paid forty sous per day. Twenty-four thousand men were to be armed, and they would be remunerated for the time lost from work by the proceeds of a thirty-million livre tax on the wealthier citizens. Meanwhile, the revolutionary committees were asked to draft a list of patriots under arms.[50] After the removal of the Girondin deputies, the Convention provided the necessary funds. In addition to these measures, the Comité central took control of the post office, ordering its commissioners to open letters addressed to suspects or mailed by the Girondin deputies under attack and imposing censorship on outgoing mail. Among the postal employees it relied on was the Enragé Théophile Leclerc.[51]

That the newly appointed commissioners worked diligently is apparent in their communication asking the Conseil général révolutionnaire for relief as they had not budged since the previous evening and were "dying of hunger."[52] The commission had stayed up all night sorting mail and had set aside letters considered suspect, such as those of Buzot and others. Before opening them, however, the commissioners asked for specific orders to do so.[53]

Although the Evêché assembly was the parent body of the sections in revolution, it was explicitly stated that the sectional assemblies could recall or reelect their commissioners at their pleasure. These commissioners were to be superior to the regularly elected constitutional authorities. The Comité central was to communicate its decisions to the regularly constituted bodies before putting them into practice, however, and it was to submit a report to the assembled commissioners every month. The Committee stated specifically, "This Commission shall always be subordinated to the sections from which it emanates." Finally, it provided that half of its members would be in session at all times and that two of them would be available for business throughout the night.[54]

The Comité central révolutionnaire declared to the Convention that a great plot against liberty and equality had been uncovered by the general assembly of the forty-eight sections (the Evêché assembly). Paris had risen for the third time to foil the counter-revolutionaries. The committee urged the legislators to remain calm because "the republican sans-culottes" had taken all property under their protection, and it announced that the commissioners of the forty-eight sections had decided to allocate forty sous per day to the workingmen who could not otherwise afford to sacrifice their time.[55] This made it clear that the Comité central révolutionnaire spoke for the sections in revolt. All real power was in its hands, not in those of the General Council of the Commune or of any other constitutional authority. All measures of security were under its control.[56]

While taking these strong measures, the Committee exerted a moderating influence by opposing the forcible seizure of deputies proposed for the purge. It was informed every half hour what was transpiring in the Convention and stood ready to render aid to that body.[57] Meanwhile, the sections were actively carrying out a variety of revolutionary measures.

Observatoire learned of the Evêché's decree to guard the barriers of Orléans and Saint-Jacques shortly after hearing the alarm at 3:30 A.M.[58] At
6:00 A.M. section Unité proclaimed that the tocsin was "la voix du peuple
en courroux" (in wrath) as it assembled under arms and sent off two
commissioners with supreme powers to the Evêché assembly. In section
Réunion the assembly took steps against a hawker who was crying out
that a decree had been passed condemning to death those responsible for
sounding the alarm; there was not one word of proof for this claim in the
journals he was peddling. The assembly of Amis-de-la-Patrie proclaimed
that the commissioners of "forty-five sections" had met to resist the oppression of a part of the Convention, which had created the need for "une
révolution salutaire," and asked that its guards disarm all who resisted the
will of the people.[59]

What was the reaction of some of the deputies who were to be proscribed? During the night of 30 May Louvet, Buzot, Barbaroux, Guadet,
Bergoeing, and Rabaut-Saint-Etienne went to a secluded room, evidently
prepared in advance, to await events. They heard the tocsin ring at 3:00
A.M. and came down into the street at about 6:00, well armed. On 31
May they had dinner together; at this meal Louvet insisted that only an
uprising of the departments could save France, that it would be foolish to
return to the Convention, where they would be only hostages of the
Mountain, and that they must depart one after another for Bordeaux or
Calvados to organize the departments.[60] History will note, wrote Louvet,
that the "comité révolutionnaire" of the Commune (he means the Comité
central révolutionnaire) was almost entirely made up of foreigners like
the Spaniard Gusman, the Swiss Pache, the Italian Dufourny, and Marat,
who was from Neufchâtel.[61]

While the insurrection was developing in the Evêché, the Commune,
the clubs, and the street, the Convention witnessed a sharp division between the Montagnards and the Girondins. Some one hundred deputies
must have been in the hall when Mallarmé took the chair as they heard
the tocsin ring at about 6:00 A.M. Demands for the suppression of the
Commission des Douze made by Couthon, Augustin Robespierre, Thuriot, Danton, Cambon, and Garat were placed on the immediate agenda
by spokesmen of the municipal authorities and the mayor. Meanwhile,
the Girondins—Valazé, Vergniaud, and Guadet—supported by delegates
from section Molière et la Fontaine, continued to attack Hanriot and the
"factionalists" in the Convention. The need for the Commission, they
insisted, was greater than ever. When Guadet asked oratorically if at such
a time an insurrection was necessary, he was answered by a universal shout
from the galleries, a loud "oui!" Interruptions and shouts punctuated the

proceedings throughout this session. While the Girondins insisted that the Convention was not free, the Montagnards contended that there was no insurrection, that whatever trouble was apparent was due solely to the reestablishment of the hated Commission.[62]

One question must be posed: Why did Vergniaud move that the sections of Paris had "merited well of the country"? After all, most of them were bitterly opposed to all that he and his colleagues represented. It is possible, of course, that like others on that day, Vergniaud was confused and unsure of just what was taking place. Again, he may have mistaken the support given by such sections as Molière et la Fontaine as indicating a new trend in favor of the Girondins.[63] (The outcome of the clash between section Butte-des-Moulins and Faubourg Saint-Antoine had not yet become known to the Conventionnels.) When he made an effort to walk out of the Convention only to return (Jaurès calls this "la fausse sortie de Vergniaud"), he may have been seeking support from the sections by appealing to their sympathy or sense of fairness. Aulard thought Vergniaud was appealing from the Commune to Paris proper.[64] In any case, there was little he could do.

When members of the Left, on the invitation of Levasseur, joined their colleagues of the Right while petitioners from the municipal authorities and their supporters occupied the benches left vacant by the Montagnards and their sympathizers, the deputies and the people became so entangled (physically and politically) that even if the Girondins had wanted to follow Vergniaud they could not have done so.[65] Nevertheless, many Jacobins realized the danger in Vergniaud's move, since the mass of sans-culottes was not free of illusions. On the other hand, others immediately saw through this maneuver. A citizen Mittié declared in the Jacobins, "I myself regard [it] as a way of thanking the aristocrats for having prevented the patriots from giving to the insurrection the character that it ought to have had."[66]

While this was going on, a new delegation of commissioners from the forty-eight sections presented itself at the bar of the Convention in the name of the people of Paris. Speaking as those who had risen against tyranny on 14 July, 10 August, and 31 May, they presented seven demands: the formation of a paid revolutionary army; a decree of accusation against the twenty-two Girondin deputies and the Commission des Douze; a price ceiling on bread; the establishment of arm manufactures; the dispatch of commissioners to Marseilles; the arrest of Clavière and Lebrun; and the renewal of the administration in the post office. Although this petition was signed by Dorat-Cubière as secretary-registrar of the Commune, it too had emanated from the pen of Loys; his original address, however, was much more extensive than the one presented to the Convention. It began, "Le peuple de Paris levé en masse," and continued, "The time for moderation has passed, that of the sovereign justice of the people has begun." It stressed certain economic demands in favor of the sans-culottes and asked the Convention to occupy itself with problems of the poor, the old, the weak, and the wounded. Loys demanded workshops *(ateliers)* to assure work to the unemployed and a subsidy for the dependents of soldiers at the front. Finally, he asked for a purge of the institutions and government committees.[67]

This program obviously went much further than the removal of the Girondin deputies. A number of the demands were not to be granted by the Convention until after the demonstration of 4–5 September 1793, and the general *maximum* was not enacted into law until 29 September. The expulsion of some two dozen deputies was hardly worth such an effort. It is no wonder that many members of the Evêché assembly were disappointed by their own success. Their goals, expressed in Loys's address, went far beyond those to which the Montagnards and the Jacobins aspired.

Other petitions followed, among them a powerful address delivered by Louis-Marie Lulier (or Lhullier), the *procureur-général-syndic* of the Paris department. Demanding a bill of impeachment against the Commission des Douze and defending Paris against her accusers, he spoke of a "mouvement extraordinaire" in Paris that ought to be considered "une insurrection morale."[68] Lulier (1746–1794) was a bachelor of law and had a distinguished revolutionary career: he was a representative to the Commune from district Saint-Jacques-l'Hôpital in 1789; a member of the Commune of 10 August, over which he presided for some days; was elected a substitute to the Convention; and finally became *procureur-général-syndic* of the department. He was arrested as an Hébertist and committed suicide in prison before the trial of his colleagues.[69]

After his oration delegates of the department, followed by a crowd, mixed fraternally with deputies of the Left. Then Robespierre, speaking in support of Lulier's demands, asked not only for the suppression of the Commission but for the arrest of its members as well.[70] In addition, he strongly opposed disarming the people and giving the Convention control of the armed forces, as had been proposed by various Girondins. It would be only in the hands of traitors, he declared. Vergniaud shouted, "Concluez-donc," and Robespierre replied, "Yes, I shall conclude, and against you."[71] When the debate was over, Barère's motion to suppress the Commission des Douze was adopted.[72]

With the suppression of the Commission des Douze it appeared that the main goal of the insurrectionists had been achieved. But was this true?

When the alarms and excursions of the day had come to an end, the real goal of the revolution—to purge the Convention—had not been accomplished. Billaud-Varennes stated bluntly in the Jacobin Club that the suppression of the Commission was not enough; the country had not been saved. Not only must a decree of accusation be passed against the Girondin ministers, he insisted, but the right wing of the Convention had to be destroyed. Until this was done, the insurrection had to continue. Furthermore, he had heard a Montagnard [Marat] say that the country needed a dictator, something he vehemently opposed.[73]

Marat explained his proposal to the Jacobins the next day, 1 June, not by letter but in person. He termed the accusation against him a calumny. A delegation of several sections came to him for advice as to what measures to take, and he replied that it was impossible to save the people without a "chef" who would direct their action. When they asked him if he was suggesting a "chef," he replied in astonishment: "Non . . . je demande un guide et non pas un maître, et c'est bien différent."[74] It seems to have been his use of the word "chef" instead of "guide" that caused the confusion among his followers. There is no indication that he had anything more sinister in mind—though it should be noted that in time of uncertainty and frustration, a "guide" can turn into a master.

In commenting on the events of 31 May, Marat remarked that despite the beating of the general alarm and the great activity that seemed to have taken place, nothing had really happened; the storm just passed. True, the Commission des Douze had been quashed, but its members were as free as before. In fact, Valazé had demanded that Hanriot be punished for having sounded the alarm.[75]

The potential for decisive action remained, of course, but the insurrection thus far had been blunted or turned aside. No one expressed this disappointment more forcefully than did Robespierre's own section, Piques, which

> proposed consequently to decree that the Commission révolutionnaire [Comité central révolutionnaire] and the General Council of the Commune [Conseil général révolutionnaire] are unworthy of the confidence of the section. If, within twenty-four hours, the country is not saved, the sections will be invited to elect new commissioners worthy of their confidence, who will meet in the Evêché, and who, invested with unlimited powers, shall be charged with taking sweeping measures which alone can save public affairs.[76]

The militant Gusman accused the Jacobins of wanting to pull back from the insurrection. "Never has one played more indecently with the majesty of the people," he complained.[77]

Jean Varlet objected that the mayor had not been instructed for the past twenty-four hours and even accused Dobsen of impeding the work of the Comité central. Pache replied that "this is what happens . . . every time you place a Varlet at your head; he will go beyond you."[78] Hébert refuted the opinions of Varlet, arguing that the insurrection of 31 May was one of the most "beautiful" of the Revolution, and congratulated the citizens with the words, "Paris always counted on the force of reason rather than on that of arms."[79] Despite these self-congratulatory expressions, however, the insurrectionists must have agreed with the Enragés: the Girondin deputies remained in their place, and there was no evidence that the Convention was planning to remove them. Its Committee of Public Safety wanted "order" above all, and it expressed uneasiness at the way things were unfolding in the capital. The Committee urged the municipal authorities to multiply their precautions and informed the General Council that although the minister of foreign affairs, Lebrun, had lost his effectiveness, the Convention had resolved to guard all ministers and to assure their "independence." It admonished the Commune to help the Committee in this task and to communicate with it should it have any anxiety over such matters.[80] It was obvious that the Committee of Public Safety, despite individual members' sympathies for the insurrection, was fearful that the municipal authorities would go beyond the "insurrection morale." It assured Mayor Pache in a letter of the Committee's good wishes and asked that he transmit its sentiments to the General Council, on whom it counted for "enlightened and civic conduct."[81] These brief notes clearly express the Committee's disquiet as it sought to restrain the General Council from going beyond the limits of what the Committee felt was necessary to resolve the political crisis. It hoped to do this by maintaining cordial relations with both the mayor and the Commune. This was critical because the armed force was in the Commune's hands.

The dilemma of the Mountain remained. It realized that the struggle was now to the death; it had to triumph or be crushed. Once the insurrection had begun, neither party could compromise. But if it embraced the Evêché committee and the revolutionary Commune, it stood in danger of encouraging Varlet, Gusman, and other radicals, and perhaps unleashing a civil war with the departments.[82]

Thus everything seemed at a standstill—until the Evêché committee once again fanned the flames of revolt. It decided to adopt two plans, one secret, the other public. By ordering the arrest of Roland during the night, it made clear to the Convention that should that body refuse to move against the proscribed Girondins, it would not hesitate to do so on its own. (Roland was not at home when the police arrived, but Mme. Roland was arrested and taken to Abbaye prison at 7:00 A.M. on 2 June.) It also prepared the address of 1 June urging the sections to go all out against the Girondins. In addition, it agreed to press the Convention to go much further than it had thus far. Hanriot was to envelop the legislature with loyal troops and prevent the armed forces of the moderate sections from coming near it. This plan was undoubtedly the secret measure that the commissioners to the Evêché assembly did not want to share with the Commune.[83]

The Commune reconvened on 1 June at 6:00 A.M. Hanriot reported that all necessary measures of security had been taken and all sensitive posts were being guarded. Only now, on the second day of the insurrection, did the General Council decide to give an official title to the Comité central; it was to be known officially as the "Comité révolutionnaire crée par le peuple du département de Paris." After this came the exchange between Varlet and Hébert as to Dobsen's role, but no decisive steps had been taken when the Council adjourned at 3:00 P.M. for a two-hour break. When it was reported that the Convention had suspended its session without having arrested the Girondin deputies, Marat urged the Council to rise up and present the address adopted in the previous session. Above all, he pressed the gathering not to allow its delegation to depart from the Convention until it had received the answer the Commune wanted. The effect of his plea must have been heightened by Chaumette's report that although the Comité central was deliberating on measures of public safety, "all proposals to arrest [the Girondin deputies] were to be rejected."[84]

The Convention, meanwhile, was in no hurry to satisfy the demands of the petitioners. It asked its Committee of Public Safety to report within three days, and postponed for a week action on the question of whether Roland was free to leave Paris. Furthermore, it decreed that the postal administration must explain its censorship of mail in violation of the law. Finally, it hastened to assure the departments that although the sections had risen, the insurrection was peaceful.[85] The delay was becoming serious because the poor sans-culottes who were still under arms had not been paid and could not continue in their present state. Should they be forced to leave, others would take their place, but they could hardly be considered defenders of the Republic—so warned the revolutionary committees of Montreuil and Quinze-Vingts.[86] The General Council was helpless in this crisis and turned to the Comité central with the request that it provide some means of resting the armed force, a rest that by this time was much needed.[87]

A member of the Council must have expressed the general feeling when he stated shortly thereafter that although the Convention had adjourned, the people would take the necessary salutary measures themselves. Among these measures were the Council's decrees to prohibit nobles or priests from holding public office and to expel petitioners of eight thousand and twenty thousand from the general assemblies, plus the conservative clubistes of Sainte-Chapelle.[88] Furthermore, without waiting for the Convention, the Commune decreed that Roland, Clavière, Lebrun, and others be found and arrested and that all suspects be disarmed. It joined the Comité central in ordering that the alarm cannon be fired and that the sections beat the general alarm.[89]

The Jacobins, meanwhile, heard Hassenfratz read his reply to the Lanjuinais's accusation against him. The general alarm was heard shortly thereafter. It was reported that the Convention had been surrounded by thousands of men. While some members suggested that they remain in place, others urged that the post for patriots was in the General Council of the Commune, and the young Enragé Théophile Leclerc called on them to join the people.[90]

The address prepared by Barère to the departments and adopted by the Convention sought to give the impression that order reigned in the capital and that all authorities were held in proper respect. While most benches were still empty as the representatives reassembled for the evening session of 1 June, the general alarm was heard again. To the inquiry why the tocsin was sounding, some replied that it was because the Convention had failed to act on the petitions demanding the removal of the Girondin leaders. The Convention was about to entertain still another delegation from the revolutionary and the constituted authorities, at whose head was Hassenfratz. He had presented his address to the General Council at 5:00 P.M., had had it adopted by that body, and now was prepared to read it to the Convention in the name of the departmental authorities whose delegation he headed.[91] "Save the people, or we declare to you that they will save themselves," he warned.[92] The now-familiar demands were raised once again: a decree of accusation against the Commission des Douze and the accomplices of Dumouriez, and the impeachment of twenty-seven deputies (not the original list of twenty-two), some of whom he named.[93]

While Hassenfratz and his fellow delegates were preparing to deliver their petition, all the avenues leading to the Convention were occupied by huge crowds. It was reported that the spokesmen of the Commune had been badly received but that Hassenfratz had told the representatives bluntly that his delegation had no intention of leaving until the act of accusation had been decreed. Robespierre, it was said, had admitted that although the deputies denounced by the petitioners could not be (legally?) arrested, nevertheless, because the people had risen, the Convention had to complete the work demanded of it. Until this happened, therefore, the insurrection would continue. The General Council, it was added, had adopted measures to assure order while the Comité central révolutionnaire took secret revolutionary measures that could not be publicized until they had been accomplished.[94]

Although pressure was mounting on the deputies to sacrifice the Girondin leaders, the fear of violating the independence of the legislature held many in check. Barère's proclamation on how calmly Parisians were conducting themselves hid more than it disclosed. Marat reported that when he told Barère that the only way to reestablish tranquility was to mete out "justice to the traitors," he was rebuffed "by a mocking smile."[95] Cambon demanded an immediate report on Hassenfratz's petition, and Legendre went much further, proposing that all who had voted for the appeal to the people during the king's trial be arrested.

These proposals were a response to the pressure of the Commune, the sections, and the Evêché committee. Masses of men and women had come out into the street once again, many complaining about the Mountain's lack of vigor[96] and clamoring for the arrest of the "traitors" in the Convention. Large crowds at the Carrousel were repeating the cries.[97] Marat's motion that the Committee of Public Safety report on the proposed arrests within three days seems strangely indulgent, considering the immediacy of the crisis.[98] A short while later, Marat moved that the Committee of Public Safety report the next day regarding the accusations against members of the Commission and the denounced deputies; but the decree adopted was on the previous motion, that the report be heard within three days.[99] He did manage to modify the original list and was to do so again the following day. Meanwhile, he removed the less obnoxious deputies but stripped several of their dignity: Jean-Joseph Dussaulx he characterized as "a driveler of nonsense"; François-Xavier Lanthenas was "pauvre d'esprit"; and Jean-François Ducos was "too young" (he was twenty-eight).[100]

Before the decisive *journée* of 2 June began, the last issue of the *Patriote Français* was hurriedly being put together. It was a sharp attack on the Commune and called on the Convention to close the Jacobin and Cordeliers clubs if it wanted to avoid being subjugated.[101] But this call came too late. More than two weeks earlier, Dutard had warned Garat, "If the Convention allows the committees of surveillance to substitute [themselves] for its authority, it is lost . . . and I don't give it more than a week."[102] By now, even if the Convention had decided to adopt such drastic measures, it would have been ignored.[103] All Paris was up in arms. The only question was how far the insurrection would go. Would it stop at the removal of some two dozen Girondins, or would it dissolve the Convention itself?

VII

The Insurrection Completed

This was the best organized *journée* of the Revolution.

Georges Lefebvre, *La Révolution française*

The 2d June 93 contained within it both Fructidor and Brumaire, as well as all the coups d'état that followed.

Jules Michelet, *Histoire de la Révolution française*

THE SECOND of June was a Sunday. Thousands of Parisians who would normally have been at work were out in the streets, adding the pressure of their presence and voices to that of the armed men who were about to surround the Convention. Within the hall, the sharp internal crisis of that body was giving the deputies a feeling of great uneasiness. Letters were read describing the seriousness of the Vendée rebellion, underscored by that in the department of Lozère. In Lyons a counter-revolution had taken place; some eight hundred patriots had been massacred, reported Cambon. The mood of the Convention can be gauged by the demand of Jean-Bon Saint-André to invoke martial law in the rebellious departments and to outlaw all aristocrats. It is against this background that the final clash between the Gironde and the Mountain must be viewed.

Lanjuinais, spokesman for the Gironde at the moment, must have exacerbated the situation still further when he chose to ignore the growing threat from the rebellious departments, and instead turned on the "anarchy" (as he called it) outside. "A rival power" was menacing the Convention, he declared. When several voices shouted that he wanted to "light the flames of civil war," Lanjuinais continued undaunted. "A usurping authority has fired the alarm cannon," he accused. Legendre, a former butcher and now a leading Jacobin deputy, threatened to "slaughter" him unless he came down from the tribune. Lanjuinais retorted, "Decree that I am an ox and you may slaughter me." While the galleries chanted, "A la Vendée," Lanjuinais continued to demand the dissolution of the Evêché assembly and its committees.[1]

The Paris Commune had been convoked at nine on the morning of 2 June in order to carry yet another petition to the Convention. Marchand of the Comité central entered the Convention hall at the head of a large delegation. Once again he demanded the arrest of the accused and threatened to have the people save public affairs should the Convention refuse. While the galleries shouted their support, Billaud-Varennes and Tallien demanded that the Committee of Public Safety report on the petition immediately. Deputy Richon cautioned, "They [the petitioners] have warned you of the dangerous consequences of a long postponement of the decree they demand."[2] The Convention nevertheless refused to act on Billaud-Varennes's motion, referring it to its Committee of Public Safety. Once again the delegates of the Evêché and the Commune departed amidst a violent tumult without having succeeded in imposing their demands on the divided Convention.

The final decision no longer rested with that body, however. Continued pressure from the insurrectionary forces, coupled with a sympathetic response by the deputies of the Mountain, forced the Convention to yield.[3] "It was clear," wrote Jaurès, "that the vital impulse was neither in the Convention, nor in the Commune, nor with the Jacobins."[4] How had this "vital impulse" manifested itself? The General Council had invited all citizens to remain under arms, but it did not deliberate on the insurrectionary measures to be taken. This decision was referred to the Comité central, which took action between 2:00 and 4:00 A.M. on 2 June. It drafted a list of the names and addresses of thirty deputies to be arrested in the expectation that the Convention would not vote the decree of accusation.[5] It had already given Hanriot power to activate the armed forces, decreed the sounding of the general alarm, ordered the sections to arrest suspects, and resolved to pay the sans-culottes under arms.

At eight o'clock on the evening of 1 June the Comité central ordered the tocsin to cease ringing and appointed four of its members to confer with the Committee of Public Safety on how to resolve the crisis. It also ordered its envoys in the post office to open all letters. To avoid another "September" incident, it had armed forces distributed around the prisons and decreed that commissioners of the General Council proceed into the streets with torches to proclaim the resolutions adopted and to invite the citizens to take up arms. It decreed "that the deputies of the Convention [that is, the Girondins] shall be placed under house arrest, and that the Commander of the guard shall be charged with execution of this decree, under the surveillance of members of the Comité central révolutionnaire, during the *journée* of tomorrow Tuesday [Monday?]." At 4:00 A.M. on 2 June the Comité central decided to send commissioners to the Committee of Public Safety to demand that it report to the Convention on that day (not waiting the three days agreed upon) so that the leaders of the "faction" could be arrested. Finally, it ordered the commanding general to surround the Convention with a respectable armed force in order to arrest the accused deputies should the Convention refuse to act on the demands of the people.[6]

To carry out the instructions of the Comité central, Hanriot ordered four hundred men from section Droits-de-l'Homme together with its company of cannoneers to be placed at the Carrousel, along the Tuileries, and in the Place de la Révolution. Another battery of thirty-two cannons was installed in the court of the Palais Royal under Petit, commander of section Bon-Conseil's cannoneers. On the evening of 1 June Hanriot announced to the General Council that all sensitive posts had been secured by his armed men.[7]

Yet the revolutionary authorities were faced with a dilemma. On the one hand, they wanted to bring sufficient pressure on the recalcitrant Convention to make it surrender the "guilty" deputies and the Girondin minister without resorting too openly to an "insurrection brutale." On the other hand, they were aware of mounting criticism not only from Enragés like Jean Varlet but from those who like Marat were demanding a purge of the Convention as well. There was also the danger of conflict with the armed forces of moderate sections that still supported the Girondins. Thus there had to be pressure put on the Convention to expel the proscribed deputies but also measures taken to protect it from the radicals on the Left and from the moderates who might come to the assistance of their partisans. This pressure must not endanger the safety of the Girondins, it was agreed. How was this to be done? The answer lay in surrounding the Convention with cannons and eighty to one hundred thousand armed men, with an inner ring of five to six thousand Parisian Guardsmen under the direct command of Hanriot. The Comité central révolutionnaire decided that "the General in command [Hanriot] will surround the Convention before morning by a respectable armed force, in such a way that the leaders of the faction can be arrested in light of open day in case the Convention should refuse to carry out the demands of the citizens of Paris."[8]

Meillan wrote that seventy-five thousand of the eighty thousand armed men who surrounded the Convention had no idea why they were there, but that Hanriot had placed his "elite troops" immediately adjacent to the doors of the Convention to "protect" the deputies.[9] Du Maillane concurred, writing that among the hundred thousand armed men were three thousand cannoneers with 163 guns. He added that he saw a military man on horseback distributing five-livre *assignat* notes to the soldiers.[10] Mortimer-Ternaux was convinced that the soldiers had been plied with wine and food and that the great masses of the public were mere onlookers, indifferent and only curious as to whether the Convention or the Commune would win.[11] Michelet wrote that in some sections the National Guard was mobilized without being told the true intention of this action: in Observatoire, the cannoneers were assured that their guns were to be taken to the Panthéon rather than to the Carrousel; in some sections the Guard was told it was to defend the Convention against royalists; in Halles and in other neighborhoods, sectionnaires were promised that a schedule of food prices was to be obtained.[12]

Jaurès differs with the above estimates as well as with Michelet's assertion that few voted and that Paris was passive. He emphasized that all Paris was united on 10 August 1792 on the need to destroy royalty, though few voted. On 31 May the sentiment to be done with the Girondins and with "traitors" was widespread. *Révolutions de Paris* wrote, "What an imposing spectacle does Paris offer! Almost 300,000 citizens under arms . . . 300,000 citizens, we repeat, assembled at the first sound of the tocsin." Faubourg Saint-Antoine had mobilized twelve thousand men. It is true that many were uncertain of their duty—hence the contradictions and vacillations—but there was neither inertia nor indifference, concludes Jaurès.[13]

Whatever the motives of the huge crowd around the Convention, there is no question of its size and the pressure that it exerted on that body to carry out the removal of the accused deputies. A report by the Jacobins catches this movement: "The people occupied all the avenues leading to the Convention. The intriguers will be accused; if the decree is not passed, we shall pass it ourselves . . . The Convention is in reality surrounded by a formidable force. All deputies were surrounded to the point where they could not leave, even to do their business *(même pour faire leurs besoins)*."[14] Mortimer-Ternaux adds that "the circle of iron which was strangling the Convention from all directions was so constraining that the Committee of Public Safety took fear." What did the Committee fear? The answer— a most significant one, it might be added—was that the revolutionary authorities (Mortimer-Ternaux says "representatives of the Hôtel de Ville") would do away with the whole representative body.[15] Just how universal this fear was it is difficult to say. Some deputies thought that the National Guard was favorably disposed toward them and reported as much. Michelet found evidence that the Committee of Public Safety was convinced the Jacobins were now in control of the Evêché committee and therefore would do no harm to the Convention.[16] Yet he admits the danger indirectly by citing Gusman, who repeated on 2 June what he had declared on 31 May, "that the insurrection was betrayed by those who had prepared it," and who was now demanding "une grande mesure de salut public."[17] Add these views to those of Varlet and it is obvious that there was opposition to the course the insurrection had taken since 31 May. Nor could anyone be certain just how things would turn out with so many armed men pressing against the Convention, many of them certainly ill disposed toward those who had been branded as traitors to their country by journalists, Jacobins, local authorities, and their own colleagues. The insurrectionists had to tread a fine line indeed: they must protect the Convention with Hanriot's "reliable troops"[18] yet bring sufficient pressure upon it so that it surrendered the accused.

Before Barère presented his report, Lacroix moved in the name of the Committee of Public Safety that a revolutionary army of six thousand men be formed for the department of Paris, to be paid at the rate of forty sous per diem.[19] This motion carried but was not implemented until September 1793. The proposal having been disposed of, Barère gave his long-awaited speech. It was surprisingly mild, considering the nature of the crisis. The Committee of Public Safety, he began, does not believe it should adopt a decree of arrest against the accused; rather, it appeals to their generosity and patriotism to suspend their powers voluntarily for the good of the republic—and only for a limited period.[20] Cries of refusal were heard mingled with demands for the arrest of the accused. Levasseur observed that a suspension of powers was no solution at all, that it was a denial of the petition presented by Hassenfratz. Even so, Lanjuinais and Barbaroux refused to go along with the solution proposed, even though Isnard, Lanthenas, and Fauchet resigned, followed by Dussaulx. The original list of deputies accused was to be modified by Marat,[21] but meanwhile another crisis had arisen.

A number of deputies reported that they had been barred from leaving the hall by companies of armed men. Several on their way to dine had been turned back, and Grégoire was escorted by four armed men as he went to the toilet.[22] Worse yet, Boissy d'Anglas had his scarf torn to shreds, Duperret had been stopped by two gendarmes (who had subsequently disappeared), and Lacroix, a member of the Committee of Public Safety, had also been molested.[23] "The majesty of the Convention," in the words of Danton, "had been outraged."[24] Lacroix therefore had the Convention adopt a decree that the armed force surrounding it be immediately withdrawn. When this message was brought to Hanriot, he shouted, "Tell your f_____ president that I f_____ him and his Assembly, and that if within one hour, he doesn't deliver to me the twenty-two, I'm going to blast it."[25]

This was a harbinger of the confrontation between the general and Hérault de Sechelles as Hérault led the deputies toward Hanriot's men.

When this response became known, even the Mountain was indignant. Barère denounced the Comité central révolutionnaire as "une autorité usurpatrice et dangereuse pour la liberté." This tyranny was in the revolutionary committee of the Commune, he repeated, and he demanded that the head of the armed force (Hanriot) appear before the Convention. Then, resorting to demagogy, he stated that the whole incident was due to the role of a "Spaniard, Gusman, who appears to have been paid to excite trouble" in order to promote the counter-revolution.[26] The Mountain was obviously embarrassed by the pressure from the street, as Hérault de Sechelles took over the presidency from Mallarmé. A Captain Lesain of section Bon-Conseil, called on to explain this threat to the Convention, admitted that he and his officers were helpless before "des gens à moustache" who controlled the exits.[27] It was then that Barère made his proposal that the deputies march outside the hall and mingle with the armed force to demonstrate that they were indeed free.[28]

According to Barère, Robespierre whispered to him, "What are you doing? You're making a mess of it." He allegedly replied that the mess was in the Carrousel and called Robespierre a hypocrite for not speaking up.[29] Surely Barère must have recognized the danger to the deputies in confronting the troops of Hanriot. If a few hotheads among the Conventionnels had made a threatening move and their counterparts among the troops had fired on them, the whole Convention could have been massacred on the spot.[30]

About a hundred deputies of the right, joined by most of the Convention including some Montagnards, followed Hérault down the great stairs of the Tuileries and into the garden. Here they met Hanriot on horseback commanding a group of armed men, mostly cannoneers. Witnesses report the following confrontation between Hérault and Hanriot:

"Herault, we know that you are a good patriot, that you are of the Mountain. Swear to me on your head that the twenty-two members will be surrendered within twenty-four hours."—"No," replied the president. —"In that case," resumed Hanriot, *"I shall not say anything,"* and he stepped aside, and gestured to his troops. One heard the cry: "To arms! Cannoneers, to your guns!" The cannoneers took up the match, the cavalry drew their sabres, and the infantry took aim at the Convention.[31]

The helpless deputies turned back and meekly returned to the hall.[32]

As the deputies turned away from Hanriot's men, cries were heard: "Vive la Montagne!"; more rarely, "Vive la Convention!"; and occasionally,

"Vive Marat!"[33] Mortimer-Ternaux reports, however, that the cries were "Vive la Montagne! à la guillotine Brissot, Guadet, Vergniaud! purgez la Convention! tirez le mauvais sang!"[34] Lanjuinais reported that the soldiers shouted, "Vive la république! Vivent les députés! La paix! la paix, des lois, des lois!" A small number cried, "Vive la Montagne, vive les bons députés!" A few called for guillotining the Girondin leaders.[35] These conflicting reports are obviously irreconcilable. The first group is nonpartisan and pro-Convention as a body; the rest are directed against the Girondins and are supportive of the insurrection. Whether Hanriot knew that Montagnard deputies were among the mass his cannoneers turned back, or as Michelet thinks was unaware of this,[36] is of little importance. He could hardly have acted differently had he recognized some Montagnards among the crowd with Hérault. The cries of the armed forces, however, are revealing of their true feelings, for they must have been spontaneous and unrehearsed. In any case, the Convention as a body had been humiliated and forced to submit.[37]

As the deputies were turned away by Hanriot's troops, they took the route through the garden and toward a bridge called Pont Tournant, not knowing that this passage, too, was blocked. It was then that Marat arrived and asked "that the faithful deputies return to their posts." The Montagnards led the way as the rest followed silently behind.[38]

Some thirty Montagnards had remained in the hall while the rest followed Hérault. As the balance of the deputies returned and took their seats, sectionnaires mingled with them. Couthon announced that now that the Convention had been convinced the deputies were free, it should vote the arrest of the accused. Mallarmé was back in the chair as the vote was taken. It is not known whether the Right voted at all.[39] The arrested numbered twenty-nine,[40] twenty of the twenty-two originally denounced, plus the members of the Commission des Douze (except for the two who had opposed the arrests of Hébert and Varlet) and the ministers Lebrun and Clavière.[41] Marat amended the final list before the decree of expulsion was discussed by the Convention.

After Couthon's motion, Vergniaud rose and suggested that the Convention offer him a glass of blood to appease his thirst.[42] It was to temper such sentiments that Danton supported a proposal made by Garat to the Committtee of Public Safety that the departments be given hostages from the Convention to guarantee the safety of the arrested deputies.[43] Danton volunteered to go to Bordeaux, and the department of Paris offered to furnish an equal number of hostages to the departments.[44] Nothing came of this, however, after Robespierre denounced the suggestion as "a trap." It is difficult to say how many Conventionnels voted to arrest their Girondin colleagues because the original *procès-verbal* seems to have been reedited.[45] The Mountain voted as a bloc, but most of the others abstained.[46] Even after the vote had been recorded, no one was permitted to leave the hall until a *huissier* brought an order from the Commune to rescind its previous decree and to leave the passage free.[47] "Here ends a major period of the revolution," wrote Thiers.[48]

Two important witnesses have described precisely what took place in the gardens of the Tuileries on 2 June while the Convention made its crucial decision. Chaumette wrote, "All armed Parisians bend their steps toward the hall of the Convention. Their numerous phalanxes inundate the avenues, fill the approaches, surround from all sides the premises of the Convention. *Indignation and respect are painted on all faces.*"[49] The last sentence is most revealing. The sans-culottes were determined to force the Convention to do their bidding; hence their indignation that the deputies still had not expelled the Girondins. Still, these were representatives of the people; hence the respect. Chaumette describes further how when the deputies rose to go out among the crowds of ordinary citizens and armed men, the armed force opened a wide path to permit them to walk about freely. No one touched or menaced a single deputy, he writes.[50] This statement is not quite true, but there can be no doubt that the sans-culottes still retained a certain awe for their representatives.

Months later, Hébert related this incident to the Cordeliers: It seems that when the Convention was surrounded by the armed mass, Lacroix complained of having been insulted. A cannoneer standing nearby replied, "You would like to be insulted very much, scoundrel, but we will not give you that pleasure."[51] Although this remark bespeaks more indignation than respect, respect is not totally lacking in it. A member of the General Council reported that he saw a deputy (Lacroix?) about to draw his pistol, but that the people assured him they had no desire to insult him and calmed him down.[52] It seems that though the sans-culottes retained their respect for the Convention, they were unhappy with its vacillations, its factional disputes, and its lack of decisive action against the Gironde.

When the revolution was launched on 31 May the Comité central révolutionnaire could not be sure of its success. It was not until three days later, after all, that its demand that the Convention be purged of Girondins was carried out. Undoubtedly, this uncertainty was an important factor in its moderation and avoidance of violence.[53] On 31 May section Quinze-Vingts warned against "excess that could be committed under the instigation of aristocrats,"[54] and section Sans-Culottes repeated the warning against "les malheureux excès" of which the Convention could be the first victim.[55] Several days after the purge, the Comité central révolutionnaire admonished the administrators of police in a document signed by Marquet, "Citizens! The law demands that suspects be placed under arrest, but it desires that persons presumed to be such should be treated in a manner worthy of free men."[56] It referred to complaints of various citizens from section Buttes-des-Moulins and urged the police to conduct themselves in a manner that would not excite further complaints.[57] The revolutionary committee of section Piques showed an unusual sense of responsibility when it asked the Comité central if it thought it prudent to conduct Clavière, whom it had arrested, to the Hôtel de Ville, in view of the large crowds gathered there.[58]

At times, the lack of a clear policy on how to deal with the deputies and ministers arrested bordered on the comical. The revolutionary committee of section Beaurepaire reported to the Comité central that it had delegated two commissioners to join the four mandated by section Cité to arrest Roland. He refused to comply with the wishes of the commissioners to place himself under arrest, arguing that since he had a report to make to the Convention he would obey only that body. A commissioner was then dispatched to the Evêché Committee for orders on how to proceed while the other five waited patiently for his return. When he reappeared at about 9:00 P.M. after a long wait, he had no new orders. It was then decided to have Roland write his reply, which he did. One commissioner of Beaurepaire stated that he was not authorized to use force and persuaded the others to leave with him.[59] Later, the Commune criticized these men for their irresolution.[60]

When the report came that Roland had finally been arrested, it became known that section Beaurepaire had taken him under its protection.[61] The General Council then appointed six commissioners to proceed to Beaurepaire (probably to its revolutionary committee) and take Roland and Mme. Roland (evidently released after her first arrest), under its care.[62]

A number of other sections also became involved in the *affaire Roland.* The revolutionary committee of section Panthéon-Français interrogated Roland's maid, Mignot, who had quit his employment some two weeks earlier. She reported hearing a conversation in which Roland planned to cede Brittany to the English and to surrender Artois and Lorraine to Emperor Francis II of Austria—after which all would be well and the sansculottes would be silenced.[63] The revolutionary committee of section Marais searched the home of Angran d'Alleray, where Roland had lodged before the Revolution. Although it found nothing suspicious, the committee placed d'Alleray under house arrest.[64] A certain Paquier, who had an engraving of Roland, whom he had known since childhood, was interrogated by the revolutionary committee of Muséum.[65] By the time these investigations were concluded, Roland and his wife presumably had been found.

That some of the docility that characterized Beaurepaire and other sections was endangering the insurrection must have been sensed by the Evêché committee. Dispatching a letter to the revolutionary committees of the sections, the Commune, and the department, it acknowledged the care and consideration that inhibited them from arresting suspects because such action was contrary to the behavior of a free government. Nevertheless, the Comité central insisted, they had to remember their responsibility and the fact that public tranquility rested largely upon how they acted; it could not be established without disarming their enemies. Because the people had risen and had no intention of returning to their previous state, they would hold their authorities responsible if they failed to carry out their duty, it warned.[66]

The revolutionary committeemen of section Contrat-Social dispatched a panicky letter to its citizens with a copy to the Comité des Neuf informing them that one of their members had just been disarmed (by moderates?) and that they were ready to die at their post. Meanwhile, it warned of "the greatest evil—public opinion is misled; much prudence is needed."[67] The revolutionary committee of section Marseille (Théâtre-Français) wondered how it could recognize suspects and how it could place their papers under seal when none of them was home.[68] On the other hand, section Unité continued to express itself boldly and firmly. It objected vigorously to the order of the Comité central releasing Louis-Marie Prudhomme, publisher of the *Révolution de Paris,* as being unjust to others held under arrest.[69] The committee called Prudhomme a counter-revolutionary who attacked friends of the people and charged that he had been released because he was rich. In addition, it accused Chaumette of being a "messmate" of Prudhomme's.[70]

Prudhomme was released by the Comité central but was rearrested and brought to the Abbaye prison. He was released again by order of the Committee, an order brought in person by Chaumette and Hébert; at the same time the seals were removed from his papers. This brought on a long discussion in the revolutionary committee of section Unité, a discussion in which Prudhomme took part.[71] On 8 June Lacroix reported to the committee on the contents of the papers seized at Prudhomme's residence. He was to be interrogated on a number of them.[72] In contrast to this zealous persecution of the journalist, the revolutionary committee of section Unité reported without objection that several Girondin deputies (among them Pétion, Brissot, and Guadet), supposedly being guarded by the committee in the Hôtel du Patriote Hollondais, were permitted to visit their wives.[73] The Comité central decided to assign two sans-culottes to each gendarme guarding an arrested deputy and adopted a formal resolution to this effect on 4 June. Not until 24 June did the Convention resolve to transfer the Girondins to Luxembourg prison, and then it failed to carry out this resolution promptly.[74]

In other sections the conflict between Girondins and Jacobins persisted. Where a revolutionary committee was in the hands of the Gironde, it could ignore the directives of the Comité central to arrest suspects. Section Finistère continued its factional dispute for some time after the insurrection. The president of its revolutionary committee was not permitted to enter the premises of the Comité central, was told that he had been replaced, and was reminded that his section had supported the "aristocrats" in the past. Despite these sanctions, its revolutionary committee refused to arrest anyone, and it reported as much to Mayor Pache.[75] Some days later it was revealed that placards had been torn down in the section, evidence of support for the local Girondins.[76] The revolutionary committee of section Piques imprisoned several people for "incivisme," including a former attaché at the Department of Foreign Affairs.[77] Panthéon-Français ordered the arrest of one Lavigne for having turned over a resolution of section Sans-Culottes to the Commission des Douze, and it imprisoned a poet by name of Roucher because he was allegedly "un des coryphées de la Saint-Chapelle," the reactionary club.[78] The Committee of General Security ordered the immediate release of prisoners who had been arrested by the revolutionary committee of Croix-Rouge, and to make sure that they remained free it decreed that its civil committee must place a guard in the home of each person released.[79]

Mayor Pache sent a circular to the sections asking how many people had been arrested by the Comité central as of 8 June. The administration of the Police Department reported the same day that contrary to accusations in the *Journal de Paris* it was not true that some ten thousand citizens had been imprisoned by the Committee. It revealed that a total of 1,310 persons was being held, among whom were fabricators of false *assignats,* thieves, murderers, and other such criminals.[80] How many of the total reported were political prisoners it is difficult to say, but they probably numbered a few hundred, certainly not in the thousands as the *Journal de Paris* surmised. The arrests reported by the sections seem to have been confined to leading individuals; their followers were not seized, though they were sometimes harassed in the general assemblies and in some cases excluded from them.[81] The victory of the sans-culottes did not automatically spell the end of moderate opposition in the sections. It was only when terror became "the order of the day" that Girondin sympathizers had to lie low; only after Robespierre's fall did they rise again.

How do historians view the insurrection and the resulting fall of the Gironde? Buchez and Roux wrote:

> The insurrection of 31 May differs greatly from the famous *journées* carried out earlier, first against the absolute monarchy, then against the constitutional monarchy. It differs entirely as to form and as to the incalculable difficulties over which its authors triumphed. It was neither a disturbance nor an engagement. Not a drop of blood was spilled. It was, as expressed then, an act of popular sovereignty brought about this time with all the regularity of government, a coup d'état of the people organized in sections, and supporting its wishes by the deployment of the social power itself.[82]

Michelet, in contrast, saw the overthrow of the Gironde as "sad" and the events of Fructidor and of Brumaire as being embodied in the coup of 31 May–2 June.[83] Lamartine wrote that the Gironde "fell because of weakness and indecision, like the king whom it had overthrown." He admits that the Girondins lacked "the imagination *(pensée)*, the unity, the politics, the resolution" and had made the Revolution without wanting it. They did not know how to rule. The insurrection of 31 May was illegal, but so was that of 10 August, he remarks; such an action may be justified by the right of self-preservation. Lamartine concludes, surprisingly, that this uprising saved the nation.[84]

Blanc criticizes Lamartine for thinking that the fall of the Girondins was largely their own work. They were not "the *only* artisans of their own ruin," he writes, nor does he accept Michelet's argument that the Gironde fell because it had been defeated by the priests in the Convention. The party was at first astonished by the challenge of the Mountain and then made angry. The Montagnards were willing to compromise, but the Girondins stubbornly refused. Blanc writes, "Thus fell the party of the Gironde, so great in enthusiasm, in eloquence, and in courage. Attracted toward the enlightened side of new things, whose charm is associated in their minds with the most beautiful recollections of antiquity, and seizing power forcefully, they used it to crush the nobles, proscribe the priests, undermine the throne, make popular the *bonnet rouge,* encourage *sans-culottisme,* and defy all Europe."[85]

Quinet is aware that the Jacobins accused the Girondins of favoring a republic governed by the bourgeoisie, but he neither accepts this criticism nor denies it. He seems to agree, however, that the Girondins recognized no talents or virtues outside their own party; nor does he believe that they would have erected the Terror into a system because it was repugnant to their "spirit." Still, he admits that they did dream "of purging the left wing," but he is "certain that this [type] of violence was impossible for them." Since they were overthrown, Quinet says, for arresting Hébert (quite a simplification), he finds it inconceivable that they would have dared lay a hand on the leaders of the Mountain.[86] Why a party that could establish links with counter-revolutionaries and foreign powers would hesitate to purge the Left he does not discuss. Moreover, words can take on a life of their own, as the twentieth century knows only too well. If "anarchistes" were indeed a threat to liberty and property, why should not those who advocated "anarchy" be purged in the name of saving French society and civilization? Quinet is too optimistic in holding that "the spirit" of the Girondins was fundamentally different from that of the Montagnards.

Carlyle expresses the Gironde's fall dramatically, and like Quinet he seeks the answer in its "spirit" or outlook. He writes, "Thus fell the Girondins, by Insurrection; and became extinct as a Party: not without a sigh from most historians. The men were men of parts, of Philosophic culture, decent behavior; not condemnable in that they were but Pedants, and had no better parts; not condemnable, but most unfortunate. They wanted a Republic of the Virtues, wherein themselves should be head; and they could only get a Republic of the Strengths, wherein others than they were head."[87] Mignet agrees that the Girondin party had great talents "and generous ideas . . . disgust of anarchy, the love of order, of justice and of liberty." Its members had been chased from one institution and post after another, so its demise was predictable. The results were not foreseen by anyone, and ultimately everyone lost.[88]

Not one historian takes seriously Cambon's charge that the Gironde was linked to a secret attempt to place Louis XVII or the Duc d'Orléans on the throne.[89] Mortimer-Ternaux comments, "The second of June was thus a veritable coup d'état directed against the national representatives. The ultra-revolutionary school that believes that the end justifies the means glorified it; the fatalistic school that proclaims the legitimacy of the fait accompli recorded it without protest." This coup, he continues, installed a kind of Caesarism under the guise of democracy.[90] Pariset also believed that the insurrection was a coup. It had little in common with the preceding journées of 14 July and 10 August, and it became a prototype for Napoleon's eighteenth Brumaire.[91]

Jaurès argues that the Convention's Committee of Public Safety could neither endorse the insurrection nor act against it. To counter it would have been to play into the hands of the Gironde, which had rejected all compromise. It pretended, therefore, that it knew nothing about it. Danton was informed of the movement, says Jaurès, and maneuvered so as to terminate the session of the Committee on the night of 30–31 May to allow the insurrection to develop.[92] If Danton favored the insurrection, he surely was opposed to its plebeian character or, to use the terminology of the day, to an "insurrection brutale." Jaurès concludes that "the Gironde had become a mortal peril for revolutionary France. It had to disappear. On 2 June its political power collapsed."[93]

Mathiez summarizes the reasons for the fall of the Gironde in one perceptive paragraph. The Girondins had unleashed the foreign war but did not know how to procure either victory or peace, he writes. They did not know how to overthrow the king and establish a republic. They hesitated at the decisive moments prior to 10 August 1792 and 21 January 1793. Their equivocal policy gave the impression that they were cherishing selfish aims. They proposed no remedy for the economic crisis, instead opposing all efforts at reform. In short, they neglected public safety and confined themselves to the narrow class policy of serving only the bourgeoisie. The insurrection of 31 May–2 June overthrew not only a party but in a sense a whole social class, the *haute bourgeoisie*.[94]

Lefebvre observes that a critical moment came when the Convention allowed itself to be persuaded to leave the hall in the hope that it could impose its will on the armed force surrounding it. The slightest incident could have led to its destruction, he emphasizes. To the great regret of Varlet and others, however, Hanriot was satisfied merely to bar the deputies' way. They reentered the hall and voted the arrest of the accused. The revolutionary army was established in principle, but the social program of the Enragés was not acted upon. The Montagnards were victorious. They rid themselves of the insurrectionary committee and excluded Varlet and his friends from the departmental committee that took its place. They governed in the name of the Convention, but its majority never forgave them. Moreover, it never arraigned the expelled Girondins. They could not act otherwise in a regime compatible with a representative system, wrote Lefebvre. "On the opposite side, the sans-culottes remained with empty hands," he concludes.[95]

Sydenham sees the result of the insurrection as follows: "The conflict between the national assembly and the sans-culottes was not again resolved until Napoleon did what Brissot and the deputies of the Gironde had lacked the power or the decision to do, and dispersed the mob with his 'whiff of grapeshot.' "[96] This is a surprising statement. Sydenham confuses the royalist "mob" (they were much more than that) with the sans-culottes. It is true, of course, that both menaced the Convention as an expression of the parliamentary system, but they did so with quite different aims. Inadvertently, he implies that but for lack of power the Girondins would have done the same thing. Had the sections and their Commune been vanquished by a "whiff of grapeshot," what kind of republic would have been established on their bones? Surely not the "social republic" for which the sans-culottes fought, as did their descendants in the nineteenth century. As for Sydenham's belief that the Girondins did not die in vain because they "proclaimed faith in a Republic which would approve and defend individual freedom of conscience," he fails to pose the fundamental questions, What kind of republic? And who was to be master of it? Nor should it be forgotten that both the Montagnards and the sans-culottes also had faith in a republic and had their own freedom of conscience—which the Girondins, had they had the power, would have suppressed forcibly. As for Sydenham's statement that Robespierre decided to sanction the violence of the sans-culottes because it was an outgrowth of his "personal philosophy,"[97] it simply flies in the face of all the evidence mustered above. Revolutions are violent actions, the French Revolution no less than others. The violence practiced by the Thermidorians and Directorials against the sans-culottes, Hébertists, Robespierrists, and all other oppositionists demonstrates, however, that no party was immune from it, nor did any have a monopoly on it.

Unlike other historians, François Furet and Denis Richet feel that the insurrection of 31 May–2 June does not have the same importance as that of 10 August 1792. The Revolution continued in the direction whose original impulse had been given by the eighteenth century, they write. The events of June saw the disappearance of "revolutionary romanticism." In times of happy expectancy the Girondins led the Convention; in times of death and suffering it was the Montagnards; when good times returned, the Plain took over. "To see in these successive teams so many social stratifications smacks of illusion or methodological prejudice. It is not the social origin but the political conjunction which distinguishes them," they write.[98]

The insurrection introduced direct democracy and delivered a grave blow to bourgeois parliamentarism, they continue. It was more than a "moral insurrection"; the Convention found itself a prisoner and for the first time was threatened by armed force. "It matters little that this force, in order to be plebeian, had to be praetorian. The mechanism unloosed 2 June contained within it, as Michelet understood it, 'both Fructidor and Brumaire.' In this sense it was not only a defeat for the Gironde, but a defeat for the Revolution."[99]

Furet and Richet have important insights, but here they approach a strange kind of mechanical interpretation. Of course "la force des choses" is present in all historical movements, but to see the popular movement as it exploded in the 31 May insurrection as rooted in the formative trends of the eighteenth century omits the living social forces engaged in struggle. It may be true that there is a tendency on the part of some historians to exaggerate the importance of "social stratifications," to use the authors' term, but to ignore them and their personal protagonists is to be equally rash.

Albert Soboul poses the question, Which road had to be taken in order to save the conquests of the Revolution? Both the Gironde and the Mountain wanted to end the old regime and royalty; both favored the republic. The question was essentially whether to establish the republic firmly by compromise from above or by an alliance with those below. By the fall of 1792, Brissot was denouncing the "désorganisateurs" and refusing an alliance with the popular masses. The Jacobins and the Montagnards chose the second, the revolutionary way, writes Soboul, and he concludes, "Thus perished the Gironde. It had declared war but did not know how to conduct it; it had denounced the king but recoiled before his condemnation; it had cried for support of the people against the monarchy but refused to govern with it; it had contributed to the economic crisis but thrust aside all popular demands."[100]

These different interpretations express the varieties of history; at the same time, they reflect the complexity of the insurrection. Mathiez, for example, sees the overthrow of a social class as an important result, but Lefebvre notes that those who presumably overthrew it gained nothing from the insurrection. Michelet, Mortimer-Ternaux, and Pariset agree that the uprising was really a coup not unlike Napoleon's eighteenth Brumaire. Some see only institutional changes, in contrast to those who think that the triumph of the Mountain assured the victory of the bourgeoisie. Several blame the overthrow of the Girondins on their ineptitude, whereas others see their fall in the inevitable historical trends of the century. Surely one reason for this great disparity lies in the differing experiences of individual historians. Living through World Wars I and II must give one a different insight from that resulting from the experience of the revolutions of 1848 and of 1871.

The insurrection seemed successful: the Girondins had been forced to resign or were silenced, and the Mountain had established its supremacy at last and was to place itself at the head of a beleaguered nation. Yet not everyone was satisfied with the outcome. The sans-culottes still lacked bread, and neither speculation nor hoarding had been curbed. The spokesmen for the sectionnaires were groping for something more effective than a laissez-faire economic policy at a time when the normal bonds of the market economy were being severely strained by war. Representative democracy was very well in peace time, but could the general will truly be represented, especially in such critical times as France faced? Moreover, could supplies be guaranteed or inflation curbed without the direct intervention of the state? A number of militants and political activists did not think so. Among the more insistent of these critics was a group called the Enragés. Their program differed sharply from that of the Jacobins and the Montagnards, and they sensed that the overthrow of the Girondins had opened new perspectives for them.

VIII

The Enragés and the Insurrection

Let the revolutionary government perish rather than
a single principle.

Jean Varlet, *Gare l'explosion* (Paris, 1794)

Liberty is but a vain phantom when one class of men can
starve another with impunity. Equality is but deceit when
the rich, by their monopoly, can exercise the right of life or
death over their fellow men.

Jacques Roux, "Le Manifeste des Enragés" 1793

MATHIEZ says flatly that "the revolution of 31 May–2 June was made
by . . . three men: Varlet, Jacques Roux, and Leclerc d'Oze," and that "to
save themselves and to triumph, the Montagnards were obliged . . . to lean
frankly on the masses led by the Enragés."[1] Without denying the important
role played by the Enragés, I have shown that the movement to overthrow
the Gironde was more complex. Nevertheless, it must be admitted that
the Enragés and other militants hoped to go beyond a simple removal of
some two dozen Conventionnels: they aspired to replace the parliamentary
system with one based on direct democracy under which representatives
would become mere proxies or mandatories of the people's will (actually,
of the primary assemblies). This doctrine was embodied in the term *mandat
impératif*. The right to convoke primary assemblies without prior permission of higher authorities, embraced in the word *permanence,* was also an
article of faith among them. Included in direct democracy was the right
of what we call initiative, referendum, and recall. In short, the introduction
of direct democracy would have ended the system of representation, which
is why both the Girondins and the Montagnards feared the Enragés and
why the revolutionary government ultimately suppressed them.[2]

Jaurès raises the question whether Robespierre feared that the Enragés
would be victorious after the insurrection just as the Paris Commune had
been after the overthrow of Louis. Was it he who persuaded the depart-

ment to reorganize the insurrectionary committee and thereby to reduce the role of the Evêché assembly, "where Varlet had triumphed"? he asks. Michelet thought so, he informs us, though Mortimer-Ternaux believed the opposite, that there was a close understanding between the Evêché assembly and the department. Jaurès concluded that there was both rivalry and agreement between the two bodies. Although they differed sharply on the direction of the movement, they agreed on the action necessary *"in order not to be overthrown by the Enragés."*[3]

Lefebvre observes that the Montagnards did not want to see the Convention dispersed or the September massacres repeated. A premature rising would have opened the possibility for the Commune and the leaders of the sans-culottes to seize power; besides, the departments would not have tolerated such a change. It was essential, therefore, that the Convention be maintained and that it accept the dictatorship of the Mountain.[4] Rudé agrees essentially with this statement in writing that although the Mountain was willing to use the popular movement for its own ends, it had to be careful not to let it pass into the hands of the Enragés or those of Hébert. "Besides, they feared that a premature rising would entail too drastic a purge of the Convention, whose Rump would be powerless to resist the economic demands of the sans-culottes."[5] Whether the Enragés or the Hébertists could have held power once they seized it from the Convention and the Jacobins is a different question, of course. It should be noted, however, that modern historians, no less than those of the previous century, clearly pose the growing influence of the Enragés.

In addition to being committed to direct democracy, the Enragés were tireless advocates of various social measures that would ease the suffering into which the war, shortages, and high prices had plunged the sans-culottes. They were among the first to demand the *maximum* and to curb profiteering, speculation, and engrossment, especially in foodstuffs. It was their agitation that made the greatest impression on the sans-culottes. Although it is true that both Marat and Hébert also attacked monopolizers and profiteers, their specific remedies were more moral principles than practical economic measures. Considering the primitive state of economic theory in the eighteenth century and the lack of experience in laissez-faire economics, the suggestions offered by the Enragés for dealing with shortages and high prices were surprisingly advanced. They were forcefully put forth in the journals of Roux and Leclerc and in the brochures of Varlet.[6]

The Enragés also insisted that the *assignat* should be decreed fiat money. They recognized, of course, the havoc wreaked on the economy and especially on the consumer by the steady decline of this bond. Making it mandatory tender for all debts public and private would, they hoped, ease the plight of the consumer, that is, the sans-culotte. In light of the monetary policies followed by governments of our own day and the acceptance of paper currency that has nothing to back it but the governments' promise to pay, the demands of the Enragés do not sound so extreme. Whether shortages could have been eased by such a policy is a different question. The Revolution was paid for in part by the confiscated estates of the church and of that portion of the nobility condemned by the revolutionary tribunal. But the greater share was paid by the sans-culottes and other urban consumers through inflation. Organizations of *compagnons* never had the power to raise wages to match rising prices, and besides, combinations of sans-culottes for such a purpose were strictly forbidden by the Le Chapelier Law of 1791. The need to hold prices was obvious to all consumers. It was for this purpose that the Enragés proposed to establish the *assignat* as fiat money. Whether such a policy could have worked in light of the demands made by the war, the traditional reluctance of peasants and farmers to surrender their produce for paper, and the general uncertainty is a different question. Nevertheless, the appeal of the Enragés for common sacrifice and their suspicion of newly acquired wealth won many to their side.

Who were the men and women dubbed by historians the Enragés? Three were men: Jacques Roux, an ex-priest in his forties; Jean Varlet, a college graduate still in his twenties with an independent income; and Théophile Leclerc, an ardent journalist and an activist in his early twenties. The other two were women: Claire Lacombe, an attractive actress of great spirit and political understanding; and her friend Pauline Léon, cofounder and early president of the women's club Républicaines révolutionnaires, still in her early twenties and the future wife of Leclerc.

Jacques Roux was born on 21 August 1752 at Saint-Cibard-de-Pransac in the diocese of Angoulême, the second of twelve children. His father, Gratien Roux, was a lieutenant in the infantry and later became a *juge assesseur,* a position that enabled his son Jacques to attend the seminary of Angoulême. Upon graduation Roux became a canon at age fifteen, was involved in a student riot that led to his arrest and imprisonment for six weeks, taught philosophy and experimental physics, became a curate and then a chaplain, and was pursuing his vocation at Saint-Thomas-de-Conac when the Revolution broke out. He was then thirty-seven years of age.[7]

The turning point in his life came on 29 April 1790 when the peasants of Saint-Thomas-de-Conac staged a *jacquerie* against the payment of feudal dues. The king's commissioner, Turpin, blamed the riot on the vicar of Saint-Thomas, "le Roux,"[8] a charge the latter denied. Roux insisted that he had departed from Saint-Thomas before the troubles began and blamed the disorders on three causes: the unjust division of taxes, the refusal of the noblemen to pay their just share, and the nobles' mistreatment of the mayor of a neighboring parish.[9]

During the opening months of the Revolution, Roux's loyalty to Louis XVI was no different from that of other Frenchmen, deputies and priests alike. By the end of 1790 Roux had arrived in Paris, where he was destined to spend his few remaining years. He sought out Marat shortly after his arrival,[10] and he probably became a Freemason and a Cordelier.[11] By the beginning of 1791 he had become well enough known to merit some laudatory comments in Prudhomme's *Les Révolutions de Paris*.[12]

What sort of man was Roux? In a remarkable graphological study by a Dr. Fritz Tögel certain basic character traits are revealed:[13]

> The nature of the author is simple, uncontrived, not in the least intellectual or academic. Its [Roux's handwriting] leading characteristic is the combination of an enthusiastic, strong, outflowing feeling and perceptivity with indefatigable strength of will. This lends him an unusual degree of inner stability, which can also manifest itself as a lack of flexibility. It seems impossible to influence J. R. [Jacques Roux] against his will or to dissuade him from an acquired opinion or purpose. His uncompromising constancy of purpose can lead to inflexibility.
>
> J. R. was not a light, sociable person. Since everything inauthentic is foreign to him, he does not hide behind deceptive facades or veils in any situation. He appears this way in relations to both superiors and inferiors, according to his nature. His manner of thinking is uncommonly quick. Reflection in thought out of context, purely theoretical concepts, and empty hair-splitting are foreign to him. He reacts to immediate demands, which can lead to acceleration of tempo. It is difficult for him to keep something to and for himself. He needs and seeks activity, contact, and continuity, is capable of extreme enthusiasm, is open, hearty, even amicable, toward the world and humanity, toward enjoyment, toward a joyous drive for life. Here one comes upon elements of a certain weakness and gentleness—his manner of dealing and relating is therefore variable. He is completely free from the need for isolation, coldness, apathy, and withdrawal—as well as being free from egotistical calculation and intent, although he possesses a strong sense of worth and a great ambition which drives him to seek success, recognition, and admiration, not to seek a career for itself, but rather to realize a feeling of a 'calling,' a great task predetermined by fate itself.
>
> He allows himself to be neither deterred nor commanded. One can consider him modest only in the material sense. Not burdened by wavering or moodiness, he is yet neither quite unpedantic nor a schemer. Never evil or hateful, rather of good will, he lacks, however, a trait of adaptability and sympathy for people and conditions—his zeal may blind him. Too great a burden elicits apathy, resignation and fatigue. But he forces himself on to

overcome such feelings at once. Perhaps he wreaks havoc with himself, since he is not to be considered of a robust nature.

Roux's daily work brought him into contact with the poor of his section, Gravilliers. He saw the contrast between the sans-culottes who lacked bread and the speculators and engrossers who vulgarly flaunted their newly gained riches. Roux could not accept this state of things and became almost obsessed with its injustice. Roux was personally kind and compassionate; he had adopted a fifteen-year-old youth, Masselin, who had been orphaned by the death of his father on 10 August 1792 at the Tuileries, and he never ceased taking up collections for the poor. Nevertheless, he demanded a policy of terror against the rich and the counter-revolutionaries, whom he linked. "Realpolitik" had no room in his life; hence his refusal to compromise politically. "This ambitious priest certainly was sincere and had character," wrote Mathiez.[14] If he was ambitious, it was not only for himself but for those around him as well.

Sharing his commitment to the poor and the sans-culottes was a young revolutionary named Jean-François Varlet. His activity and writings became well known not only in his section of Droits-de-l'Homme, but among Jacobins, Cordeliers, representatives to the Commune, and ordinary citizens as well. It was because of his popularity that Varlet was elected to the Comité des Neuf and in the temporary absence of Dobsen signed the order to launch the insurrection of 31 May.[15] He was born in Paris on 14 July 1764 to a family of some means and attended the College of Harcourt, where he studied the humanities and belles lettres. His professors predicted that he would be either a saint or a devil. Upon graduation he found employment in the post office. His mother had become a widow at age thirty-six but was left affluent enough to provide him with an income of 5,800 livres a year.[16]

Varlet participated in all the memorable days of the Revolution. He was present at Versailles when the Declaration of the Rights of Man was adopted, had helped prepare the Champs de Mars for the festival of the Federation in 1790, sang and composed patriotic songs, published revolutionary pamphlets on political and social questions, and harangued crowds at the Terrasse des Feuillants in the Tuileries gardens. After Louis's flight to Varennes he became a republican and bore petitions against "the perjured king."[17]

Varlet consistently advocated direct democracy as a practical alternative to the newly established parliamentary system, which he found corrupt and neglectful of the needs of the sans-culottes for whom he spoke.[18] He dreamt of universal democracy and the establishment of a temple, a Panthéon François that would embody the ideals of this democracy.[19] He always signed his political pamphlets as "Varlet, libre," "Varlet, apôtre de la Liberté," or "le Républicain Varlet." This jealous republicanism led him to attack Lafayette in a placard that carried the challenge: "Sovereign People, Lafayette is, was, and always will be a scoundrel, a traitor to his country. I accuse him. A citizen who is not afraid. Signed, Varlet."[20] By the spring of 1791 he had joined the Société fraternelle de patriotes de l'un et de l'autre sexe séante à la bibliothèque des Jacobins and had become a member of the Jacobins and the Cordeliers.

On the eve of Louis's overthrow, Varlet became well known in the capital for his frequent harangues, his numerous pamphlets, and his incessant resolutions. His petition to dethrone Louis, to convoke the primary assemblies, and to introduce universal manhood suffrage was adopted without opposition by section Roi-de-Sicile (the future Droits-de-l'Homme).[21] The establishment of the republic did not satisfy him, however, and after the treason of Dumouriez had implicated the Gironde, he attempted with a few like-minded militants to stage a coup against the Girondin-led Convention. This attempt of 10 March 1793 was aborted, however. Because he was unable to persuade the Commune to join him, Varlet accused it of being "infected with aristocracy."[22] Chaumette and Hébert replied that Varlet and his fellow agitators were linked to Prussia and Britain, and the General Council condemned him as "an intriguer."[23] None of this discouraged the young revolutionary, and by April he was a prime mover in encouraging his section to take the initiative in launching the Evêché assembly.[24]

Varlet's actions in March appeared suspicious to many patriots. Marat disavowed him, and even Roux called for his arrest.[25] The Jacobins expelled him "for excess of *civisme*" on 12 March 1793,[26] an act that reflected their own vacillation. Eventually, the Enragés helped win them over to the insurrection, however. The police spy, Dutard, saw two parties within the ranks of the Jacobins: the "legalists" like Robespierre, Santerre, and most of the Montagnards; and the Cordeliers and the followers of Marat. "Le peuple anarchiste," he wrote, followed Marat.[27]

As to what people thought of Varlet and his followers, Dutard reported that those he spoke with claimed that they were bored with them and called Varlet's disciples "minor barking dogs" (*aboyeurs subalternes*) who, if silenced, would let them rest, which would make things go better. Jaurès wrote that Varlet's arrest caused no stir and that some people even approved it.[28] This is an exaggeration. Undoubtedly, some did approve his arrest, but the clamor for his release in the sections and the linking of Varlet to Hébert did involve many militants in his fate. In a few cases the petitions asking for their release placed Varlet's name ahead of Hébert's. Moreover, the *Patriote Français* was aware of Varlet's role, calling him "the agitator of the gutters of Paris" and describing how he had arrived at the head of a delegation from section Sans-Culottes to take over the general assembly of section Panthéon-Français at 11:30 P.M. According to this journal, Varlet "preached at length the sweetness of a new insurrection and of a general massacre."[29] Furthermore, Lefebvre wrote that the Evêché assembly had established a "commission insurrectionelle, dont la cheville ouvrière [mainspring] fut probablement Varlet."[30] This key role of Varlet could hardly have been possible if the unconcern about his fate after his arrest had been widespread.

Lamartine was hostile toward the Evêché assembly, as could be expected, calling those who sat in it "ces hommes de sang." He was especially inimical to Varlet, whom he characterized as "plus dépravé que cultivé par les lettres" and accused of dreaming to repeat the September massacres.[31] Michelet, on the other hand, demonstrates Varlet's popularity in his own section, Droits-de-l'Homme. "This section," he writes, "one of the most violent, hesitates however when it is asked to elect commissioners with unlimited powers." Then Varlet arrived and the assembly elected him with enthusiasm,[32] whereupon he is reported to have said, "We have . . . unlimited powers; we are the sovereign [body]. We shall break the [established] authority; we shall reconstruct it and give it sovereignty. It will smash the Convention. What is more legal?"[33] Thus the commissioners of the section sitting in the Evêché are recognized as representing the sovereign powers of the people.

To prove that this was indeed so, when the Convention ordered the mayor to appear before it and give a report on the state of affairs, "Varlet and the more violent *did not want him to obey.*" Dobsen and the others, however, decided in accord with the Commune to comply and have Pache submit his report.[34] There is no indication that the question whether the mayor should obey the Convention was ever posed in the Commune, writes Jaurès. Varlet was probably absent from the General Council when the call to the mayor by the Convention was discussed. Moreover, the distrust of Pache he expressed on 1 June did not appear when the insurrection began the day before.[35] By the second day, however, Varlet was not the only one to feel frustrated by the course of events. But his frustration was not due to lack of popularity. On 8 June, for example, when he was asked to speak to the Commune on a "déclaration des droits de l'homme" that he had published, he was received with much applause, proof yet again of the regard in which he was held.[36]

One reason for this popularity lay in his well-known sympathy for the sans-culottes. In a brief historical sketch, Varlet described this feeling eloquently:

> If I can flatter myself for having conceived any useful ideas, I should thank the People Sans-Culottes for them. For four years, always on public squares among crowds of people, among the sans-culotterie, among the ragged whom I love, I learned that innocently and without coercion the poor devils of the garret, reason more surely, more boldly than the best gentlemen, the great speech-makers, the groping savants; if they wish to attain true knowledge, let them go as I among the people.[37]

The fact that "the people" among whom he was known gave him support enabled him to play the key role in preparing the insurrection. It was evident, however, that he favored going beyond an "insurrection morale," and even beyond an "insurrection brutale" if that were limited to removing the Girondin deputies from the Convention. This led to an ultimate clash between him and the Jacobins, which caused him to reevaluate the whole course of the Revolution.

The third leader of the Enragés was Jean-Théophile-Victor Leclerc, born in Montbrison in December 1771, youngest of the five children of Grégoire Leclerc and Antoinette la Boulaye. His father was a civil engineer who provided an education in belles lettres for young Théophile until he reached the age of eighteen.[38] When the Revolution broke out, Leclerc enrolled in the National Guard of Clermont-Ferrand, and in March 1790 he embarked from Bordeaux for the island of Martinique as a merchant's agent to join his two brothers.[39] There the young Enragé joined the patriots against the reactionary governor. He was imprisoned on board a vessel by Admiral Behague, who had been sent by the government to pacify the colonies, and was transferred to France in the summer of 1791. He was without resources or friends until rescued by members of the popular society of Morbihan, where he had debarked. When seventeen grenadiers of the regiment serving in Martinique were condemned by Narbonne, minister of war, Leclerc volunteered to defend them. He raised money, won over a popular society to their cause, and pleaded their case in person before the National Assembly, which exonerated them.[40]

Shortly thereafter Leclerc volunteered for the Army of the Rhine. He carried out a mission as a spy and was allegedly betrayed by Philippe-Frédéric Dietrich, mayor of Strasbourg. Returning to Paris, he found employment in a hospital. In February 1793 he was transferred to the headquarters of the Army of the Alps in Lyons. Here he joined the Jacobin Club and became reacquainted with Joseph Chalier, whom he had met earlier in Paris. The Jacobins of Lyons sent him as their envoy to Paris, where he arrived on 9 May. On the thirteenth Leclerc addressed the Jacobins: "Citizens, you are termed free, and yet you are slaves of poverty . . . We must establish a popular Machiavellianism. We must erase from the surface of the earth all that is impure. Without this you will be nothing but children."[41]

Three days later Leclerc was presented to the General Council, where he revealed that plans were afoot to murder patriots and complained that the Montagnards were too weak to deal with the crisis. There was only one way to save the republic, he asserted: "It is essential that the people themselves mete out justice, because justice always lives in the midst of the people, and they are never fooled."[42] During the night of 29 May he was elected a member of the Comité révolutionnaire of the Club central, and on 31 May he was made a member of the Commission des postes that censored mail.[43]

After the insurrection, on 4 June, Leclerc made a provocative and revealing speech in the Paris Commune. It was false to think that the Revolution was finished, he asserted. For one thing, suspects had not been imprisoned. "Why are you afraid to spill a few drops of blood?" he asked. Universal indignation recalled him from the tribune and he was called to order by the president. Hébert, too, denounced him. Shortly thereafter the General Council decreed that anyone who proposed to shed blood was to be considered "a bad citizen."[44] Why had Leclerc made such a brutal proposal? A partial answer lies in his personal experiences in Lyons, where the alleged weakness of the Jacobins had provoked a conservative reaction that led to a bloody civil war. Leclerc was aware of the forces that had imprisoned Chalier, forces that according to him had been encouraged by the spineless conduct of the revolutionary government. Moreover, he saw the ravages a policy of laissez-faire had perpetrated among the sans-culottes.

Within a few brief months he was to experience a complete change of heart, however, and to abandon his former defense of "spilling blood." On 27 June he had dared defend Jacques Roux and to attack Danton and his follower Louis Legendre for discouraging the Cordeliers from taking "revolutionary measures" on 31 May. This led to an assault on him by Robespierre and Collot d'Herbois and to the expulsion of both Roux and Leclerc from the Cordelier Club.[45] The Jacobins were not going to allow the Enragés to reexamine their role in the "sacred insurrection" of 31 May–2 June.

In addition to the three men who led the Enragés, there were two young women, Claire Lacombe and Pauline Léon. Lacombe was born on 4 March 1765 in Pamiers, near the Spanish border, to Bertrand Lacombe, a merchant, and Jeanne-Marie Gauché.[46] She was described as being five feet, two inches tall, with chestnut-colored hair, brown eyes, an aquiline nose, an "ordinary" mouth and forehead, and a round chin and face.[47] She was considered a beauty and a fine actress. As late as 9 April 1797, d'Anglas, director of the Grand Théâtre de la République, agreed to pay her five thousand livres in specie for her services during the year.[48] After appearing in the theatres of Lyons, Marseilles, and Toulon, Claire Lacombe left for Paris on 30 March 1792 with a testimonial from the mayor and commune of Toulon on the purity of her morals.[49] One reason for her departure may have been her outspoken republicanism, which neither her director nor her colleagues shared. Upon her arrival in the capital she plunged immediately into political work, and by the summer of 1792 she was ready for a leading role in overthrowing the monarchy.

A number of provincial towns had already established revolutionary societies of women. The society of Lyons, Amies de la liberté et de l'égalité, had been founded in October 1792, some eight months before a sister society was organized in Paris. On 10 May 1793 Claire Lacombe together with Pauline Léon founded the Société des républicaines révolutionnaires.[50] Jacques Roux paid the society a compliment in the General Council by attributing to its members "en partie, la gloire d'avoir sauvé la République dans les journées des 31 mai et 2 juin."[51] Of course, Lacombe had her critics as well. Buzot slandered her in the following passage:

> A society of lost women, collected from the dirty alleys of Paris, whose brazenness was equaled only by their lewdness, monstrous females who possess[ed] all the cruelty of weakness and all the vice of their sex . . . these women played a great role in the Revolution of 1793. An old street walker of Paris commanded them, and their daggers belonged to whoever would pay them more. It seems that Lacombe, their chief, had great authority; and in the debates that arose between Robespierre and his friends and Danton and his, this lewd female would often tip the balance in favor of that party for which she would declare herself.[52]

Not only does Buzot exaggerate the influence of Lacombe and her society, but by the time the dispute between Robespierre and Danton erupted, the Femmes révolutionnaires had ceased to exist. Nevertheless, his grudging admission of Lacombe's power is not without interest.

On the eve of 31 May 1793, a delegation of the feminine society appeared at the Jacobins and was addressed by their orator, Citoyenne Lecointre. She affirmed that her companions were no longer "servile women, domestic animals" but had formed themselves into a phalanx to destroy the aristocracy.[53] The Jacobins praised them for a few brief months, only to damn them unreservedly before the summer was out; yet during this short-lived period, Lacombe's women had the admiration of all. The authorities of the Paris department and commissioners of the sections lauded their deeds in ringing phrases. On 30 June 1793 they adopted the following resolution, which they communicated to Lacombe: "The Républicaines révolutionnaires have merited well of the Country; their zeal is indefatigable; their surveillance sees through plots, their activity exposes them, their wariness averts intrigues, their daring warns of dangers, their courage overcomes them; they are, in short, republicans and revolutionaries."[54] "They have frightened the traitors and prepared the revolution of May 31," they continued, and had given aid to the Convention and the magistrates.[55]

The co-leader of the femmes révolutionnaires was Anne Pauline Léon, who married Théophile Leclerc on 18 November 1793. She was born in Paris on 28 September 1768, the daughter of Pierre Paul Léon, a manufacturer of chocolate, and Mathurine Teloliau. When the Revolution broke out, Léon was engaged in helping her mother, a widow with five children, to promote the chocolate business left by her father. The fall of the Bastille inspired her enthusiasm for the Revolution, and she worked day and night to organize the people "against the partisans of tyranny," as she wrote. Lafayette had aroused her suspicions early, and they were confirmed by the events of 5 and 6 October. In February 1791 she led a group of women to the home of Ann Française Fréron, sister of the Abbé Royo, who edited the royalist journal *Ami du Roi*. Breaking in, the women tossed a bust of Lafayette out into the street. Shortly thereafter, Léon was introduced to the Cordeliers, the Société fraternelle de deux sexes, and Mutius Scaevola.[56]

In a powerful harangue on 6 March 1791, Pauline Léon demanded that the National Assembly arm and drill the three hundred women who had petitioned for this right. It was impossible to pretend that the Rights of Man did not apply to women, she argued, or to consent to permitting themselves to be butchered like lambs without defending themselves. Why should women not supplement the defense of the men? she asked. It would be cruel to await a shameful death in their homes; the women would rather die than live in slavery. She concluded, "A dagger aimed at their bosom would deliver them from the ills of slavery! . . . They will die regretting not the loss of their life . . . but the futility of their death, bemoaning not having been able, first, to dip their hands in the impure blood of the enemies of the country, and avenging themselves on some of them."[57]

After Varennes she spoke out boldly against the treason of the king.

On 17 July 1791 she signed the petition to suspend the monarchy, and she barely escaped with her life from the Champs de Mars. Upon her return from the demonstration (in which her mother was a participant as well), she was menaced by her neighbors and threatened with imprisonment by her section.[58] She passed the night of 9–10 August 1792 in the hall of section Fontaine-de-Grenelle and the next day armed herself with a pike. It was only after some desperate pleading by the men around her that she finally agreed to surrender her weapon to an unarmed sans-culotte.

Léon signed many patriotic petitions, including one demanding the death penalty for Louis. After founding the Société des républicaines révolutionnaires with Claire Lacombe, she spoke before other popular societies and addressed large crowds in Faubourgs Saint-Antoine and Saint-Marceau. On the eve of 31 May she orated at the Club central before commissioners of the sections and members of various popular societies, urging "the sacred insurrection that would deliver the Mountain from its shackles." Shortly thereafter she exhorted her listeners on the Champs-Elysées to rally to the defense of their country, and with the adoption of the new constitution she expressed her satisfaction to the Convention in the name of her section.[59]

A week before the insurrection, Roux drafted an important address, *Discours sur les causes des malheurs de la République française,* whose principal ideas were to appear in his better-known petition of 25 June 1793 that attacked the newly proposed constitution for not proscribing speculation and hoarding.[60] Some of the same phrases and even whole paragraphs were to appear in his journal, *Le Publiciste de la République française, par l'ombre de Marat, l'Ami du peuple.* It seems that he composed this oration in two parts: the first and more essential portion was written between 21 and 31 May; the second portion between 2 and 10 June.[61]

In the first part of his address, Roux exposed "the treacheries" of the aristocrats, priests, and deputies who were responsible for the war, and he attacked the Girondins. In the second part he blamed profiteers for the wretched condition of the laboring classes. The rich, he accused, exercised the right of life or death over the working people; he asked if it were for this aristocracy of wealth that Frenchmen had broken the scepter of kings. Large property holders opened or closed their granaries according to "the thermometer of avarice," he wrote, and enriched themselves at the expense of the widow and the orphan. High prices were due to bad faith, to cupidity, and to speculation, and he assaulted "the faithless representatives" for favoring this "trash" of society. He was especially bitter against profiteers and engrossers: "Your sudden fortune attests without retort to your larcenies, your treacheries, your crimes . . . Before the seizure of the Bastille, you were covered only with rags, and today you insult by your luxury the poverty of the public."[62] Rejecting the idea that high prices were caused by the war or the falling *assignat,* he put the blame on merchants, manufacturers, and bankers.

In the final portion of his address, entitled "Sur les moyens de tourner la cours des malheurs publics," he advocated the arrest of suspects and a levy on the rich to make them pay the cost of the war. "Ah, reflect that almost all the rich are by principle the abettors of crime and by habit the accomplices of kings," he charged, calling them "assassins of liberty, friends of royalty, and supporters of counter-revolutionaries."[63] On 29 May he addressed the Montagnards:

> Deputies of the Mountain, we implore you to save the country. If you can and do not want to do so, you are cowards and traitors. If you want to but cannot, say so. This is the purpose of our mission. One hundred thousand men are armed to defend you.[64]

When the insurrection began, Jacques Roux was appointed along with three colleagues to record its history.[65] On 31 May he proposed in the General Council to arrest all refractory priests, ex-nobles, and signers of "anti-civic petitions." This suggestion was referred to the Comité central.[66]

Meanwhile his section, under the guidance of its revolutionary committee, began to arm the sans-culottes, to send out patrols, and to arrest suspects. Upon the request of Léonard Bourdon the committee furnished six guns with bayonets to arm the citizens who inhabited his house. Shortly thereafter it entered into a "correspondance fraternelle" with section Panthéon-Français and accepted the proposal of section Arsenal to disarm all suspects. The committee also called to order the commander of the section's battalion for not relieving the guards at their posts, but realizing the pressure under which he was operating it named two adjutants to assist him. On 1 June it disarmed a deserter.[67]

Many were dissatisfied with the results of the insurrection. Perhaps the most critical of all were the Enragés. They continued to demand a law that would make speculation and engrossment of the necessities of life a crime. To appease them, the Convention enacted a law on 26 July 1793 making profiteering a capital offense.[68] The hastily and poorly drafted law was, however, extremely harsh and ill defined.[69] Nevertheless, the sans-culottes continued to press for its enforcement. Because too many merchants were being acquitted, they demanded that only sans-culottes compose the juries. "The sans-culottes," they argued, "are rich in virtue, and hence can best apply the law."[70] Throughout the months of July and August, both Roux and Leclerc carried on a running attack on profiteers and monopolizers. Roux repeated some of the phrases he had used in May:

> The proprietors open or close, according to the thermometer of avarice, the granaries of subsistence; the goods of the clergy and the national estates have almost entirely passed into the hands of people enriched by the blood of the widow and the orphan. The gentlemen of the robe and the sword have engrossed the yield of the earth and have become masters in all branches of commerce . . . Speculators, show me your pocket-books; your sudden wealth will attest without retort to your larcenies, your betrayals, your crimes. Before the capture of the Bastille, you were covered with nothing but rags; today you inhabit palaces; you owned but a plow and now you are rich landlords. You engaged in petty commerce, often on the street, and now you possess immense riches.[71]

Leclerc, too, continued his exposure of speculators and monopolizers. To pardon them would mean that the revolutionaries had joined them, he wrote. The republic, he argued, possessed enough to feed everyone, and the harvest of 1793 promised to be abundant. If grain sold at four or five times its value, that was due to speculators. He proposed therefore that the state purchase all grain and other essentials. Like others, he suggested storing the surplus in public granaries and selling it at moderate prices, to be fixed by the Convention; the poor, however, should obtain their grain free of charge. The Convention ought also to requisition essential goods, paying the cultivator a just indemnity. No one, he concluded, had the right to possess more than he could consume from one harvest to another.[72]

The Montagnards could hardly have embraced such a policy of nationalizing the distribution of goods. It was one thing to give concessions to the sans-culottes in order to mobilize them against the Gironde; it was quite another to transform an economy based on laissez-faire. Besides, the growing demand for centralizing the war effort left little room for dissent. In a few short months after the successful insurrection, the Enragés fell victim to the revolutionary government.

As Mathiez puts it so eloquently,

> The authorities yielded in order to avoid trouble, and the same day that they gave in, they began against the Enragés a repression without mercy . . . At the very same time that they voted the laws inspired by [the Enragés], they put them in prison, they sentenced them and dispersed their partisans. And, the better to destroy them, they turned against them the law of suspects that they were the first to demand against the monopolizers. They were the first victims of the Terror which had been their work.[73]

The tragedy of the Enragés, as Mathiez says, is that they became victims of instruments that they had forged against the counter-revolutionaries. They recognized that state power had been wrested from the privileged classes in favor of the new property holders. The sans-culottes remained powerless, however. How was it possible to curb the *négociant,* the bourgeois, or the *laboureur* and still retain the essential features of the new economy? The Declaration of the Rights of Man had proclaimed property to be "a sacred and inviolable right" (number 17). Moreover, feudal obligations had been abolished by the summer of 1793, not only in word but in deed. Under such circumstances, could the Convention reintroduce limits, adopt regulations, or impose restrictions on the accumulation of this "sacred and inviolable right"? The Enragés answered in the affirmative; but every master worker, petty shopkeeper, or ambitious entrepreneur, not to mention every landlord, large farmer, or government contractor, would have opposed efforts to shackle his newly gained freedom to invest, to profit, or to exploit.

Furthermore, the revolutionary government, faced as it was with conducting the war against the Coalition without and the counter-revolution within, could ill afford to create more enemies. Like dissenters everywhere and at all times, the Enragés were undermining the unity of the government, that "single will" of which Robespierre spoke as he defended the harsh measures of the Terror. The split between the Convention and its Great Committees on the one hand and the sans-culottes on the other, so brilliantly discussed by Albert Soboul in his masterful treatise *Les Sans-culottes parisiens en l'an II,* could not in the end be compromised. The suppression of the Enragés, followed by the arrest and trial of the Hébertists, put an end to opponents of the Mountain's dictatorship. Its ultimate consequences, however, were Thermidor and Prairial.

IX

Anatomy of the Insurrection

On 2 June . . . the insurgents scored only a partial
and precarious victory.

Albert Mathiez, *La Révolution française*

The 2d of June was, thus, a veritable coup d'état directed
against the national representation. The ultra-revolutionary
school, which believes that the end justifies the means, glorified it; the fatalistic school, which proclaims the legitimacy
of a fait accompli, recorded it without protest.

Louis Mortimer-Ternaux, *Histoire de la Terreur 1792–1794*

THOSE HISTORIANS who like Michelet think that the events of 2 June
had "unleashed what the Evêché wanted"[1] are profoundly mistaken, in my
view. The tactics of the Jacobins were aimed precisely at frustrating such
a possibility. One key to these tactics lay in their success not only in
isolating such men as Varlet, Gusman, and Loys but also in subordinating
the whole Comité des Neuf to a larger committee of twenty-five, the
majority of whom were officials, members of the Jacobin Club, or in
sympathy with the Jacobins' aims. Eleven of them were members of the
Directory from the department of Paris, and four were from the Paris
Commune. As to where and when the decision was made to establish this
enlarged committee, and who were the principal figures proposing it, these
questions cannot be answered because no documents exist that would
shed light on the exact origin of what became the Comité central révolutionnaire. Indirect evidence leads us to believe, however, that there
must have been consultations if not frantic discussions among leading
Montagnards, Jacobins, and departmental and municipal authorities, as
well as officers in the National Guard and police officials. In addition,
some memoirs, accusations, and confessions enable us to reconstruct early
developments. It is possible also to guess at some of the answers by
examining the order of events and their outcome.

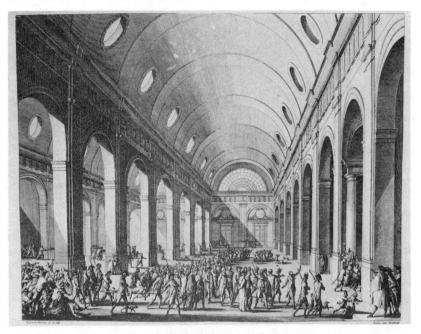

The end of the Girondins

It should be noted that the departmental authorities who called the meeting out of which the Comité central révolutionnaire would emerge did so on the initiative of the Jacobins. The delegates chosen by the sections, the department, and the Paris Commune met in their hall. This new center of the insurrection was created, in the words of Louis Blanc, in order "to destroy the prestige of the Evêché committee." Once the Comité central took control of the insurrection, it ended "the influence of the violent on the Hôtel de Ville."[2]

Jaurès points out that the Comité central révolutionnaire acted as an autonomous power. It made no allusion to the decree of the Comité des Neuf, signed by Varlet, that had annuled the powers of the constituted authorities of the Commune and of the department. It "seemed to oppose" the revolutionary committee of the Evêché (the Comité des Neuf), he writes.[3] "Seemed" is hardly the proper word; there was no question that the Jacobins, with the connivance of the departmental authorities, aimed at subordinating the Evêché committee to their own.[4] It should be noted, moreover, that the call convoking the delegates from the sections, the department, and the Commune went out on 29 May, that is, two days before the insurrection began. This means that the Jacobins and the local and departmental authorities must have been aware of the possibility, and from their point of view the danger, implicit in the Evêché assembly. Whatever their desire to remove the Girondin authorities, they surely must have recognized the peril to their own leadership that arose from the meeting of the sections. Hence even before the insurrection was launched they had already made arrangements to control it by subordinating the Evêché committee to their own organs of power. There was always the danger that an insurrection that called out masses of armed men, once set in motion, could take on a life of its own. The limited goal of removing some two dozen Girondin deputies was hardly what a Varlet, a Gusman, or a Loys aimed at. The *Chronique de Paris* admitted as much when it wrote, "*Many* misguided men, distinguishing between neither Plain nor Mountain, accused the whole Convention of stupendous increases [in the price] of foodstuffs, and believed they would find an end to their ills in its dissolution."[5] The arrest of the Girondins would hardly have been sufficient motivation for these "many misguided men."

How did it happen, moreover, that the original Comité des Neuf became a Comité des Dix with the arrival of Dobsen? His early career, on the eve of the Revolution, had placed him in a strategic position. Dobsen had founded Masonic lodges in the Champagne before the Revolution and, together with the Abbé Fauchet and Nicolas de Bonneville, had helped launch the Cercle Social in Paris.[6] Having risen to the highest degrees in the Cercle, he established amicable connections with moderate *parlementaires* before the Revolution and with leading Girondins and Montagnards after 1789. The Evêché assembly had not elected him to the Comité des Neuf; he had been imprisoned by the Commission des Douze during the time when the assembly was meeting and was not freed until 31 May. He must have been co-opted by the Comité des Neuf or appointed by the Comité central, that is, by the enlarged committee that met in the Jacobins. In any case, a change in tactics is visible once Varlet had been removed as president of the Comité des Neuf.

When Varlet gave the signal for the insurrection, it should be recalled, the directives signed by him and Fournerot suspended the powers of the constituted authorities;[7] they said nothing about reinstating them. Two early decrees are dated before midnight on 30 May, before Dobsen had joined the Evêché committee. At about 9:00 A.M. on 31 May the Evêché committee, with Dobsen at its head, went to the Hôtel de Ville, where it was joined by the fifteen commissioners from the assembly convoked by the Directory of the Paris department. This enlarged committee abrogated the powers of the General Council and immediately reinstated them. Thus the new, official power took over control of the insurrection.[8]

Writing in the fall of 1794 from his prison cell, Varlet charged that among those elected "to save the country" on 31 May were true republicans but also a number of emissaries from "the most destructive of factions." This "League of Caligula" saw nothing in the overthrow of the Brissotins but the possibility of a vast scope for its ambition. He continued, "The insurrectionary committee [the Comité des Neuf] contained the germ of a revolutionary government, conceived secretly at the start . . . The false insurgents substituted Robespierre for Brissot: for federalism [they substituted] a revolutionary dictatorship, decreed in the name of public safety. As for me, I was too sincere to be initiated into it; *I was set aside.*"[9] Gusman was also "set aside." He was arrested after the attacks on him by various Conventionnels, notably Barère. His section, Piques, intervened in his behalf, however, and freed him the same day.[10] His removal from the Comité des Neuf meant that the original committee elected by the Evêché assembly was reduced to a total of eight members—and this assumes that the latter were united in the tasks before them.

In April 1794 Sebastien-Marie Bruno de Lacroix was turned over to the revolutionary tribunal, reproached like other extremists for "un crime d'avoir, au 31 mai, faillit passer la ligne où la révolution s'était arretée" ("for a crime, on 31 May, of having nearly crossed beyond the line where the revolution had halted").[11] It seems that Lacroix did make "certains projets fort violents" in the Commune, proposals of such a nature that Dobsen forced him to leave the tribune.[12] Speaking in the Jacobin Club on 21 August 1793, Loys accused Dobsen of treachery. He charged "that Dobsen . . . abandoned his post in the Commune at the time of the insurrection of 31 May" and affirmed that "the man who conducts himself in this way can be nothing but a traitor."[13]

Another revealing episode is worth recording. On 12 March 1794 Moynin (or Monnin), aide-de-camp to Hanriot, rose in the Cordelier Club to speak about a faction in the Convention that had already appeared at the time of the 31 May insurrection. According to his account, François Chabot and Léonard Bourdon confronted the Comité central. Moynin then introduced an unnamed member of the former Comité central to tell the Cordeliers what had transpired. This witness revealed that the two Jacobins demanded to know the motives under which the committee was acting and threatened to call in the departments if the insurrectionists dared lay a hand on a single deputy. Furthermore, they insisted that since the leading Girondins had resigned, the insurrection was no longer necessary. He then revealed that he had visited the Committee of Public Safety as a representative of the Comité central and that Barère had asked him if his committee had thought through the goals of the insurrection. He replied, "What's it to you? Do your job and let us do ours." He concluded by saying that being discontented with the way he had been received by the members of the Committee of Public Safety, he returned to the Comité central and had it take "the great measures that everyone knows." Hébert arose after this recital and attested to the truth of what had been reported.[14]

It would be interesting to know the name of the member who recounted this episode. Despite some confusion as to precisely when Chabot and Léonard Bourdon arrived to confront the insurrectionary committee and whether it was the Comité des Neuf or the Comité central that they attacked, there seems to be little doubt that they were trying to abort the insurrection. Barère's opposition needs no further proof.[15] Whether the "resignation" of the chief Girondins was used as an argument before it actually occurred is not clear, for the reporter speaks of the Comité central's taking "great measures" after his meeting with the Committee of Public Safety. In any case, some leading Jacobins were opposed to the insurrection whether it was to be unleashed by the Comité des Neuf or by the Comité central. Among them was Legendre, whose expulsion from the Cordeliers for opposing the insurrection was demanded by Leclerc. When a number of Jacobins proposed on 17 May 1793 that a committee of public safety be established by the society, Legendre had opposed it, asserting that "if you organize a committee of public safety, they will say that it is a committee of insurrection."[16] This was the whole point of the proposal, of course, as it was of Thuriot's suggestion that the society declare itself to be in permanent session.

From whom was Dobsen taking his orders? A partial answer may lie in the following events. On the morning of 1 June, he and Loys were sent by the Comité central to the Committee of Public Safety in order to deliberate "on means to save the country."[17] It may seem surprising that Loys was sent along with Dobsen in light of his criticism in the Jacobins two months later. In any case, he must have had an opportunity to judge Dobsen's actions, assuming that he was critical of the president of the Comité des Dix from the beginning. Thus Dobsen must have played a key role in transmitting the decisions of the Convention's committee, decisions to which he could very well have contributed.

Nor was he the only one to play this role. On 15 April 1794 Robespierre, speaking in the Jacobins, sharply attacked Louis-Pierre Dufourny, president of the Directory of the Paris department. "On 31 May," Robespierre charged, "Dufourny was introduced into the committee of insurrection [the Comité central révolutionnaire]; when he saw that the popular movement would succeed, he left the committee and sought means to make it impotent."[18] On 7 June, Dufourny spoke in the Jacobins on the great debt the country owed the Comité central but warned that the committee could not continue to enjoy powers that tended toward dictatorship. He then offered his resignation and alerted the citizens present that the Comité central would assemble in the hall of the Jacobins at nine the next morning to deliberate on measures of public safety. He invited "the patriots" (that is, the Jacobins present) to join with the Comité in the discussion of its future. Calvet points out that his plan was to initiate a full or plenary meeting of the constituted authorities, largely open to all, to receive the decision of the Comité central.[19]

In October 1794 Dufourny published a defense of the 31 May insurrection and attacked the proposal to readmit the seventy-three expelled Girondin deputies. In the course of his defense he linked the "moderates" with Hébertists, Robespierrists, and "les Vandalistes." Then he made this revealing confession:

> There were on 31 May conspirators and their agents! Yes, without a doubt, there were such men as Guzman and several other men of blood. I made it my duty to spot them, to draw attention to them, to remove them . . . It was then that the triumph of patriotism was assured . . . Fearing, with reason, that the powers delegated temporarily by the people not be debased or treacherously used by a dictatorship . . . I took steps for a new convocation of the people, which, suppressing the Comité central révolutionnaire, replaced it by a Comité de Salut public for the Department . . . Robespierre . . . reproached me at the Jacobins, on 16 Germinal last, . . . for having *shackled the popular movement at that time*.[20]

Calvet finds this statement impudent since on 3 June Dufourny and his colleague Dufresne in an address to the department of Paris called the arrest of the Girondins a "mere dilatory measure that will muffle the revolutionary movement" and praised the Commune as being both "energetic" and "bold."[21]

Equally revealing is the incident that took place on the morning of 31 May when the newly elected commissioners who had met in the Jacobins joined their colleagues in the General Council of the Paris Commune. Delegates of the important women's club the Société des républicaines révolutionnaires asked to be admitted in order to deliberate with the commissioners on public affairs and on the course of the insurrection. They were refused on the pretext that "the committee [the Comité central révolutionnaire] was not a club, but rather, that it was composed of delegates from the forty-eight sections."[22] Technically speaking this may have been true, but the informal nature of the elections and the extra-legal organization they created should not have excluded the women from discussing the crisis with delegates of the sections. On 2 June the women appeared in the Convention and asked to be heard on an "important project" but were refused the floor as the Convention was preoccupied with its own crisis.[23]

Once the Girondins had been expelled, the Committee of Public Safety demanded that the Commune get rid of the "dangerous elements" on the Comité central. This was to be done by allowing only commissioners who had been elected by the departmental authorities to remain on the new committee, with the power to co-opt others and to report to the Commune.[24] The General Council acknowledged this complaint and adopted the following resolution: "The General Council, after receiving the complaint from the Committee of Public Safety, Resolves in consequence that only the citizens elected by the constituted authorities will form the Comité révolutionnaire and will co-opt assistants who shall be known to the Council."[25]

On 3 June Mayor Pache, accompanied by two members of the Comité central and an adjutant of Hanriot, presented himself before the Committee of Public Safety to assure it that the provisional authorities would surrender their insurrectionary powers. Furthermore, they would do all in their power "to halt the general movement, to hand over without danger, without shock and without agitation, the full and free exercise of the administrative and municipal functions to the constituted authorities alone."[26] There could hardly have been a more complete capitulation to official authority. Despite this surrender, the Comité central sought to justify its actions by assuring the Committee of Public Safety of its good faith.

It could have no illusions, after all, that the arrest of the twenty-nine Girondins had been a popular act of the Conventionnels. They had forced the Assembly to do their bidding and thereby had humiliated it. Although the Montagnards were its friends, it had many enemies.[27] Furthermore, there is little doubt that within the very bosom of the Comité central and of the General Council there were those who hoped to dissolve the Evêché committee. Hassenfratz seems to have played a moderating role, softening the measures proposed by his colleagues. He even struck from the list some of the Girondins proposed for the purge, and he played a key part in the dissolution of the Comité central.[28]

The same day Pache and his comrades visited the Committee of Public Safety, the Comité central reported on the tasks it had undertaken and accomplished. At its conclusion it offered to resign, a proposal the Commune neither accepted nor refused.[29] The General Council expressed its gratitude, however, for the Comité's important work. The Evêché committee also drafted an address congratulating the Convention for the arrests it had decreed and asking it to draft a republican constitution.[30]

On 4 June the Comité central appointed Jean Varlet and two colleagues to draft the act of accusation against the arrested deputies, and the young Enragé read the act to the assembled members on the following day. At the same time it advised the commissioners in the post office to continue their censorship of the mail. It also instructed Loys to report to the General Council on his meeting with the Committee of Public Safety and to inform the Jacobins of the Comité's operations.[31]

Although the capitulation of the municipal authorities to the Committee of Public Safety was without reservation, the Comité central's delegates did ask the committee to provide the subsidy voted for the men who had borne arms during the three days of the insurrection. In return, they promised to surrender their powers.[32] They could hardly have done less for the sans-culottes who had followed them. Robert Lindet reported that he would consult Danton on the method of paying the men and that he foresaw no difficulty in meeting this obligation.[33] Was Lindet sincere? If so, he must have agreed to the request only after the Comité central had indicated that it would accept the demands of the Committee of Public Safety. According to that committee's *procès-verbal,* the delegates of the Comité central were told bluntly that it would not provide funds for the revolutionary army until the Comité central révolutionnaire had laid down its powers.[34] This report is buttressed by an unsigned and undated note drafted by the Comité central that reports the meeting with the Committee of Public Safety.[35]

On the same day, 4 June, the Comité central decreed that the authorities of the Paris department should convoke the commissioners of the sections (that is, the Evêché assembly) to revoke the "unlimited powers" that had been granted them by their respective sections. The reason for this act was stated quite bluntly: it was dangerous to leave them with such powers for too long.[36] Lulier informed the Comité central that same day that the General Council of the Paris department had called a meeting for 6 June.[37] It was to this body that the commissioners of the sections were to surrender their powers. The address drafted by the delegates in the hall of the Jacobins left little doubt as to where their sentiments lay: "Faithful to principles, submissive to the law, the Department of Paris supports the worthy representatives of the people, at the price of their [own] blood."[38]

Rumors about its supposed usurpation of power reached the Commune during its session of 4 June. At the same meeting its reporter noted, "several representatives of the people, and notably those of the Committee of Public Safety, have expressed their uneasiness on this subject." There followed a universal protest. The *procès-verbal* reported that "at these words, a cry of indignation arose from the members of the Council, as well as from the galleries, and this loathsome charge is unanimously disclaimed." The offer of the Conseil général révolutionnaire to resign, made the day before, permitted the indignant response of the Paris Commune to accusations that it was aspiring to a dictatorship.[39]

The following day the Conseil général révolutionnaire and the commissioners of the forty-eight sections adopted a resolution expressly reaffirming their desire for a Republic "one and indivisible," swearing to defend the inviolability of the Convention, and promising to execrate any individual who would dare propose a dictatorship.[40] There is no need to challenge the sincerity of this resolve. Nevertheless, the persistent existence of the Comité central, and the support it received from the sections and the Paris Commune as a result of the successful insurrection, continued to threaten the peace and security of the deputies. Only its elimination or transformation into a legal agent of state power subordinate to the Convention would satisfy its opponents.

On 6 June the Committee of Public Safety presented a decree to the Convention seeking to end the independence of insurrectionary committees that represented a challenge to that body. All "extraordinary committees" were to be suppressed in favor of the regularly constituted surveillance bodies established by the law of 21 March 1793. Official authorities were to be expressly forbidden to recognize such extraordinary committees, and the armed forces were not to obey them. Furthermore, any interruption of the postal service would carry a penalty of ten years in prison.[41] Two days later the Convention opened a discussion on these proposals drafted by Barère.

The Committee of Public Safety and its reporter twisted and turned. On 31 May, it will be recalled, the Convention had voted that the sections had merited well of the country; no opposition seemed to have developed in the Committee. Danton had declared on the same day, "Il faut donner justice au peuple," and Barère had proposed a soothing address that spoke of "order and [the] respect" shown to constituted authorities and the representatives of the people. On 2 June Barère reversed himself, however, and warned of the danger to the Convention surrounded by bayonettes. "It is not for slaves to draft laws . . . The movement with which we are threatened, that menaces us, belongs to London, to Madrid, to Berlin."[42]

On 2 June Barère took the floor only once, to denounce the leaders of the insurrection and to menace them with the threat to avenge the "outraged majesty" of the Convention. As a result, he became unpopular among the sections. An observer wrote, "Such appeared to me the state of mind [of the sans-culottes], that I could not but be frightened by the vision of the head of Danton mounted on a pike along with that of Clavière, and I would think to be infinitely more secure than Papa Pache if I were but the doorman of his *hôtel.*"[43] On 7 June Danton was denounced in the Jacobin Club but was defended by Desmoulins, who maintained that "Danton is always the same," which was by then doubtful. Months later, on 6 April 1794, Robespierre too accused Danton. "The *journée* of 31 May," he stated, "without contradiction saved the country, . . . Danton, Hérault, Lacroix wanted to halt the insurrection in order to turn it against the people."[44]

The attempt to repudiate the Evêché assembly and by implication the insurrection was too blatant, however. Robespierre came to the defense of the revolutionaries and asked if the suppression of revolutionary committees [insurrectionary committees], "created by the people themselves," would not encourage the aristocrats and the malevolent. Barère was forced to retreat, and in so doing he demonstrated the uncertainty and vacillation of the government. Finally it was agreed to table the project by referring it to the Committee of Public Safety for further study. It was never reintroduced.[45]

The Comité central révolutionnaire was transformed into the Comité de Salut public du département de Paris on 8 June.[46] At first it met in the Jacobins, later moving to its permanent quarters in the Collège des Quatre-Nations. Many of its members had served on the original Comité central, and its first president, Marquet, had presided over that committee as well.[47] The Comité central had done an immense amount of work, from drafting an act of accusation against the Girondin deputies to censoring the mail—in short, it was the moving force in the insurrection.[48] Together with the Commune, the commissioners of the sections, and the communes of the Paris department, it reported proudly that Parisians had conducted themselves with such discipline that not one drop of blood had been spilled during the days of the insurrection. Traitors were in hiding and suspects had been arrested, it wrote, but a spirit of concord reigned supreme.[49] In an address to the eighty-five departments, the Comité central explained that Paris had risen in insurrection because the security of individuals and the liberty of the press had been violated while the Commission des Douze promoted the counter-revolution.[50] What it failed to say was that it had forced the Convention to do its bidding. Nevertheless, the resolution adopted by the Convention read, "The national Convention declares that during the *journées* of 31 May, 1st, 2, and 3 June, the Revolutionary General Council of the Commune and people of Paris contributed powerfully to save the liberty, the unity, and the indivisibility of the Republic."[51] Thus the attempt to discipline the Comité central, the Commune, and the sections came to nought.

The last session of the Comité central took place on 5 June. It was no mere formal gathering; the Committee acted upon important matters and continued to work on the public business before it as it had during the insurrection.[52] The Comité central did all it could to force the Convention to move against the arrested Girondins. Despite the support that an act of accusation against them received from the Committee of Public Safety, the Convention refused to adopt such an act for a long time. On 5 June the Comité's members charged with correspondence wrote the Commune that they had failed to receive supporting pieces of evidence against the Girondins. The Commune submitted this letter to the Comité central, which explained that its heavy schedule had made it impossible to get on with the work of gathering evidence against the arrested deputies.[53]

The last act of the Comité central was to warn the administrators of police of the Paris department that prisoners were to be treated with the dignity due free men. This was in reply to a complaint of citizens of section Butte-des-Moulins. On 6 June Clémence was given an official notification by Raisson, secretary of the Assemblée des autorités constituées du département et des section de Paris, citing the cessation of the Comité's powers. This was the assembly that had met under the presidency of Dufourny. It praised the actions of the Comité central, but was seconded by the Convention only on 13 June on a motion of Couthon.[54]

The insurrection was celebrated officially until Thermidor. On 8 December 1794 the seventy-three expelled Girondins were readmitted into the Convention. On 10 and 11 March 1795 the sections began to address the Convention, formally repudiating the insurrection. Mont-Blanc was the first to congratulate the Convention for condemning the insurrection, followed by section Unité. Gardes-Françaises resolved on 10 March 1795 to proclaim to the Convention that it had not taken part in the *journée* of 31 May and that a band of conspirators had acted in the name of the majority. Other sections followed soon after.[55]

Did the sections meekly acquiesce in dissolving the Evêché committee? The answer appears to be a qualified no. An unknown section held a discussion on this question shortly after the insurrection at which a spokesman gave an eloquent appeal to maintain "the union" of the sections, which alone gave them power and made "the people invincible." He then suggested certain measures that were adopted by the assembly.[56] The general assembly of this section then resolved the following: (1) that the Comité central révolutionnaire sitting in the Commune be composed of one member from each section; (2) that this member be selected from the comité de surveillance of the section; (3) that he report back to the comité de surveillance, which would present his report to the general assembly; (4) that the comité de surveillance place great emphasis on demanding this report and in case of its neglect so inform the general assembly; (5) that the commissioner so delegated be changed any time the section found it necessary.[57]

The same ideas may be found in the register of deliberation of the general assembly of section Halle-au-Blé dated 4 June. It asked the sections to elect commissioners with unlimited powers to attend a meeting in the Evêché in order to install a new Comité central révolutionnaire. The appeal of Halle-au-Blé was widely disseminated. "It attests that many sectionnaires wanted to maintain the Comité central in reorganizing it and in controlling it very tightly," wrote Calvet.[58]

Dufourny presided over the assembly of constituted authorities on 8 June when the Evêché committee surrendered its powers. But under pressure from sections like Halle-au-Blé, Lulier proclaimed in the name of the Paris department that all constituted authorities of the department would be convoked on Thursday "the seventh of the present month [read sixth]." From this assembly arose the Comité de Salut public du département de Paris.[59] The effort of sections like Halle-au-Blé to maintain a Comité central that would reflect the desires of the sections failed. Even if they had won this demand, it could have been only a temporary victory. It is doubtful whether the revolutionaries who supported this effort could have withstood the growing pressure for centralization. By December 1793, whatever remnant of independent power the Paris Commune still exercised had been surrendered. The Convention and its Great Committees had proved too powerful.

How did the participants who left records of their reactions view the events described? As might be expected, not one embraced the cause of the Evêché assembly or its committees. All Conventionnels felt embarrassed and threatened by the Comité des Neuf and the Comité central; none made a distinction between the two. The Montagnards felt that the Girondins had brought retribution on themselves by their stubborn refusal to adopt the drastic measures that alone would have responded adequately to the crisis. Had they been more perceptive or more honest, they would have admitted, as Robespierre understood, that the Revolution could not succeed without the active involvement of the sans-culottes. To involve them, however, would have meant extending economic and social concessions that would have satisfied their most pressing needs. The Girondins viewed the *journée* as the result of a plot, a conspiracy between the Jacobins and the Paris Commune. They made no distinction between Montagnards and Enragés, between Robespierrists and Maratists, between the Jacobin Club and the Evêché assembly.

Barère blamed Danton and Jean-François Lacroix for conspiring with the Paris Commune. In fact, he accuses "the whole party of the Left [which] was in on the secret." Barère describes an incident, probably fictitious, that allegedly took place when the deputies led by Hérault de Sechelles confronted Hanriot and his cannoneers. According to him, an aide-de-camp of Hanriot approached Danton and Lacroix, as Barère and a cousin of his, termed simply Hector B., heard him say, "C'est bien cela, cela va bien," as Danton pressed his hand.[60] Strange that only Barère and his cousin witnessed such a revealing incident. Barère also claims that he tried to rally the deputies to join him in combatting the acts of violence against them but that many cited the Girondin impeachment of Marat that had flouted the principle of inviolability. As for Danton's offer to act as hostage, it was a result of his bad conscience because he was responsible for the proscriptions, writes Barère. The Federalist movement was launched by the departments, he says, because they disapproved of these proscriptions.[61] He refuses to acknowledge the prior revolt of Lyons or the steps taken by several departments against Paris. Equally revealing is his confession that "I had to act according to the wishes of the Convention, and to believe (as it believed, or as it appeared to believe, and had the French believe) that it approved the events of 31 May, and that it accepted their results in order to conform to the general opinion of the nation."[62]

Lanjuinais blamed the uprising on Danton, Marat, and Robespierre, who were supported by Pitt and the émigrés in London. Moreover, the insurrectionary committee was composed of foreigners drawn from the Cordeliers and elevated by the Commune and the Jacobins into a "comité d'insurrection."[63] Louvet was convinced that 31 May had resulted from the desperation of the Mountain as it saw its followers being defeated in Marseilles, Bordeaux, the Jura, the Midi, and finally in Lyons. When it received news from Lyons, the Mountain sensed that "there was no longer any safety for it but in a coup of despair."[64] To the question how it was possible that all Paris could be subjugated by "four or five thousand brigands," Meillan replied that "all the reins of power were in the hands of the conspirators, and that the people were apathetic." They did not dare act against the lawful authorities who were the "principal actors in the conspiracy . . . Everyone was frightened; no one dared speak up."[65]

Needless to say, the Montagnards had a different explanation for the insurrection. "Do you want to know who sounded the tocsin?" asked the younger Robespierre. "I will tell you: it was the treason of our generals, it was the perfidy that delivered the camp of Famars, it was the bombardment of Valenciennes, it was the disorder that was sowed in the army of the North."[66] Levasseur admitted that the Montagnards were in a dilemma: they did not wish the deaths of their colleagues, but neither could they allow them to do more mischief. The departmental guard proposed by the Girondins was similar, in essence, to the armed force that Louis had intended to establish in order to make himself master. Levasseur admitted further that "a kind of stupor" had seized the Convention before the deputies voted the arrest of the Gironde. Everyone was depressed and disturbed by "the long and sad session of 2 June." Yet he praises the courage and principled behavior of Barbaroux and Lanjuinais and concludes that the Girondins had brought on their fate by their own actions.[67]

Conclusion

THE CONFLICT between the Gironde and the Mountain was an intraclass struggle with overtones of a classic combat between two contending elites. Political parties and those who lead them develop a momentum of their own, however. Not every position, party plank, or platform embodies the historic or even the momentary interests of a social class. If an ideology is a "false consciousness," party leaders who promote it do so at the expense of reality. The Girondins had tasted power and were unwilling to share it with their rivals. There was nothing in their class structure that dictated a repudiation of Danton's efforts to compromise. The vitriolic attacks of the *Patriote Français* on the "anarchistes" encouraged the counter-revolution, objectively speaking, no less than did the *Père Duchesne*'s denunciation of the "aristocrates" in the sections. Supporters of the Mountain were no more anarchists than the defenders of the Gironde were aristocrats. In politics, it has often been noted, whoever says "A" must say "B" as well. Revolutionary politics are no different. It is hardly conceivable that had the leaders of the Gironde been willing to compromise with their opponents, the Montagnards would have repudiated them. Both groups were committed to the parliamentary system, after all. In the long run, its weakening undermined both factions equally.

It may be true, as Hamlet says, that "there's a divinity that shapes our ends, rough-hew them how we will." Without embracing the belief in geographic determinism, we cannot ignore it altogether. Those who were born in port towns could hardly disregard the interests of commerce; commercial interests in turn tended to neglect the needs of sans-culottes in the urban centers as well as those of agriculturalists in the countryside. But the Revolution needed the support of more than *négociants*, merchants, and wealthy bourgeois. This meant that the sans-culottes had to be given their due. The *maximum*, forced loans, laws against speculation and engrossment, encouragement of an egalitarian spirit—these were concessions and compensations for the sacrifices made by the people for *la patrie*. A commitment to the belief in laissez-faire economics and in the absolute freedom of the individual to pursue his own interests struck, obviously, at a regulated economy, the forced levy, and the government's traditional responsibility to maintain the price of necessities at certain levels. Here is the tragedy of history embodied in the phrase *la force des choses*. The defense of various economic interests develops a politics and a psychology of its own. Factional disputes embittered by personality conflicts encourage irreconcilable political positions. Compromise becomes less and less possible. A "moral insurrection" seems the only way out. Moral insurrections, as our century knows, lead to brutal insurrections—brutal in the sense that political parties or their leaders must be removed by force. *La force des choses* exerts its influence yet again.

The differences between the two parties in terms of age, property, ownership of national estates, education, and birthplace should not be minimized, but it must be borne in mind that not one of these categories predetermines individuals' political views. There has never been a direct relationship between youth and radicalism, for example, or between a small income and popular views; such factors cannot account for a deputy's support of the Gironde or the Mountain. Too many personal variables tend to interfere with such neat explanations. It would be equally false, in my opinion, to ignore the obvious social and psychological differences that such disparities give rise to. An average income of ninety-one thousand livres may be a qualitatively different influence on an individual than one of only thirty-nine thousand livres. A young man in his twenties does see the world—and a revolution—through different eyes from those of a colleague in his fifties.

It is best to acknowledge that it is impossible to know precisely the number of Girondins in the Convention. The absence of many deputies when important questions were being considered, the changes in various individuals' voting patterns, the abstentions, and the reversals all indicate the fluid nature of party politics in eighteenth-century France. In addition there is the evolution or in some cases the retrogression of individuals on various social or political measures. Moreover, if one asks the nature of the republic that the parties wanted to establish, a numerical distribution cannot provide the answer. That there was a hard core of Girondins balanced by one of Montagnards is not in doubt; it was the floating allegiances of the Plain that determined the victory or defeat of parties in the Convention. This analysis must of course be modified if we add the pressures of the sections, the Commune, and the popular societies on the legislative body. Parliamentary majorities depended ultimately not on the votes of deputies alone but on the weight exerted by these additional forces on the representatives.

This is not to say that opponents of the sans-culottes lacked political principles. Far from it. The men arrested by sectional revolutionary committees were often zealous defenders of the Gironde. Yet they were certainly not aristocrats, sometimes not even as that term was defined by the sans-culottes. Le Tellier of section Unité is a good example: had he not befriended Girondin deputies, he might have been left alone. His verses against the leaders of the Mountain, his intemperate self-description as "an enemy of anarchists," and his open contempt for the sans-culottes must have irritated the revolutionary committee. Whether he really extolled kings as his one accuser charged is questionable, however.

Despite his lowly social position, Caudel was popular enough to have been elected sergeant of his armed company. It is possible, of course, that his ownership of some property and his domestic service made him sympathetic to the moderate party, but they hardly rendered him an "aristocrat." Chazot was certainly not a Jacobin, but his personal service in the National Guard in the early days of the Revolution, his preference for a citizens' militia rather than a professional armed force, and his financial contributions to various revolutionary appeals and causes mark him as a supporter of moderate republicanism.

The political biography of Grapin demonstrates his devotion to the Revolution from its early beginnings, and his service both in the armed forces and on various sectional committees shows that he was an activist who was generous with his time and energy for the popular cause. It is interesting to note that despite the successful overthrow of the Gironde, the moderate party remained strong in section Contrat-Social and continued to show its confidence in Grapin and his moderate allies. To determine whether he was "un véritable sans-culotte," as his wife swore, or to what degree he was a moderate despite his own denial of this term prior to the installation of the Directory, is less important than to recognize that he was a republican.

Tassin, despite his profession of banking, was devoted to the Revolution during all its early stages. He was certainly public minded and served section Mail loyally. The charge that he had impeded recruitment of volunteers for the Vendée—an accusation repeated, incidentally, against all the moderates—is made without proof of a single specific act to sustain it. However strong the moderates' opposition to the Mountain in Paris, they did not join the counter-revolution. Whether they would have remained loyal to the revolutionary government had Federalism gained more popular support is a different matter. There is something tragic in his sigh that he could hardly imagine doing more for the Revolution than he had.

Tranchelahausse was more fortunate than Tassin, but only because he lived through the events of 9 Thermidor. There is little doubt of his devotion to republicanism, and if he failed to cure the wounded and the ill with his magic medicine, he must have given them some comfort at least. Few in section Mail held so many posts or carried out so many public duties. It is unfortunate that Brichet's letter denouncing him to the revolutionary committee of the section fails to specify the charges against Tranchelahausse. This makes it tempting to believe that the accusations may have had more to do with personal hostility than with politics. In either case the arrest and imprisonment of a popular president must have angered his followers, and to paraphrase Macbeth, though they could not utter their curses out loud, they must have expressed them deeply.

What especially strikes an observer of the struggle between the moderates and the sans-culottes is that those who had expressed themselves forthrightly in favor of the Girondins paid the price—but rather late in the game. Grapin was imprisoned in September 1793, Caudel in October, Chazot in December, Tassin and Tranchelahausse in February 1794. Le Tellier was arrested as late as May 1794. It is difficult to argue that the revolutionary government needed their heads, especially after crushing the Federalist revolt and repelling the foreign invaders by the winter and spring of 1794. Terror against counter-revolutionaries was one thing; against moderate republicans, it was something else. In this respect, the fraternization movement demonstrates that despite its slogan, the French Republic was neither one nor indivisible.

What essentially was the so-called fraternization movement? From the viewpoint of the sans-culotte militants, it was an action of like-minded men determined to suppress the "aristocrats" of the sections. They were especially resentful of the better-educated, more articulate, and socially superior sectionnaires whose politics were more moderate than theirs. These people were often accomplished professionals; some were men of property, and all were literate. These advantages made them more persuasive in the general assemblies, which must have given them an edge in winning the unattached or the neutral over to their policies or programs. This was another reason for the resentment felt by the less educated and articulate sans-culottes and their spokesmen. To overcome their disadvantage, they had to combine their forces among several neighborhoods and take over a moderate or conservative section by adding their votes to those of the "patriotic" minority of a general assembly.

There was nothing democratic in this type of action, of course. If the Girondins in the sections were not outvoted, they were often intimidated by the militants who came armed with a variety of weapons, from clubs to sword sticks. It is obvious that no assembly could express its will under such circumstances. One can be sympathetic to the desires of the sans-culottes and can understand the desperate plight in which they found themselves as the Girondins discouraged the recruitment of volunteers for the Vendée or obstructed the forced loan. At the same time, one must be critical of attempts to discourage the general will of moderate sections.

In light of the Gironde's defeat, it is doubtful whether establishing the Commission des Douze was a wise decision. The Commission lacked the power to intimidate the sections or the Commune, and it could do nothing to obstruct the plans of the Evêché assembly. Had the Convention been united behind the Commission, it is conceivable that it might have had sufficient moral force to overawe its enemies. Failing this, however, the Commission only irritated the Montagnards and lost the Plain. Furthermore, it became a focus for the mounting sectional movement, which suppressed or neutralized whatever support the Girondins had in the sections. The arrests of Hébert and Varlet only aggravated the strife and further exposed the hollowness of the Commission's power. Garat, who was in a position to know the relative weight of the forces engaged in struggle in the capital, understood this fact.

Had the Girondins been able to persuade the Convention to concentrate the armed forces of the capital in its own hands and had the deputies succeeded in doing so, the balance of forces might have changed in the Gironde's favor. Barring such an outcome, which would have implied the complete capitulation of the popular forces to the Commission, the Girondins had to adopt a more realistic policy, one that denoted a willingness to compromise with the Montagnards. Such a policy would have meant an end to provoking the Mountain, to threatening the "anarchistes," and to attempting the arrest of their leaders. It would have necessitated a willingness to relinquish some of the power Vergniaud, Buzot, Gensonné, and Brissot had enjoyed. Anything short of this kind of compromise would have meant a confrontation with forces far superior to their own.

As for the threat to destroy the Mountain by using troops from the departments, it contained in itself the element of defeat for any party that dared to utter it. Just as in the summer of 1792 the Fédérés who had come to defend the Revolution were won over by the Jacobins, the Cordeliers, and the Enragés, so many of the departmental volunteers who came to support the Girondins were persuaded by the popular forces to change their loyalties. The threat of unleashing a civil war against Paris could not but undermine whatever lukewarm support for the Girondins remained among members of the Plain as well as among the sectionnaires who championed Girondin policies on a local level. In the end, the Federalist revolt only gave a further impetus to the patriotic feelings of many Frenchmen and strengthened the centralizing tendencies inherent in the concept of a "république, une et indivisible." The fact that it never was very united made little difference once terror became "the order of the day."

It is unlikely that the insurrection would have occurred had the duly constituted authorities remained in place. The Commune, despite its radical language, made no plans to remove the proscribed Girondins. Chaumette was certainly opposed to revolutionary action, and Hébert showed signs of vacillation. It is true, of course, that once the insurrection had begun, the Conseil général became the Conseil général révolutionnaire, signifying its adherence to the uprising. Nevertheless, the hesitations, vacillations, and retreats of that body before the insurrection and in the first hours of the action demonstrate that it was neither united on the tasks before it nor certain how to initiate the overthrow of its enemies. Fiery resolutions and enthusiastic resolves were hardly substitutes for determined action. That action had to come from a completely different kind of body.

The Evêché assembly was an insurrectionary body that developed the initiative to put an end to the crisis. It alone could give the signal for the revolt. Its first action, the suspension of the regularly constituted authorities, was initiated, appropriately enough, by Jean Varlet, the young Enragé who was devoted to direct democracy. An assembly, no matter how revolutionary, cannot undertake the exacting work of an executive organ; this can only be done by a small and a secret body. The Comité des Neuf proved adequate to the task. If it failed to remove the Girondins on the first try, it succeeded admirably on the second. By then, of course, the original committee had been dissolved into a larger body.

A careful examination of the mechanics of the *journée* demonstrates how the Comité des Neuf gave place to the Comité central révolutionnaire. In a sense this transformation was the decisive step in the insurrection; to it is due the relative smoothness of the uprising. Had Varlet and his colleagues remained at the head of the Evêché, it is doubtful whether Robespierre and those Montagnards who followed him would have supported the uprising. The lack of their support would hardly have encouraged the vacillating members of the Commune. Could the original Comité des Neuf have staged a successful uprising? Probably not. Even if it had been successful in the early stages of the revolt, the opposition of the Convention, the Commune, the Jacobins, and the moderate sections would have doomed the insurrection.

This in no way undermines the argument of the Enragés, however extreme their pronouncements must have sounded to the bourgeoisie, the professionals, or the master workers. There is evidence that they had the support of many sans-culottes. Roux, Varlet, and Leclerc uttered some harsh truths, while Lacombe and Léon shocked many Jacobins and Cordeliers alike. Varlet's contention that the Comité central had shackled the insurrection could scarcely be refuted. Removing some two dozen deputies from the Convention hardly solved the problems of shortages and high prices, the continuing plunge of the *assignat,* or the lack of popular education. Friedrich Engels' warning that there is no greater tragedy than the coming to power of a party before its time applies to the Enragés. It is inconceivable that they could have governed without the aid of the bourgeoisie or the peasantry—assuming that they had the universal support of the sans-culottes, which was far from the case. The paradox remains: as Jacobinism triumphed and as it made concessions to sans-culottism, it excluded the Enragés from its triumph.

The ideas that "corrupt deputies" had to be expelled, that the country had to be saved, and that certain economic and financial measures had to be taken—all these originated in the more radical sections of Paris. The journals of Marat and Hébert, the brochures of Varlet and his colleagues, the orations of Roux and the more radical Cordeliers and Jacobins, and the accusations of the leading Montagnards against the Girondins—all these polemics served to radicalize public opinion in the capital and prepare the insurrection. The most active participants in the preliminaries, however, remained the sections whose resolutions, demonstrations, and votes led first to the Evêché assembly and from it to the Comité des Neuf. Ultimately, therefore, the Comité was an emanation of the sections and remained such throughout the days of the uprising. When spokesmen of the sections warned the deputies, including the Montagnards among them, that if they were unwilling or unable to save the country they would do so themselves, it was no idle threat. The insurrection was their work, just as the pressure exerted on the representatives to purge the Convention was their creation. It was the sectionnaires who composed the armed force that surrounded the National Assembly. It was their insistence that forced the Convention to bow before them.

The concept of an "insurrection morale" versus an "insurrection brutale" should be modified. Much depends, of course, on one's definition of brutality. It can be argued that any violation of the Convention's sovereignty, any interference with its deliberations, any forcing of the deputies' will was a brutal act. But this assumes that representatives of the people are aloof from their constituents' concerns. Pressures can be exerted on representatives by means other than threats of armed force. If the Convention had been left free to deliberate without interference and its majority had ruled in a detached, philosophical manner that in order to save

France the leading Girondins had to be expelled, would this have been a less "brutal" act? Would not such a decision have violated the parliamentary immunities of the purged representatives? Where is the morality in such an act? To argue that such a sacrifice was needed to save the country is to beg the principle inherent in the question. Unless the Girondins had voluntarily agreed to be purged, a patent absurdity since it implies that they no longer wanted to be what they were, it is inconceivable that no pressure would have been brought to bear upon them. They could have been voted down, of course, but their continued presence would have reminded the Convention that the problem had not been resolved.

In the sense that the "insurrection brutale" forced the Convention—that is, the institution as a whole—to do the bidding of outside forces, it can be argued that it was a brutal act. Its majesty had been outraged, as Danton declared. Yet the institution as such had not been destroyed, direct democracy had not been put into effect, the deputies remained representatives rather than mandatories of their electors, and even the arrested Girondins were allowed wide freedom. The Evêché committee and its successor, the Comité central révolutionnaire, had been dissolved and transformed into an administrative organ without power. The threat to the Convention's existence disappeared like a puff of smoke. The more savage attempt to dissolve it came not from those who wanted to broaden what we today call participatory democracy but from a resuscitated royalist opposition. When this menace was suppressed, its independence disappeared. The forces engaged in struggle—the social antagonists in the real world—were bound neither by the idea of an "insurrection morale" nor by that of an "insurrection brutale." They reacted pragmatically to the politics of the day. In doing so, they may have saved the Revolution.

Abbreviations
Notes
Bibliography
Index

Abbreviations

Archives and Libraries

AP   Archives de Paris

AN   Archives nationales

APP   Archives préfecture de police

BHVP   Bibliothèque historique de la Ville de Paris

BN   Bibliothèque nationale

BVC   Bibliothèque Victor Cousin

Published Works

AP   M. J. Mavidal, M. E. Laurent, et al., eds., *Archives parlementaires de 1787 à 1860; recueil complet des débats législatifs et politiques des chambres françaises. Imprimés par ordre du sénat et de la chambre des députés* (Paris: Librairie Administrative de Paul du Pont, 1879–).

Moniteur   *Réimpression de l'ancien Moniteur depuis la réunion des Etats-Généraux, jusqu'au Consulat (mai 1789–novembre 1799)* (Paris, 1858–1863).

B & R   P. J. B. Buchez and P. C. Roux, eds., *Histoire parlementaire de la Révolution française* (Paris: Paulin, Libraire, 1834–1838).

Notes

I. Montagnards versus Girondins

1. Edgar Quinet, *La Révolution,* 6th ed. (Paris, 1869), I, 446. Quinet is convinced that had the two factions had a common religion, ancient or modern, they would not have split (ibid., p. 445).

2. Albert Soboul, *Girondins et Montagnards* (Paris, 1980), p. 7. A. Kuscinski, *Dictionnaire des Conventionnels* (Brueil-en-Vexin, 1973), pp. 400–402, lists Marie-Joseph Lequinio (1755–1814) as the deputy and Jacobin. Unlike Soboul's work, Kuscinski's does not contain an entry for a Laquino.

3. M. J. Sydenham, *The Girondins* (London, 1961), p. 59.

4. C. Perroud, *La Proscription des Girondins (1793–1795)* (Toulouse and Paris, 1917), pp. 2, 3–4. The author cites Aulard, who quotes Thiers and C. Nodier as having coined the name Gironde between 1823 and 1831, but he refutes this claim.

5. B. Barère, *Mémoires de B. Barère* (Paris, 1842–1843), II, 43.

6. Quoted in Sydenham, *Girondins,* p. 34.

7. René Levasseur, *Mémoires de R{ené} Levasseur* (Paris, 1929), I, 254, 264.

8. D[ominique] J[oseph] Garat, *Mémoires sur la Révolution, ou exposé de ma conduite dans les affaires et dans les fonctions publiques* (Paris, 1795), p. 110. The Minister of the Interior compared the fatal division between the parties to the differences between Aristides and Themistocles (ibid., p. 138).

9. Alison Patrick, *The Men of the First French Republic* (Baltimore and London, 1972), p. 118. The author is convinced that even before 2 June 1793 there was a large group of deputies who accepted the political line associated with the Mountain and that it was this group that "did a disproportionate part of the actual work of government" (p. 130).

10. George Rudé, *The Crowd in the French Revolution* (Oxford, 1959), p. 120.

11. Neither the Mountain nor the Gironde formed a political party in the modern sense. Like our own Federalists and anti-Federalists in the early days of the Republic, both were opposed to the very concept of a "party" or "faction." Robespierre wrote that he was against all factions because a faction was contrary to the public interest, a common belief in the eighteenth century. M. Robespierre, *Oeuvres complètes de Robespierre,* ed. Eugène Deprez et al. (Paris, 1910–1965); *Le Défenseur de la constitution, Les Journaux,* ed. Gustave Laurent (Nancy, 1939), IV, 44.

12. Soboul, "Les Girondins," *Girondins et Montagnards,* pp. 20, 23–26, pas-

sim. This essay, in my opinion, is one of the most perceptive studies of the differences between the Mountain and the Gironde.

13. Ibid., pp. 27, 28, 30–31; Sydenham, *Girondins,* p. 190.

14. Robespierre, *Oeuvres, Discours,* ed. Deprez, IX, 88, 5 November 1792, "Réponse de Maximilien Robespierre à l'accusation de J. B. Louvet."

15. Chaumié, in Soboul, *Girondins,* p. 38; Albert Mathiez, *Girondins et Montagnards* (Paris, 1930), pp. 7, 8, 9–10; Sydenham, *Girondins,* pp. 187–188, 189–190.

16. Robespierre, *Oeuvres,* ed. Deprez, IX, 112, "Opinion de Maximilien Robespierre sur les subsistances," 2 December 1792: "What is the primary objective of society? It is to maintain the imprescriptible rights of man. What is the first of these rights? That of existence." The same passage may be found in Albert Laponneraye, ed., *Oeuvres de Maximilien Robespierre* (New York, 1970), III, 34–35.

In his *Défenseur* no. 4, Robespierre wrote, "Has one not seen, from the beginning of this revolution, an attempt to frighten the rich, by the idea of a *loi agraire,* an absurd bogy offered to stupid men by perverse men?" *Oeuvres,* ed. Laponneraye, I, 388.

Marat too rejected the *loi agraire.* He wrote, "They accuse me of preaching the agrarian law. It is a deceit without precedent . . ." He called it "this deadly doctrine [*cette doctrine funeste*] . . . destructive of all civil society . . ." (*Le Publiciste de la république française par Marat l'ami du peuple,* "Profession de foi, par Marat . . . ," no. 156, 30 March 1793).

17. Quoted in B & R, *Histoire parlementaire de la Révolution française* (Paris, 1834–1838), XXX, 126.

18. Mathiez, *Girondins,* pp. 8, 10.

19. Aulard, *Histoire politique de la Révolution française . . .* (Paris, 1901), pp. 397–398. "Les Girondins furent caractérisés et perdus par leur aristocratie d'attitude, de goûts, presque d'épiderme. On peut donc dire que, s'ils furent aussi démocrates que les Montagnards par les idées, ils le furent moins par les manières." Mathiez, however, believed that the Girondins had moved toward the right and to royalism because they refused to remove the king from the throne and because they dissolved the *tribunal extraordinaire* which had succeeded the Haute Cour (*Girondins,* p. 12).

20. Mathiez, *Girondins,* pp. 8, 9.

21. Jean Jaurès, *Histoire de la Révolution française,* ed. A. Mathiez (Paris, 1924), VII, 93.

22. Ibid., VII, 515. Jaurès admits, however, that the Gironde's politics led it to rest on the support of the bourgeoisie, while the politics of the Mountain were based on the support of the people. Politics, it must be observed, does not occur in a vacuum but is itself an outgrowth of the socioeconomic conditions it reflects—or refracts. In a footnote (p. 529), Mathiez writes that Jaurès minimized the conflict of interests and of classes that quickly developed behind the politics of the Gironde.

23. Ibid., VII, 526–527.

24. Ibid., p. 527.

25. Ibid., pp. 528, 530.

26. Ibid., pp. 528, 532.

27. Mathiez, *Girondins*, pp. 4, 13–14, 15. The quote is from Michelet.

28. Ibid., p. 15. Mathiez calls these opponents in the sections "Culottes-dorées." Whether they were such is questionable, as is discussed in the chapters on the conflict in the sections. See also François Gendron, *La Jeunesse dorée épisode de la Révolution française* (Québec, 1979).

29. C. Riffaterre, *Le Mouvement antijacobin et antiparisien à Lyon dans le Rhône-et-Loire en 1793 (29 mai-15 août)* (Lyons and Paris, 1912), discusses the conflict between the Girondin-dominated department and the Jacobin municipality. Also see B & R, XXVII, 424–443, passim.

30. The Girondins flattered the people until 1791, then made a volte-face because they feared that property was in danger after 10 August, says Michelet (quoted in Mathiez, *Girondins*, p. 17).

31. BN, Lb⁴¹ 2728, *Lettre de Jérome Pétion aux Parisiens* (Paris, 1793); the quote is from p. 15. Pétion begins his letter, "Just to what point will you continue to suffer while a handful of intriguers governs you? Have you broken the yoke of despots to bend your head under a yoke even more humiliating, even more intolerable, of a few factious underlings . . . who violate all laws of morality and justice, and speak of nothing but pillage and murder?" (p. 1).

32. BN, Lb⁴¹ 142, *A tous les Républicains de France, sur la société des Jacobins de Paris* (Paris, 29 October 1792). The quote is on p. 8, which continues, ". . . who want the ordinary worker to receive the same pay as the legislator; who want to level even the talents, knowledge, virtues, because they do not possess any of these. Perfidious men!" In an atmosphere of egalitarianism and democracy, Brissot's assertion that his opponents lacked talent and virtue must have convinced few that only the Girondins possessed these attributes.

33. Cited in Jaurès, *Histoire*, VII, 243–244. Cabet added, "The bourgeois dread the popular influence and fear for their riches" (ibid., p. 243).

34. Soboul, *Girondins*, p. 13. In contrast, "the Montagnard group established its base upon a much lower level, that of the artisanate and the shop, whose upper fringe approached the bourgeoisie."

35. Aulard, *Histoire politique*, pp. 400–401.

36. Chaumié, in Soboul, *Girondins*, pp. 28, 31, 32. "Il y a chez les Montagnards une grandeur tragique qui n'existe pas chez les Girondins . . . ," writes Chaumié (p. 31).

37. Jean-Paul Marat, *Le Publiciste*, no. 201 (28 May 1793). Marat reasoned, "Car au milieu d'une nation vaine, frivole, irrefléchie, possedée de l'amour de la domination, et toujours prête à devenir la dupe du premier frippon assez adroit pour capter sa confiance . . ." Federalism would reignite the disastrous wars of the barons and reestablish a feudal government.

38. Aulard, *Histoire politique*, pp. 402, 403.

39. Jaurès, *Histoire*, VII, 518–519.

40. *Le Publiciste*, no. 201.

41. Jaurès, *Histoire*, VII, 521–522. Jaurès quotes Marc-Antoine Baudot, the Montagnard deputy from Saône-et-Loire, who said that "there was absolutely no . . . uniformity of view within the different regions and towns that rose up

against the Convention after the 31st of May." Caen refused to listen to the schemes of the Girondins; its rebels wanted to restore the Old Regime. The Lyonnais wanted a hereditary monarchy. Toulon agreed to surrender to foreigners. Marseilles fought to become the capital of the Midi. Bordeaux refused to recognize the Convention but had no plans of its own. La Vendée wanted its nobles and priests restored. The question was not one of theory—federalism versus unity and indivisibility—but rather of the restoration of a class (ibid., pp. 524–525).

42. Chaumié, in Soboul, *Girondins,* pp. 42–45, passim. "The so-called Girondin federalism was nothing but a 'départementalisme,' extreme perhaps, but with no idea of a real dismemberment" (Albert Soboul, "Problème régional et réalités sociales," in *Comprendre la Révolution* [Paris, 1981], p. 233). The Girondin texts of 1792–1793 contain no project to create an American type of state. This may be seen in the *procès-verbaux* of the Girondin commission in the departments of Calvados, the Gironde, and Gard (ibid., p. 234).

43. Chaumié, in Soboul, *Girondins,* p. 41.

44. BN, 8° Le³⁸ 39, *Opinion du Citoyen Saint-Just, sur les subsistances, imprimée par ordre de la Convention Nationale* (Paris, 1792). Saint-Just declared, "Un peuple qui n'est pas heureux n'a point de patrie, il n'aime rien: et si vous voulez fonder une république, vous devez vous occuper de tirer le peuple d'un état d'incertitude et de misère qui le corrompt" (p. 5).

45. Ibid., pp. 46, 47, 48–49. Aulard was convinced, however, that there was no essential difference in matters of religion between the two factions; if anything, the Mountain opposed atheism more sharply than did the Gironde (*Histoire politique,* p. 417). Whatever differences developed were those between Robespierre "in particular" and the Girondins, he wrote (ibid., p. 397).

46. Cited by Isabelle Bourdin, *Les Sociétés populaires à Paris pendant la Révolution française* (Paris, 1937), p. 153.

47. BN, Lb⁴⁰ 2416, *Discours, Imprimé par ordre de la Société Fraternelle de patriotes, de l'un et de l'autre sexe . . . séant aux Jacobins* (Paris: November 1790).

48. BN, Lb⁴⁰ 2456, *Guerre aux Intrigans. Réponse de la Société Fraternelle du Panthéon . . .* (Paris, 1793–1794).

49. AN, T 1001² (dossier Lacombe), and AN, F⁷ 4774⁹ (dossier Léon); Alphonse Aulard, *La Société des Jacobins* (Paris, 1889–1897), V, 406–408; B & R, XXIX, 115–120; *Réimpression de l'ancien Moniteur* (Paris: 1840–1845), XVII, no. 264, 21 September 1793, 604–606; Alexandre Tuetey, *Répertoire Général des sources manuscrites de l'histoire de Paris pendant la Révolution française* (Paris, 1890–1914), IX, no. 1234. The dissolution of feminine popular societies is treated more fully in the chapter on the Enragés.

50. Chaumié, in Soboul, *Girondins,* pp. 50–51.

51. *Le Patriote Français,* no. 1211 (4 December 1792), 637, for example. A letter from Bordeaux in the issue of 5 December 1792, no. 1212, pp. 642–643, speaks of "les anarchistes et les agitateurs qui pèsent sur Paris." The paper's slogan was "Une gazette libre est une sentinelle qui veille sans cesse pour le peuple." It appeared four times a week in an eight-page edition costing twenty-four livres; later it was published daily in quarto and cost thirty-six livres by subscription. During the last half of 1792 and the beginning of 1793 it reflected the growing

struggle between Brissot and Robespierre, and it is thus a record of the Girondin party. From the end of 1791 on its chief editor was Girey-Dupré, who defended Brissot and shared his fate. Eugène Hatin, *Histoire politique et littéraire de la presse de France* (Geneva, 1967), V, 36, 43–44, 46, 52.

52. Perroud, *La Proscription*, p. 22; Durand du Maillane, *Histoire de la Convention nationale* (Paris, 1825), in *Collection des mémoires à la Révolution française*, ed. Saint-Albin Berville and Jean François Barrière (Paris, 1820–1828), XXIII, 45.

53. *Le Patriote Français*, "Supplément," no. 1213, 649–651; Louvet attacked the Jacobins for their "idolatry" and "system of calumny" and accused them of responsibility for the September massacres. How was Marat able to pay for so many placards? he asked (no. 1179, 31 October 1792). See the especially bitter attack on the Jacobins in issue no. 1184, 6 November 1792, which denounces them as "artisans of discord" and "anarchists." J.-B. Louvet de Couvrai, "Mémoires de Louvet de Couvray" in *Collection des mémoires*, ed. Berville and Barrière, XXXIV, 35. Louvet argued that "federalism" existed from the moment one Montagnard deputy did what he pleased in a department (ibid., p. 48).

54. Louis Mortimer-Ternaux, *Histoire de la Terreur, 1792–1794* (Paris, 1868–1881), VII, 215–216, citing no. 1360 of the *Patriote Français*.

55. Cited in Jaurès, *Histoire*, VII, 224. Condorcet was one of the contributors to this journal, first appearing in it on 17 November 1791. He continued to write for it until 9 March 1793. The insurrection of 31 May 1793 finished the journal (Hatin, *Histoire*, V, 247, 252).

56. Alphonse de Lamartine, *Histoire des Girondins* (Brussels, 1847), VI, 64–71, passim.

57. *Geschichte der Revolutionszeit von 1789 bis 1795* (Düsseldorf, 1877), II, 271. He calls it "der kommunistischen Pöbelherrschaft."

58. Durand du Maillane, *Histoire*, pp. 71, 109.

59. Cited in Georges Lefebvre, *La Révolution française*, vol. XIII of *Peuples et Civilisations*, ed. Louis Halphen and Philippe Sagnac (Paris, 1951), p. 337.

60. Ibid., p. 336.

61. Garat, *Mémoires*, p. 84.

62. Durand du Maillane, *Histoire*, p. 47.

63. Ferdinand Brunot called Hébert "l'Homère d'ordure" (quoted in Gérard Walter, "Table analytique," in Michelet, *Histoire de la Révolution française* [Paris, 1961], II, no. 1442).

64. Hébert was especially venomous in attacking Mme. Roland, whom he compared to Pompadour or du Barry. Brissot was her "Master of the Horse"; Louvet, her "Chamberlain"; Buzot, "the Lord Chancellor"; Fauchet, her "Almoner"; Barbaroux was "the Captain of her Guards"; Vergniaud, the "Grand Master of Ceremonies"; Guadet, her "Cup-Bearer"; and Lanthenas, her "Usher." Jacques-René Hébert, *Le Pére Duchesne* (Paris, 1969), VII, no. 202.

65. Ibid., nos. 201, 237.

66. Ibid., nos. 229, 235. The latter number contained the following "preview": "Against the former financiers, *avocats, procureurs,* and the big shopkeepers who laugh up their sleeve, to see the departments ravaged. The good advice that

he gives to the women of all the Sans-Culottes who are departing for the Vendée, to arm themselves with rods (*verge,* "rod," also means the male organ) during the absence of their husbands and to patrol the former Palais Royal and the spectacles, to f—— the dance to all the *foutriquetes* (diminutive persons, an impolite expression) who preach the counter-revolution."

67. Ibid., no. 237. He continued: "Yes, f——, I swear on my mustache, Parisians, here is the infernal plot of our enemies. Disarm promptly all the traitors; put all suspects out of harm's way; it's about time f——. Better to kill the devil, than have the devil kill you. One more victory over the aristocrats and you will be at peace."

68. Ibid., no. 238.

69. Jean-Paul Marat, *Le Publiciste,* no. 201 (24 May 1793). After the defection of Dumouriez, Marat launched a continuous attack on the Girondins. In his no. 165 (10 April), he called Pétion and Valazé "swindlers and cutthroats." In the following issue he accused Louvet, Gensonné, and "their accolytes" of "nocturnal plots." No. 168 (16 April) spoke of "des hommes d'état, complices de Dumourier," and the next ten issues continued the attack on "the faction." No. 178 carried Marat's own judicial defense and no. 180 his exoneration. The following numbers continued to attack the Girondins.

70. Ibid., no. 201 (24 May 1793). In no. 203 he denounced "la faction des hommes d'état" for wanting to do in Paris what they had done in the Vendée, citing Valazé's circular asking his colleagues to come armed to the Convention.

71. Ibid., no. 204 (29 May 1793). Marat described the effort of "the aristocrats" of sections Butte-des-Moulins, Mail, and Bibliothèque, followed by those of Gardes-Françaises, to present "an anti-civic petition" drafted by Valazé and how the petitioners were hooted down.

72. Ibid., no. 207. All these groups were opposed to recruitment for the Vendée and to the forced loan, he wrote, and wanted to expel the sans-culottes from the sectional assemblies.

73. Levasseur, *Mémoires,* I, 210–211.

74. Garat, *Mémoires,* p. 90. The proposals were to "faire maison nette," as he expressed it.

75. "If they [the Girondins] did not succeed in hurling the National Guard against us, it was because they lacked the power, not their good will" (Levasseur, *Mémoires,* p. 231).

76. Aulard, *Histoire politique,* pp. 292, 393. In the vote on Marat, ninety-two were opposed to impeachment, forty-one expressed no opinion, and seven favored adjournment. A total of 129 delegates expressed opposition to the events of 31 May and 2 June. To this number Aulard adds another thirty-six Girondins, making a total of 163. He lists the Girondins alphabetically, with their departments, on pp. 393–394.

77. Mathiez, *Girondins,* p. 3.

78. On the *appel nominal* of 15 January 1793 she found 178 Girondins, 302 Montagnards, 250 Centrists (members of the Plain), and 19 unclassified delegates, for a total of 749. On the 13 April vote she cites 110 votes against Marat, but if those who were absent are included the total would be 175. On the last test, that

of 28 May 1793, she lists 128 votes for, 5 against, 33 absentees, and 9 away on mission, for a total of 175 Girondin votes (Patrick, *Men of the First Republic*, pp. 93, 111).

79. Ibid., pp. 296, 297, 299–300. "Nearly 79 percent of those who voted consistently in Louis' favor later opposed the Jacobin republic, and 87 percent of the unrelenting regicides have been placed with the Mountain," she writes (pp. 302–303).

80. Sydenham, *Girondins*, p. 205.

81. Ibid., p. 42. Sydenham gives the following figures estimated by historians for the number of Girondins: Perroud, 191; Morse Stephens, 183; Aulard, 162 (not 163).

82. Ibid., p. 165. On the vote to reestablish the Commission des Douze, 135 of the 200 Girondins voted in favor (ibid., pp. 175–176). (Patrick lists 128 votes in favor.)

83. Ibid., p. 207.

84. Chaumié, in Soboul, *Girondins*, pp. 53–60.

85. Soboul, *Girondins*, p. 11.

86. Ibid., pp. 11–12.

87. Michel Pertué, "Remarques sur les listes des Conventionnels," *Annales historiques de la Révolution française*, 245 (July-September 1981), 366–389. Barère and Cambon had been pro-Girondin in their earlier politics.

88. Mathiez gives the number of Montagnards *en mission* as eighty-six (*La Révolution française*, 10th ed. [Paris, 1951], II, 205).

89. Pertué, "Remarques," p. 375.

90. Ibid., p. 377. In "La Liste des Girondins de Jean-Paul Marat," Pertué lists 102 delegates and breaks down their votes on the king's death, the *procès* of Marat, and the decree suppressing the Commission des Douze. The final column summarizes how the names are regarded by Aulard, Sydenham, Patrick, and Chaumié.

C. J. Mitchell, in "Political Divisions within the Legislative Assembly of 1791," *French Historical Studies*, 3 (Spring 1984), 356–389, argues that the old lists compiled by Buchez and Roux and by Aulard on divisions in the Legislative Assembly are inaccurate and even misleading. This is also true of the various *dictionnaires*. He substitutes the *appels nominaux* on seven different issues and divides the Assembly into *oui*-voters versus *non*-voters in order to give a more accurate division between the Jacobins and the Feuillants, the left and the right. He concludes that "today, unfortunately, it is difficult to know where any particular deputy sat, and thus an analysis of this assembly in terms of left, right, and center must ignore most of its members . . . We cannot apply [labels] to two-thirds of the deputies." He is convinced that the distinction between *oui*- and *non*-voters gives a better description of political behavior in the legislature but cautions that "what stands revealed is more a demonstrable political inclination than a clear political commitment, more a tendency than a position" (ibid., pp. 388–389). His conclusion, it should be noted, is not very different from that of Pertué for the Convention.

91. *Moniteur*, 16, no. 96 (6 April 1793), 52–54. "I have said that I did not want to discuss at all with the friends of Dumouriez," Robespierre concluded.

92. *Moniteur*, 16, no. 100, (10 April 1793), 87; Mortimer-Ternaux, *Histoire*,

VII, 97–100, passim. The address urged the Mountain to declare war on all moderates and Feuillants.

93. B & R, XXV, 319–322. *Moniteur,* 16, no. 102 (12 April 1793), 100. Among the demands was one for a law against speculators. The petitioners asked if this were the time to send patriotic deputies to the departments so that "a corrupt majority" could pronounce on the fate of the Republic. The petition ended with the words: "Montagnards of the Convention, it is you we address: save the Republic; or, if you do not feel strong enough to do it, dare to admit it frankly: we shall undertake to save it ourselves."

94. Mortimer-Ternaux, *Histoire,* VII, 101–105, passim. Robespierre spoke at some length in defense of section Halle-au-Blé's petition and sharply attacked Feuillants, moderates, and the roles of Brissot, Guadet, Vergniaud, and Gensonné. *Moniteur,* 16, no. 102 (12 April 1793), 100, 105–108. See also Robespierre, *Oeuvres,* IV, 414, 415.

95. Mortimer-Ternaux, *Histoire,* VII, 143; du Maillane, *Histoire,* pp. 91, 94–95; Levasseur, *Mémoires,* I, 180–181 (Levasseur called Rousselin's address "forte et modérée à la fois"); Henri Wallon, *La Révolution du 31 Mai et le Fédéralisme en 1793 ou la France vaincue par la Commune de Paris* (Paris, 1886), I, 129, 131. Wallon's work is based largely on the *Moniteur.* He calls the petitioners "anarchists," without quotation marks (p. 135). Aulard (*Histoire politique,* p. 435) says the address was provoked by anti-Montagnard petitions of the departments and cites the resolution of Bordeaux adopted on 14 May to march on Paris. "Un coup d'Etat départemental se préparait contre Paris et la Montagne," he writes. Mathiez (*Histoire,* II, 205–206) wrote that the wealthy were exasperated by pecuniary sacrifices and feared the revolutionary Commune. Jaurès (*Histoire,* VII, 234–235) concluded that the Paris Commune asked that the departments be consulted out of timidity, and that in so doing it risked fragmenting all France and disorganizing the Revolution. The Commune replied in advance to those who accused it of wanting to "federalize" the departments by advertising its desire to correspond with the forty-four thousand municipalities of the country "qu'elle n'adopte que cette seule espèce de fédéralisme." AN, C 355, 1865, 23 April 1793.

96. Jaurès, *Histoire,* VII, 235. Wallon argues that the proposal of the Commune was a "federalist" motion (*La Révolution,* I, 131).

97. Mortimer-Ternaux, *Histoire,* VII, 151–152.

98. *Moniteur,* 16, no. 108 (18 April 1793), 153, citing proceedings in the Paris Commune on 15 April.

99. Jaurès, *Histoire,* VII, 236; *Moniteur,* 16, no. 112 (22 April 1793), 191.

100. *Moniteur,* 16, no. 112 (22 April 1793), 190–192, and no. 113 (23 April 1793), 195–199. Pierre-François Réal, the substitute *procureur,* reported that "a certain party in the Convention" had received him and the Commune's delegates badly and had tried to place them in an unfavorable light, but that "the party of patriots" gave evidence of cordiality for them. AN, C 355, pl. 1865, 21 April 1793.

101. See C. Riffaterre, *Le Mouvement antijacobin et antiparisien;* Maurice Wahl, *Les Premières années de la Révolution à Lyon* (Paris, 1894); Jean Gâumont, *Histoire générale de la coopération en France,* vol. I, *Précurseurs et prémices* (Paris, 1924).

102. Pétion, *Lettre,* p. 15.

103. News of his death was brought by delegates of section Finistère, whose company of cannoneers he had commanded. *Moniteur,* 16, no. 117 (27 April 1793), 226.

104. Tuetey, *Répertoire,* IX, xxxv. Hébert headlined no. 231 of his *Père Duchesne:* "Against the royalists, the Brissotins, the Girondins, the Rolandins, who want to destroy all the patriots by hunger, fire, and poison, and who, after having assassinated Lepelletier and Léonard Bourdon, just poisoned the brave Lazowski, the pearl of the Sans-Culottes of Faubourg Saint-Marceau. / The services that he has rendered to the republic merit at least the honors of the pantheon."

105. AN, C 355, pl. 1865. It intended to pursue the matter.

106. B & R, XXVI, 317–318, 1 May 1793.

107. *Moniteur,* 16, no. 137 (17 May 1793), 384. On 16 May the *procureur* of the Paris Commune reported that the conference scheduled in the Evêché by virtue of the resolution of 13 May had to be postponed since only Dufourny of the Paris department had been present to represent that institution. Ibid., no. 139, (19 May 1793), 409; B & R, XXVII, 72.

108. Issue of 5 May 1793, cited in Jaurès, *Histoire,* VII, 309–310.

109. Quoted in Adolphe Schmidt, *Tableaux de la Révolution française* (Leipzig, 1867), I, 206.

110. AN, C 355, pl. 1865, 8 May 1793. This petition was signed by Pache, among others.

111. Quoted in Jaurès, *Histoire,* VII, 310–311. Garat comments that "The list of the *dozen* showed much virtue; it did not show, even in the eyes of their friends, enough wisdom" (*Mémoires,* p. 111).

112. *Moniteur,* 16, no. 139 (19 May 1793), 414.

113. AN, C 355, pl. 1859–1871, "Commission extraordinaire des Douze, crée par décret du 18 Mai 1793." AN, C 355, pl. 1866 of 8 *pièces* is entitled, "Cahier des Procès-Verbaux et Déliberations de Cette Commission." The first document (21 May 1793) lists the names of the commissioners and cites their duties. Among them were to examine the decrees of the General Council and the sections for the past month, to uncover plots against liberty, to take testimony, and so forth. See also B & R, XXVII, 131–132; Mortimer-Ternaux, *Histoire,* VII, 242–243, 244–245.

114. B & R, XVIII, 451. In *Mémoires de Garat,* the minister of the interior quotes Danton as follows: " 'Twenty times,' he said to me one day, 'I offered them peace; they did not want it.' Then he added the following revealing words: '. . . it is they who have forced us [who have] thrown us into sans-culottisme which has devoured them, which will devour all of us, which will devour itself.' " Quoted in Jules Michelet, *Histoire de la Révolution française,* I, nos. 1193–1223 (book VIII, chap. IV), discusses at some length this demarche of Danton's. See also Lefebvre, *Révolution,* p. 332.

115. Jaurès (*Histoire,* VII, 415) wrote that Danton's speech sounded "douloureusement" and was too late. Despite his conciliatory role, von Sybel wrote, Danton was repulsed because he was "the chief of the Septembriseurs," adding, "Yet he lacked the will to die: he determined to hold on to life and to crime" (*Geschichte,*

II, 284–285: "Noch hatte er nicht die Kraft zu sterben: er entschloss sich, am Leben und am Verbrechen festzuhalten").

116. Marc-Antoine Baudot, *Notes historiques sur la Convention nationale, le Directoire, l'Empire,* cited in Daniel Guérin, *La lutte de classes sous la première république* (Paris, 1946), I, 127.

117. If the above-named leaders met, wrote Jaurès, it was to try to avoid bloodshed. As late as 29 May Danton still had not given up hope for a compromise, and Robespierre did not lose hope until the day the Convention reestablished its Commission des Douze (*Histoire,* VII, 417–418).

118. Jaurès, *Histoire,* VII, 392.

119. Mathiez calls Robespierre no "ideologue" but rather "a realist" ("un esprit réaliste") (*La Révolution,* II, 208).

120. Lefebvre, *Révolution,* p. 332. With the exception of Mathiez, historians of the Revolution agree that Robespierre was a man more of parliamentary formalities than of action in the street.

121. Aulard, *Histoire politique,* p. 435.

122. *Patriote Français,* no. 1375 (20 May 1793), 559; *Moniteur,* 16, no. 139 (19 May 1793), 415–416. During the session of 19 May, Marat objected to Guadet's attack on the commissioners sitting in the Evêché. *Moniteur,* no. 141 (21 May 1793), 429.

123. In the *Patriote Français,* no. 1375 (20 May 1793), 560, Guadet denounced "a secret *revolutionary* assembly, held in the Mairie . . . during the night" (ibid.). M. Mignet, *Histoire de la Révolution depuis 1789 jusqu'en 1814,* 16th ed. (Paris, 1886), I, 379, quotes Guadet: "The evil is in the impunity of the plotters of 10 March; the evil is in the anarchy; the evil is in the existence of the authorities of Paris, authorities greedy both for money and for domination."

124. Jaurès, *Histoire,* VII, 357–358. Mignet agrees that Guadet's plan would have spread civil war and weakened the Revolution, I, 380. Mathiez thought it was foolish, *La Révolution,* II, 211.

125. Aulard, *Histoire politique,* p. 405.

126. Cited in Juarès, *Histoire,* VII, 351–352.

127. AN, C 256, 488–489, pc. 18, 23, and 24 May 1793; AN, C 355, pl. 1868, pc. 21, 22 May 1793, reported by Legrand; AN, F¹ᶜ III, Seine, 27, pc. 27, 30 May 1793, a perceptive report by Dutard for the department of Paris.

128. In Schmidt, *Tableaux,* I, 244, Dutard's report to Garat, 18 May 1793.

129. B & R, XXVII, 150, 20 May 1793. The same day a report was read in the Jacobin Club that the republicans of Lyons had formed a revolutionary army of six thousand men and had levied a contribution on the wealthy of six million livres (ibid., pp. 156–158).

130. De Meillan, *Mémoires,* "Eclaircissemens historiques et pièces officielles," Note B, pp. 176–177. [See n. 139 for full citation.] Tuetey, *Répertoire,* IX, xlix-l. Mathieu-Jean Brichet of section Mail was also arrested.

131. M. A. Thiers, *Histoire de la révolution française,* 14th ed. (Paris, 1846), IV, 25–26.

132. *Oeuvres,* IX, 540–541. "It would thus be an absurdity to hand over the armed force into their hands," he concluded.

133. See B & R, XXVII, 185–186, for Viger's proposals in eleven articles;

Moniteur, 16, no. 146 (26 May 1793), 467–471. *Moniteur,* 16, no. 145, 25 May, 459–460, continues the discussion begun on 23 May.

134. Jaurès, *Histoire,* VII, 387–388.

135. Section Lombards informed the General Council on 28 May that after 10:00 P.M. its citizens met as a club. See Soboul's many examples and discussion of this practice in *Les Sans-Culottes,* pp. 614–648.

136. The effect of this action on the Commune and on the sections is discussed in the chapters dealing with those institutions.

137. Quoted in B & R, XXVII, 225.

138. B & R, XXVII, 251–270, passim; Jaurès, *Histoire,* VII, 397, 398; de Meillan, *Mémoires,* "Procès-verbal de la Convention," note C, pp. 198–203. Garat had received a packet of papers intended to convince him that the Jacobins were preparing to assassinate members of the Convention. It was evident to him that the Girondins were urging him to arrest the Montagnards, and he was indignant to think that responsible deputies could blame Jacobins for the committee of insurrection that had been formed in the Evêché. Had he been ordered to arrest them, this act would have constituted as great a crime as the insurrection of 31 May, he wrote. Besides, he asked, "What forces were entrusted to me to make such arrests? . . . Pache and Chaumette—would they have arrested the Jacobins and the mountain?" (Garat, *Mémoires,* pp. 104–105, 106–107, 108). The second question was the key.

139. Armand Jean de Meillan, *Mémoires de Meillan député . . . des Basses-Pyrénées, à la Convention nationale . . .* (Paris, 1823), in *Collection,* eds. Berville and Barrière, XXXV, 203–205; Thiers, *Histoire,* IV, 30–32.

140. De Meillan, *Mémoires,* pp. 205–208; see also Thiers, *Histoire,* IV, 33–34; Mignet, *Histoire,* I, 383–384; Jaurès, *Histoire,* VII, 406–407.

141. Mortimer-Ternaux, *Histoire,* VII, 304–305; see also B & R, XXVII, 276–289, passim.

142. Jaurès, *Histoire,* VII, 418–419, 420. Mignet says of Danton, "He feared as much the triumph of the Montagnards as that of the Girondins; he also wanted by turns to prevent the 31st of May and to moderate its results . . ." (*Histoire,* I, 385). See also Aulard, *Jacobins,* V, 213, for a description of Billaud-Varennes's attack on Barère's call for unity.

143. Tuetey, *Répertoire,* VIII, No. 2735, 31 May 1793; AP, LXV, 646. Garat relates that the first time he heard the expression "l'insurrection morale" was from l'Huillier (Lulier), the *procureur-général-syndic* of the Paris department (*Mémoires,* pp. 102, 137).

144. Quoted in Aulard, *Jacobins,* V, 112.

145. Quoted in ibid., V, 120.

146. *Oeuvres,* IX, 451. Robespierre ended his discourse by calling for "prudence" (Aulard, *Jacobins,* V, 138).

147. *Oeuvres,* ed. Laponneraye, III, 384–385. Louis Blanc (*Histoire,* VIII, 378–379) says the following: "[Robespierre] wanted . . . to disarm [the Girondins] without violating the principle of the national representation that was so dear to him. He understood perfectly that to attack the National Convention was as dangerous a remedy as the evil itself" (cited in Guérin, *Lutte,* I, 114).

148. Michelet, *Histoire,* II, 360.

149. Garat, *Mémoires,* p. 138.
150. Aulard, *Histoire politique,* p. 437. Buchez and Roux are convinced that the Girondins were attacking the very basis of the Revolution, that they opposed the draft and the levy on the rich so as to get support from that part of the population that was egoistic and selfish. But they were greatly outnumbered and compromised by the treachery of Dumouriez, and by 31 May they were quite isolated. The Jacobins, on the other hand, were careful to do everything legally, the editors continue, because they held the power and because they wished to avoid a march on Paris by the departments (*Histoire,* XXVII, vii-ix). This view is not quite accurate, as will be seen below, and ignores the role of the Evêché committee, the sections, and the Commune.

151. *Moniteur,* 16, no. 152 (1 June 1793), 521–522; B & R, XXVII, 300–305, passim. Alexandre Rousselin (de Corbeau de Saint-Albin) (1773–1847) was twenty years old at this time. He was a protégé of Danton and favored the expulsion of the twenty-two deputies, not their arrest. He also wanted the departments to endorse this measure so as to avoid ranging them against the capital (Perroud, *Proscription,* p. 27).

II. The Fraternization Movement in the Sections

1. See the divisions among the sections in Table 1. See also Albert Soboul, *Les Sans-Culottes parisiens en l'an II* (Paris, 1958), ch. I, "Modérés et San-Culottes," especially the first two parts. See also G. Pariset, *La Révolution, 1792–1799,* 2 vols. *Histoire de France contemporaine,* ed. Ernest Lavisse (Paris, 1920), II, 95; and Henri Calvet, *Un Instrument de la Terreur à Paris* (Paris, 1941).

2. AN, C 256, pl. 488, p. 20, 25 May 1793.
3. AN, C 256, pl. 488, p. 7. These are, in order, Unité, Marais, 1792, Temple, Bon-Conseil, Faubourg-Montmartre, Droits-de-l'Homme, Marchés, Lombards, Fédérés, Gravilliers, Popincourt, Bonne-Nouvelle, Marseille, Muséum, and Bondy—a total of sixteen (including Temple itself).

4. Ibid., pl. 488, pp. 38–39.
5. Ibid., pl. 489, p. 13, italicized in original.
6. The section refused to adjourn at 10:00 P.M. as decreed by law "justified [by the principle] that it is permissible to resist oppression." Jaurès, *Histoire,* VII, 388.

7. Schmidt, *Tableaux,* I, 309. See the report of the *Patriote Français* on the fracas in the Convention after it voted to free Leroux, the justice of the peace in section Unité, who had been arrested by the section's revolutionary committee (no. 1373 [18 May 1793]).

8. BN, Lb[40] 530, *Rapport fait à l'assemblée générale de la section de l'Unité* (Paris, 28 February 1795). "Session of 27 [May]: The commander mounts the tribune to invite the citizens to report with their arms to the general quarters, etc. Decreed stating that the assembly shall be permanent . . ." (p. 4).

9. Mortimer-Ternaux, *Histoire,* VII, 216–217. The conservative address adopted by Bon-Conseil on 4 May pledged respect for the Convention: ". . . to

show all deputies without distinction the respect due their position." When president Boyer-Fronfrède congratulated them, "the extreme Left" cried out, "These are intriguers, these are promoters of civil war!"

10. AN, AD XVI, 70, *Extrait du procès-verbal de l'assemblée générale permanent de la section de Bon-Conseil . . . 5 mai 1793* (Paris, n.d.). It was reported that six hundred citizens were present at the adoption of the new resolutions.

11. Mortimer-Ternaux, *Histoire*, VII, 219–220.

12. AN, C 256, pl. 488, pp. 28, 29.

13. AN, C 256, pl. 488, pp. 8, 40. The demonstrators agreed to bear a placard with the proclamation, "Section du faubourg Montmartre reclamant la Souveraineté et les droits du Peuple, et la liberté de ses Magistrats." One of the commissioners appointed by the assembly to bear the petition was Hassenfratz, the well-known militant.

14. AN, BB³, d. 16.

15. BVC, MS. 120, fol. 135. Jacques Charavay, ed., *Catalogue d'une important collection de documents, authographes et historiques sur la révolution française depuis le 13 juillet 1789 jusqu'au 18 Brumaire an VIII* (Paris, 1862), p. 28, no. 106, letter under the signature of Dubois, president, and Varlet, secretary, 28 March 1793; BN, MSS, Nouv. acq. fr. 2647, fol. 120 (Paris, 4 April 1793); Lb⁴⁰ 1792 is the same as the preceding document, with a defense of the section's action and a renewal of its invitation to the sections to send commissioners to the Evêché, 7 April. See also AP, V. D. *9, no. 1025, 27 March, Year II "Extrait . . ."

16. BVC, MS. 120, fols. 138–141, 19 May 1793; AP, 1 AZ 159², *Procès-Verbal*, 20 May 1793; BHVP, 104.095, *Section des Droits de l'Homme. Procès-Verbal de la séance du 20 Mai, 2e* (n.d.). See also AN, F⁷* 2497, p. 24, 20 May 1793, "Extrait des Registres des déliberations de l'assemblée générale des Droits de l'Homme dans sa séance de ce jour," which contains a slightly different version of the proceedings from those found in the preceding sources. The session has been published by Walter Markov and Albert Soboul, *Die Sansculotten von Paris Dokument zur Geschichte der Volksbewegung 1793–1794* (Berlin, 1957), no. 7, pp. 24–33.

17. AN, C 256, pl. 488, p. 31.

18. BVC, MS, 120, fol. 143; AN, C 256, pl. 489, p. 26: "L'assemblée générale de la section des droits de l'homme adhere à l'adresse et invite les commissaires à reporter à l'evêché."

19. AN, C 256, pl. 488, p. 22, 25 May 1793.

20. AN, F⁷ 4580, pl. 6. Appert was a Jacobin but supported the Girondins. On 17 May 1793 he drafted a petition to the civil committee of the section requesting that it convoke the general assembly the next day at 9:00 A.M. in order to deliberate on measures to maintain "le calme et la liberté des opinion[s]." This petition was signed by sixty-three supporters. The seals on his papers were removed on 16 June 1794, and he must have been released shortly thereafter.

21. AN, F⁷ 4580, 16 June 1794.

22. AN, F⁷, 4580, pl. 6, p. 16. The committee charged "that he always ranged himself on the side of the artistocrats in the general assembly and excited and provoked trouble there and was one of those who opposed admission of sans-

culottes to the assemblies . . . that he was a royalist, that he said on the morrow of Marat's assassination: Marat has been assassinated, the republic is f———." There is no indication when Leroux was freed.

23. AN, C 256, pl. 488, p. 30. The secretary spelled Varlet's name "Warlee."

24. AN, C 256, pl. 489, p. 26.

25. AN, F⁷ 4635, 9 June 1793, and an undated document.

26. AN, F⁷ 4635.

27. Less than a week later he submitted a document, signed by the captain, lieutenant, and sergeant of his company, attesting that he had always carried out his duty. It can be assumed that he must have been freed shortly thereafter (ibid.).

28. Soboul, *Sans-Culottes*, p. 27, n. 39.

29. AN, C 256, pl. 488, p. 34, 26 May 1793.

30. *Moniteur*, 16, no. 119 (29 April 1793), 242.

31. AN, C 256, pl. 488, p. 44.

32. *Moniteur*, 16, no. 148 (28 May 1793), 482.

33. AN, C 256, pl. 488, p. 37, 25 May 1793.

34. Ibid., pl. 489, p. 17, 29 May.

35. Ibid., p. 49.

36. Ibid., pl. 488, p. 47.

37. BVC, MS. 120, cited in Soboul, *Sans-Culottes*, p. 23.

38. AN, C 257, pl. 489, p. 19.

39. AN, W 111, *Procès-Verbal de la Séance de l'assemblée générale permanente de la Section Poissonnière du 31 Mai 1793*. The anonymous citizen wanted to know "the reasons for our assembly. Upon the proposal of a Citizen to state if the General Assembly accepted or rejected the committee of ten, [and] after quite a long discussion, this Citizen withdrew his proposal motivated by the belief that the Assembly cannot approve it, not having been instructed in this Regard."

40. Ibid. The procès-verbal states that "all division [of different opinions] ought to be suppressed for the general good."

41. AN, F⁷ 4775⁴, d. Ruffier, "Tableau" of the section's revolutionary committee and Ruffier's petition to the Committee of General Security of 2 March 1794. The revolutionary committee accused Ruffier "for not having ceased to Express an opinion contrary to that of Patriots always in the most critical circumstances, and notably during the time of 31 May, when he was wholly opposed to the salutary insurrection."

42. AN, F⁷ 4775⁴, 26 February 1794. Among the many pleas of his father and friends for his release was that of one Arnaud, an "officier Municipal qui a secouru le Représentant Collot d'Herbois." The civil committee of the section testified that Ruffier "*a rempli Exactement Ses devoirs Civiques*" (underscored in the original).

43. APP, A A/266, p. 78, 24 May 1793.

44. AN, C 256, pl. 489, p. 5, "Extrait du Registre des déliberations de l'assemblée, du 25 Mai 1793 . . ."

45. AN, C 256, pl. 489, p. 32; BN, Lb⁴⁰ 1849, "Adresse lue à la Convention Nationale . . ."; BN, Lb⁴⁰ 1850, "Adresse Présentée par le Citoyen Burguburu à

la Section, & lue à la Convention Nationale le 31 Mai 1793 . . ." is almost the same as the preceding. In addition to Chazot, the section expelled seven other "plotters." The general assembly also placarded the neighborhood with its repudiation of Chazot's petition and sent copies of its refutation to the Commune, the sections, the popular societies, and the departments.

46. If the total population of section Gardes-Françaises was 12,486, then a mere .35 percent of its citizens were under arms in contrast to 5.88 percent of Gravilliers's population (total = 16,747) (population statistics as listed in AN, F⁷ 3688⁴, "Etat Général de la Population de Paris," 1 February 1795).

47. AN, F⁷ 4644, d. Chazot, 22 April 1794. Chazot's accuser (Afforly?) considered him "comme l'espion de la Section auprès de l'aristocratie."

48. Ibid., "Tableau," 29 March 1794.

49. Ibid., 13 December 1793, "Copie de l'Adresse du Citoyen Claude Chazot Présenté à la Convention Nationale le 25 Mai 1793." The two sentences quoted in full are underscored in the original.

50. AN, F⁷ 4644, "Tableau," which notes simply that Chazot preferred the regime of the National Guard rather than the proposal of Lafayette. For a clear and convincing argument against the proposal of Lafayette, see BN, Lb³⁹ 7837, *Très-Sérieuses Observations sur la Mauvaise Organisation de la Garde Nationale–Parisienne . . . par Coque (soldat-citoyen du district St. Germain–l'Auxerrois)*, 15 September 1789.

51. AN, F⁷ 4644, 28 February 1794, to the Committee of General Security.

52. Ibid., 2 July 1793. The motion demanded the recall and reintegration of those excluded from the assembly on 21 May and 3, 4, and 5 June.

53. AN, C 355, pl. 1862, "Commission Extraordinaire des Douze, Arrêtes et Déliberations du Comité révolutionnaire de la Section du Contrat Social. Du 9 Mars au 20 Mai 1793."

54. AN, C 355, pl. 1860.

55. Ibid.

56. AN, C 256, pl. 489, p. 25.

57. Calvet, *Instrument*, wrote that although Pariset defined exactly the attitude of such sections as Molière et La Fontaine and Pont-Neuf, he presented Contrat-Social as being sans-culotte and underestimated the resistance of the moderates in other sections as well (p. 31, n. 11). Dutard wrote to Garat, 16 June 1793, on a dispute over one David, a member of the section's revolutionary committee accused of incapacity and turbulence (Tuetey, *Répertoire*, IX, no. 695).

58. AN, F⁷4649, packet 3, 30 November 1793.

59. Ibid. The petition of eight thousand was circulated by politically conservative National Guardsmen in favor of the king on the eve of the demonstration against him, 20 June 1792.

60. Ibid. This story was told to representative Mont-Gilbert by Clement's brother-in-law.

61. AN, F⁷ 4732, "Etat des Citoyens détenus" and "Extrait des procès-verbaux de l'Assemblée Générale de la section Contrat-Social." Grapin spelled his name with one *p*, but it often appears as *pp* in official documents.

62. Ibid. Among the allegations against him was an undated charge by an anonymous, illiterate accuser who held Grapin guilty of "committing infidelities in the manufacture of uniforms for the troops" (ibid.).

63. Ibid., 27 April 1794.

64. Ibid., 7 August 1794. Less than two weeks after Robespierre's fall, Grapin still denied that he was a "moderate," called the insurrection of 31 May "cette belle journée," and wrote that he had been a "sans-culotte all his life."

65. Ibid. The general assembly of Contrat-Social ruled that Grapin's expulsion had been the work of "intruguers" and it characterized him as "a good citizen" (ibid., 9 June 1795).

66. AN, C 256, pl. 488, pp. 24, 26. The note appended to Unité's address merely states, "Vu en assemblée générale des gravilliers le 28 mai L'an deux de la république" (ibid., pl. 489, p. 29).

67. AN, C 256, pl. 488, p. 24, 27 May 1793.

68. Mortimer-Ternaux, *Histoire*, VII, 330, n. 1.

69. *Journal des Débats et de la correspondance de la société des Jacobins . . .* , no. 412 (14 May 1793). Since the session described was that of 19 May, either the date of this issue is in error or the proceedings took place before 14 May.

70. AN, C 256, pl. 488, pp. 35, 36.

71. Ibid. The petition proposed, ". . . create Workshops in Paris and in its Environs; employ there all arms accustomed to work in iron . . ."

72. Pariset, *Révolution*, II, 95; Soboul, *Sans-Culottes*, p. 23.

73. AN, C 256, pl. 488, p. 27 and pl. 489, p. 27 (25 and 28 May).

74. Soboul, *Sans-Culottes*, p. 29, n. 44, citing F^7 4584, and so forth.

75. AN, C 256, pl. 488, p. 31, 25 May 1793; and pl. 489, p. 17, 28 May 1793.

76. AN, C 256, pl. 488, p. 7, and pl. 489, p. 30. Marseille gave its unanimous adherence to the petition of Unité.

77. BVC, MS. 120, 26 May 1793, cited in Soboul, *Sans-Culottes*, p. 27.

78. AN, C 256, pl. 489, p. 27. Soboul points out, however, that documentation is lacking for the section (*Sans-Culottes*, p. 27, n. 39).

79. *Moniteur*, 16, no. 149 (29 May 1793).

80. AN, C 256, pl. 489, p. 30.

81. AN, C 256, pl. 489, p. 13, 29 May 1793.

82. Ibid., pl. 489, p. 15.

83. Ibid., pl. 489, p. 30.

84. AN, C 256, pl. 488, p. 21, 25 May 1793; pl. 489, p. 8, 28 May 1793. The peroration concluded, "Enfin nous jurons d'exterminer toutes les tyrans et toutes leurs partisans; tremblez traîtres à la Patrie, tremblez."

85. *Moniteur*, 16, no. 151 (31 May 1793), 506.

86. AN, W 11, d. 529, 11 February 1794.

87. Ibid., 7, 8, 9, and 10 May 1793, from the interrogations of witnesses.

88. Ibid., 9 May 1793. There is no indication that Bousquet was arrested or held for further questioning.

89. Ibid., 8 and 10 May 1793. These were Manus Polk, a *négociant*, Jean Joseph Coppeaux, an *avoué aux Tribunaux de Paris*, and Philippe Chassagnole, an

architect. All were released under the guarantee of two citizens of the section.

90. Ibid., 7 May 1793.

91. The *procès-verbal* was signed by Bourgoin, by the commissioners, and by Coquelin, *assesseur* of the judge, on 7 May 1793. The commissioners were served with summonses to appear before the police tribunal on 15 June 1793.

92. Ibid., 8 May 1793.

93. Jaurès, *Histoire*, VII, 384. Original italicized.

94. AN, C 355, pl. 1859, 24 May 1793. The address of section Fraternité, as pointed out above, was in favor of the Girondins in the Convention.

95. Schmidt, *Tableaux*, I, 294–295, 24 May 1793, "Commune de Paris. Conseil général."

96. BVC, MS. 120, fol. 143, 26 May 1793. Sectional Arsenal had requested help against its "aristocrats," and the general assembly of Droits-de-l'Homme decided to go en masse.

97. AN, W 41, d. 2764, 25 May 1793. The witnesses against the moderates referred to the latter as "meneurs et provocateurs des dits complots qui sont arrivés dans la section." They allegedly met in the home of Rodot, a wine merchant residing on rue Saint-Antoine.

98. *Moniteur,* 16, no. 148 (28 May 1793), 482; no. 149 (29 May 1793), 490. On 27 May Dutard, the police spy, noted the "cheerfulness" of the sansculottes in the section (Schmidt, *Tableaux*, I, 313). The *Chronique de Paris* reported that patriots of sections Montreuil, Quinze-Vingts, Droits-de-l'Homme, Marseille, and Arcis had come to the assistance of the section's patriots (Jaurès, *Histoire,* VII, 386).

99. AN, C 256, pl. 488, p. 46, 27 May 1793. This was in support of the petition of section Faubourg-Montmartre.

100. AN, F⁷ 4733, packet 1, 17 October 1793, the appeal written from La Force prison.

101. BN, Lb⁴⁰ 1706, *Extrait des registres des Assemblées générales de la section de l'Arsenal* (Paris, 10 March 1795).

102. AN, C 256, pl. 488, p. 48.

103. Ibid., pl. 488, p. 19. Soboul points out that Faubourg-du-Nord and Maison-Commune lack documentation (*Sans-Culottes*, p. 27, n. 39).

104. AN, C 256, pl. 488, p. 20.

105. AN, C 355, pl. 1864, "Assemblée Générale du Mail." This dossier contains fifty-one documents dating from 18 April to 24 May 1793; it is especially rich in describing the factional struggle in the section. The first document is dated 10 March 1793, after which the references are to the dates as in the above.

106. Ibid., 25 April 1793.

107. Ibid., 10 March, 15, 18, and 19 April.

108. Ibid. Boulanger was elected provisional commander by seventy-four of seventy-five votes (AN, C 355, pl. 1865, 17 May 1793). Although he took the oath of office on 18 May, the General Council submitted his name for endorsement by the sections. After sections Arsenal and Temple voiced their objection to him, Boulanger refused the position of commanding general (*Moniteur,* 16, no. 141 [22 May 1793] 426; no. 143 [23 May 1793], 441).

109. AN, C 355, d. 1864.
110. Ibid. "The aristocracy has sworn to destroy the sans-culottes just as the sans-culottes have sworn to kill the aristocracy," said the spokesman.
111. Ibid. He also declared, "We are all brothers and all patriots. Union and Peace reign among us; no Citizen is without his Card [of civic conduct] and we know and love everyone. There is but one view in section Mail, the Republic one and indivisible . . . we have declared war on tyranny and on anarchy."
112. Ibid. He then demanded that the officers of the section be composed of patriots (an obvious attack on Tranchelahausse) and that the same be true of the revolutionary committee. Italics in the original.
113. "Nous irons chez les riches avec des mandats d'arrêt dans notre poche, et en force, nous prendrons leur portfeuille, nous compterons les assignats, qui sont de dans, nous leur[s] laisserons ce que nous voudrons et s'ils [sont] raisonables" (ibid.).
114. Ibid.
115. Ibid., 22 May 1793.
116. Ibid., 26 May 1793, signed by Tranchelahausse and Le Tellier.

III. The Struggle for the Sections

1. AN, C 256, pl. 488, pp. 42, 43, 25 and 26 May 1793.
2. AN, F⁷ 4768 d. Jean Baptiste Firmin Flicourt, 7 June 1793.
3. AN, F⁷ 4699, d. Louis Nicolas Duval.
4. Ibid., n.d.
5. AN, F⁷ 4699, 22 March and 23 June 1793.
6. Ibid.: The replies to the charges against him appear in a letter of his wife without date to the Committee of General Security.
7. Wallon, *Tribunal*, V, 168, lists him among the twenty-four (out of a total of twenty-five) who were condemned on 9 Thermidor, Year II, citing the dossier W. 433, d. 973 as proof. But as late as 3 August 1794 Duval was still demanding his release. AN, F⁷ 4699.
8. AN, F⁷ 4768, 15 November and 7 June 1793; 10 June 1793. In addition to other charges he was reproached for being an enemy of Marat and for arguing that Louis was not justiciable, at the time of Louis's trial.
9. AN, F⁷ 4768, 10 June 1794.
10. AN, F⁷ 4775²⁵, packet 4.
11. AN, F⁷ 4774⁹⁹, packet 3, 7 June 1794.
12. AN, F⁷ 4774⁸⁷, 7 June 1794.
13. AN, F⁷ 4774⁶³, packet 3, 29 March 1794.
14. AN, F⁷ 4774⁶¹, packet 2, signed by six members of the committee, n.d.
15. AN, F⁷ 4774³⁰, dos. 4, "Tableau," 7 June 1794. Appeal signed by Maillet's wife, Captain Ponceau, the sergeant of his company, and others, 16 August 1794.
16. AN, F⁷ 4764, packet 1, "Tableau," 23 April 1794.
17. AN, F⁷ 4737, packet 2, "Tableau," 23 April 1794.
18. Ibid., 19 March 1794. See also Jean-Noel Dumoulin, a merchant draper,

AN, F⁷ 4687, packet 4, and Jean-François-Esprit Canaple, an armorer and craftsman in inlaid ware, age twenty-five, AN, F⁷ 4632, packet 1.

19. AN, F⁷ 4581, booklet 1, 12 February 1794.
20. Ibid.
21. AN, C 256, pl. 489, p. 9. The resolution read, "Obeissance au loix, soumission aux autorités constituées, conservation des propriétés, sûreté des citoyens, liberté des opinions pour consolider les bases de la république . . ."
22. Calvet, *Instrument*, p. 31.
23. AN, BB³ 80, dos. 5, pc. 139.
24. *Procès-verbal de la Convention nationale, imprimé*, XI, 136.
25. *Moniteur*, 16, no. 148 (28 May 1793), 482.
26. Ibid., no. 152 (1 June 1793), 517.
27. Mortimer-Ternaux, *Histoire*, VII, 308, "Extrait des registres des procès-verbaux de la société patriotique de la section de la Butte-des-Moulins."
28. AN, F⁷ 4651, n.d. Another document in his file indicates that he had written the letter in September 1794. In signing the letter, Collin spelled his name with a double *l*.
29. AN, BB³ 80, dos. 16.
30. Soboul, *Sans-Culottes*, p. 29 and p. 32, n. 55. Dutard reported to Garat a rumor that should militants from sections Contrat-Social and Bon-Conseil invade the assembly of Butte-des-Moulins, the latter would blow out the candles (Tuetey, *Répertoire*, IX, no. 695, 16 June 1793). The following day a delegation of a hundred from Unité was unsuccessful in transforming the composition of Butte-des-Moulins, which it called "royalist" (ibid., no. 699, 17 June 1793).
31. BN, Nouv. acq. fr., 2684, *Extrait des registres des déliberations de l'assemblée générale . . . Séance du 20 Mai 1793*. It exhorted the representatives, "C'est à vous, à terraser l'anarchie qui tue la liberté." Le³⁸ 260, *Adresse de la section des Champs-Elysées . . . Séance du 20 mai 1793*. See full title in Maurice Tourneux, *Bibliographie de l'histoire de Paris pendant La Révolution française* (Paris, 1895–1897), II, 7993.
32. BN, Lb⁴⁰ 1769, *Extrait du Registre des déliberations de l'assemblée générale. 2 juin 1793*. Full title in Tourneux, II, 7994.
33. AN, BB³ 80, dos. 5, 2 June 1793.
34. Pariset, *Histoire*, II, 95.
35. *Moniteur*, 16, no. 149 (29 May 1793), 490.
36. *Patriote Français*, no. 1383 (28 May 1793), 592 (italicized in original). "Obviously, it is not from the Commune paralysed by legality, it is from the most revolutionary and fiery sections, deliberating outside the control of constituted authorities, that the decisive signal will emanate," writes Jaurès, *Histoire*, VII, p. 389.
37. AN, C 256, pl. 488, p. 10, 27 May 1793. "Punish the unfaithful commission that destroys all principles by arbitrary acts," it urged, and it demanded that the Commission des Douze be turned over to the revolutionary tribunal. See also BVC, MS. 120, fol. 143, 28 May 1793.
38. BVC, MS. 120, fol. 143, 28 and 29 May 1793; B & R, XXVII, 299.
39. Soboul, *Sans-Culottes*, p. 25.

40. AN, C 256, pl. 488, p. 14.

41. AN, F⁷ 4635, packet 3, 21 May 1794.

42. Ibid., 15 March 1794. The document was in the hands of the revolutionary committee of section Fontaine-de-la-Grenelle, to which Cattin-Dubois had moved.

43. Mortimer-Ternaux, *Histoire*, VII, 236–238, and p. 236, n. 1.

44. *Procès-Verbal de la Convention Nationale*, XI, 112–113, "Extrait des registres des deliberations des assemblées générales de la Section de la Fraternité." It accused the "perfidious" and members of revolutionary committees of planning "to massacre [the twenty-two deputies] and to publicize consequently that they had emigrated."

45. *Moniteur*, 16, no. 147 (27 May 1793), 474; Jaurès, *Histoire*, VII, 366.

46. Pariset, *Révolution*, II, 95.

47. AN, AD XVI, 70, p. 56, 31 May 1793; Calvet, *Instrument*, pp. 30–31, citing Karéiev's *Documents inédits sur l'histoire des sections de Paris (1790–1795)*.

48. AN, C 256, pl. 489, p. 3.

49. AN, F⁷ 4332. On 20 March 1795, in repudiating "the terrorism of the faction that had long dominated the section," it appointed a commission of four to examine the *procès-verbal* of 31 May and 1 and 2 June. The report that resulted was published under the section's auspices.

50. AN, F⁷ 4774⁹⁷, "Tableau" of the revolutionary committee of section Brutus (Molière et la Fontaine), 3 May 1794, and Roland's petition for release of 1 May 1794.

51. AN, F⁷ 4774⁹⁷, 26 December 1793. Roland wrote that he had enrolled in the battalion of Petits Augustins and marched on 27 June 1791, but he must be mistaken as to the date.

52. Ibid., 26 December 1793 and 4 August 1793.

53. AN, F⁷ 4707, d. Fielval, 5–6 and 9 June 1793.

54. AN, F⁷ 4707, 5–6 June 1793.

55. Wallon, *Tribunal*, V, 389.

56. *Moniteur*, 16, no. 129 (9 May 1793), 326; no. 130 (10 May 1793), 334.

57. AN, C 256, pl. 489, p. 1.

58. Ibid., pl. 480, p. 33.

59. AN, C 256, pl. 489, p. 23.

60. Soboul calls it and Croix-Rouge "tepid" *(tiède)* (*Sans-Culottes*, p. 25) but points out that documents are lacking for it (p. 27, n. 39).

61. Ibid., p. 24, citing BVC, MS. 120.

62. Pariset, *Histoire*, II, 95.

63. Soboul, *Sans-Culottes*, p. 37.

64. Ibid., p. 27, n. 39.

65. See Chapter VII, "The Insurrection Completed."

66. Wallon, *Tribunal*, IV, 297–298, 24 June 1793. Le Tellier wrote, "Brillants soutiens de la patrie, / Ah! comme vous savez rendre heureux les Français! / Avec quel consolant succès / Ravaillac et Clement de leur puissant génie / Animent de Damien le digne rejeton, / Ce brave Robespierre!!! et Marat . . . et Danton!!!" (p. 298).

67. Ibid., pp. 299–301. "Depuis" was probably Jean-Baptiste-Claude-Henri Dupuy (1752–1824).

68. *Moniteur*, 16, no. 148 (28 May 1793), 485.

69. Ibid., 16, no. 251 (8 September 1793), 590. A Le Boeuf accused Le Tellier in the Commune of eulogizing kings to his students. The General Council then decided to turn him over to the department of police.

70. Wallon, *Tribunal*, IV, 303–305.

71. The *Patriote Français* reported that the Convention had freed Le Tellier during its session of 26 May (no. 1383, 28 May 1793). See also *Moniteur*, 21, no. 281 (29 June 1794), 88.

72. AN, F⁷ 4775²⁵, dossier Tassin, "Confession civique du Citoyen Louis David Tassin cy devant Banquier et actuellement à la maison d'arrêt du Luxembourg . . ." 1 March 1794.

73. Ibid., "Comité de surveillance révolutionnaire de la section de Guillaume Tell."

74. Wallon, *Tribunal*, III, 371–376. It is strange that Wallon fails to mention his brother, de l'Etang, who as a military man more likely would have appeared among the thirteen officers and soldiers. Could he have confused de l'Etang with Tassin the banker?

75. AN, F⁷ 4775³³, dos. Tranchelahausse, "Vie Politique de Cen Tranchelahausse Depuis le mois de May 1789," 24 March 1794; and "Tableau," undated.

76. Ibid., "Vie Politique."

77. Ibid.

78. Ibid., February 1794.

79. Ibid. The first part of the document is dated sometime in January-February (this is the *procès-verbal* of the interrogation of Mme. Tranchelahausse); the second portion of the document is dated 26 February 1794.

80. Ibid., "Extrait du Registre des Déliberations de l'Assemblée générale de la section du Mail à Présent du Guillaume Tell," 1 June 1793.

81. Ibid. This summary of the proceedings was transmitted to Tranchelahausse on 4 June 1793.

82. Ibid., "Extrait du Procès-Verbal de l'Assemblée générale permanente de la section du Mail," n. d. Tranchelahausse was arrested by order of the Comité central révolutionnaire on 5 June 1793 (Tuetey, *Répertoire*, VIII, no. 2918).

83. AN, F⁷ 4775³³, 24 March 1794.

84. Ibid., 11 August 1794, written from Maison d'arrêt des Angloises, rue Charenton, Faubourg Saint-Antoine.

85. Ibid., 16 February 1794, transmitted by the Committee of General Security to the revolutionary committee of section Mail. The People's Representatives wrote, "and that all suspicion of emigration ought to be removed," but asked if other motives existed for his arrest.

86. Ibid. "The committee of General Security decrees that the said citizen be instantly released and the Seals lifted . . ."

87. Ibid. In the margin of an undated document, a letter written to the Committee of General Security by Tranchelahausse regarding his relations with

one Félix Héain who had just returned from a diplomatic mission to Constantinople, the police administrator Guérin wrote that Tranchelahausse "conducted himself well in the *journées* of 12, 13, and 14 Vendémiaire."

88. AN, C 355, pl. 1864, 23 April 1793.

89. BN, Lb⁴⁰ 530, *Rapport* . . . , p. 23. The petition defended Louis after the demonstration of 20 June 1792.

90. Ibid., p. 11.

91. *Moniteur*, 16, no. 126 (6 May 1793), 302.

IV. The Paris Commune and the Evêché Assembly

1. Paul Sainte-Claire Deville, *La Commune de l'an II* (Paris, 1946), pp. 9, 10, and 11.

2. Jacques Godechot, *Les Institutions de la France sous la Révolution et l'Empire* (Paris, 1951), p. 105; Marcel Reinhard, *Nouvelle histoire de Paris. La Révolution 1789–1799* (Paris, 1971), p. 175; Sainte-Claire Deville, *Commune*, p. 9.

3. Sainte-Claire Deville, *Commune*, pp. 12–13. One reason why the Girondins could do nothing against the Montagnards, Sainte-Claire Deville argues, is that the Mountain was supported by the only organized armed force in the capital. Although Buzot and Gensonné had raised this point on occasion, nothing was done (or could be) about it (ibid., pp. 28–33, passim).

4. Mortimer-Ternaux, *Histoire*, VII, 59–60, 61–62.

5. Barère, *Mémoires*, II, 47. "The Commune of Paris and the Jacobin Club were jointly liable for all the extreme measures and ambitious projects during the revolution of 1793" (ibid., p. 68). On 30 October 1792 he demanded a decree to suspend the authority of the General Council "because its disobedience of the law has been proved" (*Patriote Français*, no. 1179, 1 November 1792). See also the violent attack on the Commune by Pétion in issue no. 1196 (18 November 1792).

6. Aulard, *Histoire politique*, p. 434, citing BN, Lb⁴⁰ 212, *La Commune de Paris aux communes de la République.*

7. B & R, XXVII, 24, 15 May 1793. Chaumette cited Roussillon, a member of the revolutionary tribunal who compared the statements of Gorsas and Brissot in their journals of early September (that is, immediately after the September massacres) with those of later dates. In the former they spoke of the massacres as "terrible justice but necessary" and quoted Brissot as writing that the people had "struck some guilty heads" (*Patriote Français*, no. 1373, 18 May 1793).

8. B & R, XXVII, 72–73; Jaurès, *Histoire*, VII, 308, 309.

9. B & R, XXVII, 115–119; BN, Lb⁴¹ 715, *Bergoeing: Député du département de la Gironde, & membre de la commission des Douze, à ses commetans, et à tous les citoyens de la République* (Caen, 1793). Bergoeing took depositions from various citizens against the "anarchistes" of the Evêché assembly. Varlet figures prominently in these reports. Bernard T . . . of Bordeaux testified that a young man [Varlet] told a crowd that before departing for the Vendée they should take care of the "noirs," and "A.M.Q." cited Varlet's promise to some three hundred women:

"Wait, in three or four days we'll accomplish something" (Meillan, *Mémoires*, pp. 186–187, 195).

10. B & R, XXVII, 120–121, where Paine is spelled "Payne."

11. Meillan, *Mémoires*, p. 181: " . . . et que l'on regarde cette motion comme non avenue."

12. Ibid. He was told this by another member of the police administration, Froidure.

13. Meillan, *Mémoires*, pp. 182, 183–184, 185. The editor hastens to add that Pache did not want to discuss such matters in the town hall, not because he was opposed to the proscription, an exact copy of what Bergoeing wrote.

14. F. Braesch, *La Commune du dix août 1792* (Paris, 1911); BHVP, 8°959751, *Articles, Notes, et Extraits d'Articles de J. L. Carra, Tirés des Annales Patriotiques . . . 1793 l'an II de la République;* AP, 4 AZ 961, 10 August 1792, "Commissaires de la majorité des sections réunis avec pleins pouvoirs pour sauver la chose publique;" AN, C 156, 304, p. 27, "L'Assemblée des commissaires de la majorité des sections réunis avec plein pouvoir de sauver la chose publique . . ."

15. Schmidt, *Tableaux*, I, 149, 10 March 1793; Mortimer-Ternaux, *Histoire*, VI, 184–185; *Journal de Paris*, 3, no. 71 (12 and 13 March 1793), p. 287. AN, AF IV, 1470, 11 March 1793, "Garde Nationale Parisienne. Commandant-Général Citᵉⁿ Santerre." Jean Varlet, who was the moving force behind the attempted coup, accused the Commune of being "infected with aristocracy." See the study of A. M. Boursier, "L'émeute parisienne du 10 Mars 1793," *Annales historiques*, 208 (April–June 1972), 204–230.

16. Charavay, *Catalogue*, p. 28, no. 106, item #2, letter under the signature of Dubois, president, and Varlet, secretary, 28 March 1793. See also BN, MSS, Nouv. acq. fr. 2647, fol. 120 (Paris, 4 April 1793); BN, Lb⁴⁰ 1792, same as preceding; A de P, V.D. *9, no. 1025, 27 March 1793, "Extrait . . . "

17. Aulard, *Jacobins*, V, 118, 1 April 1793; Tuetey *Répertoire*, IX, xxvii.

18. AN, C 355, pl. 1865, 2 April 1793.

19. Louis Jacob, *Hébert le Père Duchesne Chef des sans-culottes* (Paris, 1960), p. 172. The *Affiches de la Commune* was to be a rival of the Convention's *Bulletin*.

20. B & R, XXX, 306, 309.

21. *Moniteur*, 16, no. 302 (28 October 1792), 309.

22. Henri Calvet, "Les Origines du comité de l'évêché," *Annales historiques*, VII, pp. 12–23.

23. Schmidt, *Tableaux*, I, 218–219, points out that the General Council drafted the important resolution on preparing the insurrection on 12 May; it was adopted the following day. The *Moniteur* has nothing on it, but the *Chronique de Paris* carried it. It is reproduced by B & R, XXVI, 472. The resolution advocated the establishment of a revolutionary army to be composed of poor patriots, "true sans-culottes" who were to be paid by the wealthy for protecting their property. At the same time, suspects were to be disarmed. Of the five hundred individuals who sat in the Evêché assembly, it is estimated that about a hundred were women. Thiers, *Histoire*, IV, 38.

24. "Rapport du Dutard à Garat," Schmidt, *Tableaux*, I, 225, 14 May 1793. Dutard informed the Minister of Interior that "la faction" had formed a central

committee of commissioners from the sections and planned to disarm all suspects "that is to say, the better half of Paris." Then he wrote, "Ils emprissonneront le premier individu qui avant de parler ne criera pas *vive Marat.*"

Dutard added the following interesting observation: "In almost all the sections, it is the sans-culottes who compose the committees of surveillance. It is they, also, who occupy the chair, who arrange the interior of the room, who position the sentries, who set up the censors and the examiners" (ibid., I, 223). He warned Garat of the approaching insurrection and sought means to arrest it. Among other measures he suggested buying off a few key men, whom he termed "d'hommes à moustaches."

25. Perroud, *Proscription*, p. 30.

26. AN, AF II carton 46, dos. 158, no. 1: *Moniteur*, 16, no. 141 (21 May 1793), 429.

27. See Dutard's letter to Garat of 18 May. After describing the clash between Thuriot and Legendre, he quotes an anonymous participant in the Jacobins as declaring, "Oh! c'est celui-là [Legendre] qui est un homme! ce n'est pas un Robespierre!" (Schmidt, *Tableaux*, I, 245).

28. Ibid., pp. 188–189. See Dutard's letter to Garat of 18 May (ibid., p. 245).

29. Ibid., p. 206, entry for 23–24 May. Wallon wrote that reports of the municipal police indicate sympathy for the approaching revolution, whereas those of the police to the minister of interior deal with means of preventing it *(Révolution,* p. 205). Dutard remarked that one should encourage the bourgeoisie to help prevent the coming insurrection, because it was moderate (ibid., p. 208).

30. Levasseur, *Mémoires,* I, 222–223. He then blamed the dissension between the Convention and the Commune on the "Right wing."

31. Jaurès, *Histoire,* VII, 308, 309.

32. B & R, XXVII, 90–91. Seventy-four of seventy-five delegates voted for the appointment. Boulanger resigned shortly thereafter and was replaced by Hanriot. It was in reaction to this appointment that the Girondins established the Commission des Douze.

33. Garat, *Mémoires,* pp. 113–114; Jaurès, *Histoire,* VII, 396. Rabaut Saint-Etienne, Boyer-Fonfrède, and Viger opposed Hébert's arrest but were outvoted by their colleagues on the Commission. Levasseur added that although Garat had a horror of some sentiments expressed by journals like the *Père Duchesne,* he had been assured by both the mayor and his friend Destournelles (vice-president of the General Council) that never had Hébert proposed anything in the General Council that could not have been proposed by any good citizen (*Mémoires,* I, 224).

34. *Père Duchesne,* no. 239: "It's in the Convention, yes, f——, it's among the representatives of the people the foyer of counter-revolution now exists . . . Rise up and you will see your enemies at your feet," he wrote.

35. AN, C 355, pl. 1867, *Rapport très précis de la Commission des Douze* (n.d.). The Commission quoted Hébert, "Il avoue que ses expressions figurées dans un stile qui, sans exagerations, n'auroit aucune sel" (underscored in the original).

36. *Moniteur,* 16, no. 147 (27 May 1793), 473; B & R, XXVIII, 204; Jaurès *Histoire,* VII, 367, 368.

37. B & R, XXVII, 230–231.

38. This controversy is discussed above.

39. Levasseur, *Mémoires,* I, 226, 227. Levasseur wrote that after interviewing members of the Commission he was convinced they were imagining nonexistent plots (ibid., I, 225–226). Jaurès was especially impressed with the role played by Pache, who wrote "modestly but truthfully" about how he maintained calm and soothed all parties during these emotional events. Had he been less modest and self-effacing or had he refused to accept the role of the Evêché committee, the outcome of 31 May could have been quite different (*Histoire,* VII, 449–450).

40. B & R, XXVII, 230–231; *Moniteur,* 16, no. 147 (27 May 1793), 473–474; Jaurès, *Histoire,* VII, 370–374, passim.

41. *Moniteur,* 16, no. 148 (28 May 1793), 482. Delegates told how they had defeated supporters of Champs-Elysées, Butte-des-Moulins, and Fraternité, the three conservative sections who led the fight against the Commune.

42. Ibid., no. 149 (29 May 1793), 490. This is discussed more fully in Chapter II.

43. Ibid., no. 150 (30 May 1793), 498. The Commission was temporarily reestablished on 27 May, then suppressed finally on 31 May; its papers were transferred to the Committee of Public Safety.

44. Ibid., no. 151 (31 May 1793), 506; B & R, XXVII, 292; *Journal des Débats,* no. 423 (31 May 1793). This journal appeared three times weekly and was edited by Deflers "with an independence, almost an irreverance." It had a sense of humor and defended the right to tell the truth even if it was disliked by the Jacobins. Upon its suppression, on 14 December 1793, it was succeeded by the *Journal de la Montagne* (Hatin, *Histoire,* VI, 437–443, passim).

45. Jaurès, *Histoire,* VII, 412–413.

46. Maurice Tourneux, *Procès-Verbaux de la Commune de Paris (10 août 1792–1er juin 1793)* (Paris, 1894), "Séance du 29 mai," p. 136.

47. Tuetey, *Répertoire,* VIII, no. 2622. The resolution stated that because the rights of man, the liberty of the press, and so on were being violated, Cité called on the sections to meet the next day at 4:00 P.M. in order to deliberate on the means that ought to be taken to assure the triumph of patriotism (from AN, F7 4432, of the general assembly of section Molière et la Fontaine).

48. Jaurès, *Histoire,* VII, 420. The Commission des Douze was not unaware of what was taking place; it warned the mayor of "des motions incendaires" adopted by the Evêché assembly (Tuetey, *Répertoire,* VIII, no. 2653, 30 May 1793). Schmidt, *Tableaux,* I, 343, 344, gives the following explanation of the Evêché assembly. To begin with, there were actually two assemblies that deliberated separately on the steps to be taken during the insurrection. One was the Club electoral, a large body probably composed of commissioners recently elected by the sections, in which delegates spoke only of the Commission des Six. The other occupied itself with matters relating to the Commission des Douze. It acted as a cover for a smaller assembly made up exclusively of commissioners from the

sections that met in secret to elect the Comité des Neuf. Garat spoke of the secret assembly, which was the dangerous one. He reported that Pache had informed him that the Evêché assembly was composed of members of the Club electoral and of popular societies, plus commissioners of some sections, but that this assembly was incompetent to take any revolutionary measures. Schmidt adds that Pache was referring to the Electoral Assembly, not to the secret assembly, either because he was misinformed or because he did not want to tell what he knew.

49. Dufourny (1739–1796?) was an architect by profession. He had been president of district des Mathurins in 1789 and a "turbulent" Jacobin and Cordelier. After 10 August he became president of the Directory of the Paris department. A frequent visitor to the Committee of Public Safety, he even participated in its deliberations. He was expelled from the Cordeliers by Hébert and Vincent and was a witness in their trial. Dufourny was closely linked to Fabre d'Eglantine; he was attacked by Robespierre and expelled from the Jacobins, then imprisoned until 31 July. He was released, then rearrested and held until the general amnesty of 26 October 1795. He died shortly thereafter (Walter, "Table Analytique," in Michelet, *Histoire*, II, 1371–72). Jaurès calls him a "maratiste extreme, même communiste" (*Histoire*, VII, 426–427). This characterization is doubtful, for he played quite a conservative role in the insurrection, as will be seen.

50. Jaurès, *Histoire*, VII, 421; B & R, XXVIII, 108–126, Bergoeing's report. The visit of this commission is discussed in Chapter VI.

51. In a "Note remise à la Commission des Douze, sur ce qui s'est passé dans la journée du 29 à l'assemblée de l'Evêché," one reads, "A kind of large banner, with a red background, was [over] the seats of the hall. It carried these words: education and good morals can alone make men equal" (Schmidt, *Tableaux*, I, 338–339). Jaurès thought that this slogan was probably raised in an attempt to appease and reassure the petty bourgeoisie (*Histoire*, VII, 421).

The Jacobins reported at their session of 30 May that thirty sections were meeting in the hall of section Cité and that among the first measures taken by the assembly was "enthusiastically" to place private property under their safeguard (Tuetey, *Répertoire*, VIII, no. 2655). Hassenfratz informed the Jacobins that his section had placed property under the protection of the sans-culottes—the very first measure adopted by the general assembly. The Jacobins then swore to die rather than allow attacks on property (Aulard, *Jacobins*, V, 214–215).

52. Maurice Tourneux, *Procès-Verbaux*, p. 140, lists the thirty-three sections in the following order: Arcis, Bondy, Tuileries, Faubourg-du-Nord, Panthéon-Français, Fontaine-de-Grenelle, Quatre-Nations, Gravilliers, Quinze-Vingts, Popincourt, Marseille, Réunion, Faubourg-Montmartre, 1792, République-Française, Croix-Rouge, Marchés, Halle-au-Blé, Montreuil, Piques, Amis-de-la-Patrie, Contrat-Social, Marais, Bonne-Nouvelle, Luxembourg, Pont-Neuf, Sans-Culottes, Temple, Arsenal, Bon-Conseil, Lombards, Droits-de-l'Homme, Cité.

Sainte-Claire Deville, citing AN, BB³80 (no dossier), says that there were thirty-four sections represented by commissioners elected on 29 May who met in the great hall of the Archévêché the following day. They called their assembly "Assemblée générale et révolutionnaire de la ville de Paris." Twenty-eight sections had given their delegates unlimited powers, and six had granted limited powers only (*Commune*, p. 80).

53. *Inventaire des autographes et des documents historiques composant la collection de M. Benjamin Fillon*, Series I and II, ed. Etienne Charavay and Frédéric Naylor (Paris, 1877), p. 64, no. 546, "Paris déclaré en insurrection," items 1 and 2; AN, BB³ 80, dos. 8; Tuetey, *Répertoire*, VIII, no. 2647.

54. AN, BB³ 80, dos. 8, 30 May 1793. This carton is the most significant collection on the insurrection. Unless otherwise noted, the references are to the forty-fourth carton, which contains documents of the department of police, the General Council of the Paris Commune, the department of Paris, and the general assembly of the commissioners of the sections of Paris (the Evêché assembly), as well as individual letters, resolutions, and reports of revolutionary committees of the sections. The last group is in a dossier entitled "Etat produit par les sections qui dans les journées des 31 mai, 1er et 2 juin ont marché sous les drapeaux de la liberté."

55. Tuetey, *Répertoire*, VIII, no. 2643, citing the cahier of deliberations of section Molière et la Fontaine, AN, F⁷ 4432; Mortimer-Ternaux, *Histoire*, VII, 309, 310; B & R, XXVII, 300.

56. Tourneux, *Procès-Verbaux*, "Arrêté pris en l'assemblée des commissaires des autorités constituées du département et des quarante-huit sections . . . ," pp. 146–147, lists ten names, not eleven, whether through an omission in the original minutes or one of his own is not clear. See also BN, MSS, Nouv. acq. fr. 2716, fol. 57, 31 May 1793; Tuetey, *Répertoire*, VIII, no. 2658; Sainte-Claire Deville, *Commune*, p. 87.

57. AN, BB³ 80, dos. 1, pc. 141, 31 May 1793. The document, mistakenly dated "du 1er mai 1793," reads as follows: "Le Conseil général arrête que le Comité Révolutionnaire existant actuellement à la Maison Commune sera appelé le *Comité Révolutionnaire crée par le peuple du département de Paris*. Signé, Cailleux, vice-président par interim, Coulombeau, secrétaire-greffier" (emphasis in original).

58. AN, BB³ 80, dos. 16, pc. 49, "Liste des membres composant le comité central et révolutionnaire du département de Paris." Marquet of section Bonne-Nouvelle heads the list.

59. AN, T 604², packet 9e, b, "Mémoires de Chaumette, sur la révolution du 31 mai, premier récit, p. 179." One way of distinguishing the Comité central révolutionnaire from the Conseil général révolutionnaire is to recognize that documents signed by Varlet, Marquet, Loys, or Marchand are of the insurrectionary committee, whereas those signed by Destournelles, replaced at times by Cailleux, Marino, and Defavannes, are from the Conseil général révolutionnaire. See the explanation of Tuetey, *Répertoire*, IX, lii–lxxx, lxxxi–c, and cii–civ.

60. Pariset, *Révolution*, II, 97.

61. AN, BB³ 80, dos. 16, pc. 15, 15 May 1793. The Comité central révolutionnaire added that it would seek the best means to organize the insurrection since it recognized "de ne pas mettre toujours le peuple en mouvement." See also ibid., pc. 51, n.d., entitled "Projets d'organisation du Comité des Propositions."

V. The Comité Central Révolutionnaire

1. Perroud (*Proscription,* pp. 31–32) lists twenty-eight names on the Comité central, including three men, Bouin, Moëssard, and Furnerot, whom Tuetey excludes as permanent members. They are discussed below.

2. Gustave Laurent, "Un magistrat révolutionnaire. Claude-Emmanuel Dobsen l'homme du 31 mai," *Annales historiques,* 15 (1938), 2–11. This is a brief summary of Laurent's unpublished manuscript on Dobsen (whose name Laurent, unlike many sources, spells without the *t*), deposited in the Bibliothèque municipale of Reims, a xeroxed copy of which is in my possession. The work is 624 pages long and includes an index and a table of contents; 499 pages of it are typed and the remainder is in script. Unfortunately, pages 48–201 are missing, including Chapter VII, "La Révolution du 31 mai (mars–juin 1793)." It is strange that this manuscript, which would require so little effort to prepare for publication, still remains unpublished.

3. Laurent, "Magistrat," pp. 7–11. Dobsen seems to have played a conciliatory role and defused tensions during the early days of the Revolution. He was "at all times, the defender of the humble workingmen" and favored the reforms proposed by spokesmen of the Third Estate. Among other things, he occupied himself with the problem of shortages and how to guarantee the basic needs of the people. Many of his proposals of 1789 were to be repeated in 1793 and even in 1794 (Laurent, manuscript, pp. 33–34). A brief sketch of the judicial posts Dobsen held after 4 November 1799 is by J. Dressler, "Un magistrat révolutionnaire: Claude-Emmanuel Dobsen l'homme du 31 mai," *Annales historiques,* 145 (1956), 395–399. In April 1810 Dobsen had to combat rumors that he was unworthy of holding his judicial post. His opponents seemed to have resented his role as former vice-president of the revolutionary tribunal (ibid., p. 398).

4. Calvet, *Instrument,* pp. 68–69, citing AN, F^7 4775[44], dos. Verron [the municipal officer who had helped free him], and AN, F^7 4774[36], dos. Marquet. Marquet's signature appears on the address of 2 and 3 June congratulating the Convention.

5. Tuetey, *Répertoire,* IX, lx. Marquet left section Bonne-Nouvelle for section Luxembourg on 1 July 1793.

6. Gérard Walter, "Table Analytique," in Michelet, *Histoire,* II, 1498.

7. Calvet, *Instrument,* pp. 75–76. Except for the personal data, the dossier on Wendling is barren. Calvet cites AN, F^{7*} 2484, of the revolutionary committee as well as some documents in the Administration du Ministre de la guerre. Tuetey has no information on him (*Répertoire,* IX, lx).

8. Tuetey, *Répertoire,* IX, lx–lxl. Tuetey's sketch is based on Varlet's dossier, AN, F^7 4775[40].

9. Ibid., IX, lxj.

10. Calvet, *Instrument,* pp. 61–62, citing AN, F^7 4721; Tuetey, *Répertoire,* IX, lxj.

11. Calvet, *Instrument,* pp. 52–53.

12. Ibid., p. 53, n. 6.

13. Ibid., p. 53.

14. Ibid., pp. 53–54.
15. Ibid., pp. 54–55.
16. Ibid., p. 55.
17. Ibid., p. 53, n. 8.
18. Tuetey, *Répertoire*, IX, lxii. The large print opposite his name gives his section as Butte-des-Moulins, but the summary of his activities refers to it as being Bon-Conseil.
19. Ibid., IX, lxiij.
20. Ibid., IX, lxiij.
21. Ibid., IX, lxiij; Walter, "Table Analytique," in Michelet, *Histoire*, II, 1440.
22. Calvet, *Instrument*, p. 56, says, "Il conserva la fouguese audace et l'esprit de fronde d'un étudiant." (See also Tuetey, *Répertoire*, IX, lxiii).
23. Tuetey, *Répertoire*, IX, lxiii–lxiv; X, no. 1037; plus many scattered references in the latter volume, almost all of which deal with deliberations of the Comité de salut public of the Paris department rather than with Clémence as an individual. See also Karen D. Tønnesson, *La Défaite des sans-culottes* (Oslo and Paris, 1959), "Index des noms de personnes," p. 429. Calvet characterizes Clémence as follows: "A type of a hot-headed bohemian, quick to resort to blows and to riot, keen for police investigation and little concerned with danger" (*Instrument*, p. 57).
24. Tuetey, *Répertoire*, IX, lxiv.
25. Ibid., IX, lxiv.
26. Ibid., IX, lxiv–lxv.
27. Ibid., IX, lxv.
28. Ibid., IX, lxv.
29. Calvet, *Instrument*, p. 60. Calvet observes that many historians confuse this Marchand with others of the same name. Mathiez confused him with an Hébertist and Perroud mixed him up with the president of the popular society in section Sans-Culottes (ibid., p. 59).
30. Ibid., p. 61.
31. Tuetey, *Répertoire*, IX, lxv–lxvj; Tønnesson, *Défaite*, "Index," p. 441. Tønnesson writes that during the Thermidorian Reaction, "like its neighboring section Lepeletier, Mont-Blanc became known as an ultra of reaction" (p. 90).
32. Tuetey, *Répertoire*, IX, lxvj; Tønnesson, *Défaite*, "Index," p. 430, where he is spelled Crespin. There is evidence that he was in fairly close contact with Jean Varlet when the two were transferred from Plessis to La Force prison (Tønnesson, *Défaite*, "Index," pp. 368–369).
33. Walter, "Table Analytique," in Michelet, *Histoire*, II, 1553–54; Tuetey, *Répertoire*, IX, lxvj.
34. Tuetey, *Répertoire*, IX, lxvj–lxvij. Scipion Duroure (or Du Roure) was the godfather of Hébert's daughter, Scipion-Virginie (Jacob, *Hébert*, pp. 91, 165). Calvet seems to have confused Duroure with a Dedouvre from section Marseille (rather than the town of Marseilles) and calls him a *laboureur* from the canton of Chatillon and mayor of Gentilly. Dedouvre was a member of the club Sainte-Chapelle, hardly a likely candidate for the Comité central (see Calvet, *Instrument*, p. 70).

35. Tuetey, *Répertoire,* IX, lxvij.
36. Ibid., IX, lxvij–lxviij. On 23 October 1794 he was denounced for having declared that "he could [i.e., he had the right] to discuss a law" (AN, F⁷* 699, cited in Soboul, *Les Sans-Culottes,* p. 512, n. 35).
37. Tuetey, *Répertoire,* IX, lxviij.
38. Ibid., IX, lxviij.
39. Ibid., IX, lxviij.
40. Ibid., IX, lxix; Walter, "Table Analytic," in Michelet, *Histoire,* II, 1437. In a letter to Fouquier-Tinville on 2 April, Moëssard, Marchand, and Loys wrote that they had expelled Gusman from the committee and had him arrested as an intriguer. The testimony given to the public accuser when the Hébertists and Dantonists had been or were about to be executed is hardly a trustworthy source, however. Why was Gusman so popular among the sectionnaires as to be elected to the Evêché committee, it may be asked, if he was only an "intriguer"?
41. Calvet, *Instrument,* p. 58.
42. Tuetey, *Répertoire,* IX, lxix–lxx; Tønnesson, *Défaite,* "Index," pp. 434–435. Calvet says of him, "He appears to me rather as a street boy of revolutionary Paris, the prototype of Gavroche [Victor Hugo's street boy of *Les Misérables*]. He had youth, spirit, and courage." Although Pariset accepts Baron de Batz's description of him as an agent of the baron's grandfather (*La Révolution,* II, 153), not a single document exists to disprove his commitment to the Revolution (Calvet, *Instrument,* p. 59, n. 23).
43. Calvet, *Instrument,* pp. 73–74, says that Moëssard served on the Comité but played no prominent role. (See also Tuetey, IX, lxx.) It can be assumed that like the others he was freed shortly before or after the *journée* of Vendémiaire.
44. Tuetey, *Répertoire,* IX, lxx–lxxj.
45. Ibid., IX, lxxj–lxxij. This recital of events is based on Richebraque's "confession" after his arrest on 24 May 1795. Dobsen was formally co-opted to the Comité des Neuf under the presidency of Richebraque: "Sur l'observation d'un membre, l'assemblée a délibéré que le citoyen Dobsan [sic] serait adjoint au Comité des Neuf" (AN, BB³ 80, dos. 8, 30 May 1793).
46. Garat, *Mémoires,* pp. 102–103.
47. Who but a very young man could have written on the same page that ordered the armed forces into operation, "Bon soir ma bonne amie. Vous êtes forte jolie" (AN, BB³ 80, dos. 16, pc. 53, reproduced in Tuetey, "Ordre du comité central de mettre sur pied la force armée," *Répertoire,* IX, opposite p. lxxxix)?

VI. The Insurrection Begun

1. The myth that Marat sounded the tocsin in person has been repeated by some historians. This hardly requires refutation. He had no time even to issue his *Publiciste* from 31 May to 4 June (Jaurès, *Histoire,* VII, 442). Aulard, strangely enough, repeats the story (*Histoire politique,* p. 438).
2. AN, BB³ 80, dos. 16, 31 May 1793. Jaurès gives the time of the tocsin

sounding as between 1:00 and 2:00 A.M. (*Histoire*, VII, 460). Louvet wrote that he heard the alarm at 3:00 A.M. (*Mémoires*, p. 88).

3. Fillon, *Inventaire des autographes*. Series I and II, "Paris déclaré en insurrection," #546, p. 64, no. 1: "Délibération de l'assemblée de l'Evêché." Signed by J. H. Hassenfratz, président, and Protaix, secrétaire, 30 May 1793. See also Jaurès, *Histoire*, VII, 443.

4. B & R, XXVII, 306.

5. AN BB³30, dos. 16, 31 May 1793; Tuetey, *Répertoire*, VIII, no. 2673.

6. AN, BB³80, dos. 16. Summarized in Tuetey, *Répertoire*, VIII, no. 2648.

7. AN, BB³80, dos. 16 (several copies). These events were reported to the Convention by the mayor. Tuetey, *Répertoire*, VIII, no. 2734.

8. Sainte-Claire Deville, *Commune*, p. 86, n. 2, argues that the position of the documents in AN, BB³80 leads to the above conclusion. The resolution of the Evêché assembly, signed by Varlet, must have been passed even before the appointment of the six commissioners "de recueillir toutes les mesures de salut public." This is possible, but anyone who has examined carton BB³80 knows how unreliable is the order of the documents because of the constant examination of this collection by researchers.

9. Bachelard's report is from his deposition before the civil committee of section Luxembourg, 30 August 1795. It is in the Archives du Greffe du tribunal criminal d'Eure-et-Loir and is reproduced in Adrien Sée, *Le Procès Pache* (Paris, 1911), pp. 177–179. Bachelard describes the ceremony sarcastically: everything took place "révolutionnairement."

10. These are reproduced by Mortimer-Ternaux, *Histoire*, VII, 319–320, n. 1, under date 31 May 1793. They do not appear in either Tuetey's collection or Sainte-Claire Deville's study. Jaurès, *Histoire*, VII, 447, also reproduces the three resolutions.

11. Fillon, *Inventaire des Autographes*, p. 65, #547, 2°, "Insurrection du 31 Mai 1793," signed by Coulombeau, *secrétaire-greffier* of the General Council.

12. AN, BB³80, dos. 16, pcs. 24, 25, 38. One of the more complete documents of 31 May is entitled: "Commune de Paris. Extrait du Registre des délibérations du Comité révolutionnaire de l'assemblée générale des Commissaires des Quarante cinq Sections de Paris Séant à la Maison commune."

13. B & R, XXVII, 321.

14. Tourneux, *Procès-Verbaux*, pp. 138–139; in Tuetey, *Répertoire*, VIII, no. 2659, Destournelles's phrase reads, "by a real majority and loyally obtained," not "legally obtained" as in Tourneux. See also B & R, XXVIII, 306–307. "The president [Dobsen] declares in the name of the sovereign people, that the mayor, the vice-president, the *procureur* of the Commune and his substitutes, and the General Council of the Commune are reinstated in their functions by the sovereign people who testify to their satisfaction with their constant solicitude and true patriotism for the public good" (*Moniteur*, 16, no. 152, 1 June 1793, 517.

15. Mortimer-Ternaux, *Histoire*, VII, 319, n. 1.

16. Jaurès, *Histoire*, VII, 448–449. Pache played a fine role in accepting his subordination to the Evêché assembly, unlike Pétion after 10 August, says Jaurès. Louis Jacob, *Hébert*, passim, is critical of Pache during this period.

17. Tuetey, *Répertoire*, VIII, no. 2659, 31 May 1793.
18. Schmidt, *Tableaux*, I, 362.
19. Ibid.
20. *Moniteur*, 16, no. 152 (1 June 1793), 518. Quinet saw nothing but "unanimous" action from the very beginning: "Popular coups d'Etats, such as no other revolution provides; planned at night, like the snares of a usurper, executed during the day, by the blows of the whole people." And again: "Also such unanimity does not appear at any other time" (*La Révolution*, II, 3, 4). Michelet points out that there was a dispute over the firing of the alarm cannon. Hanriot, carrying out the directive of the Comité des Neuf, gave orders to fire it, but the Commune decided to abide by the law and countermanded Hanriot's order (*Histoire*, II, 362–363).
21. B & R, XXVII, 305; *Moniteur*, 16, no. 152 (1 June 1793), 518; Tourneux, *Procès-Verbaux*, p. 136; Tuetey, *Répertoire*, VIII, no. 2656, 30 May 1793.
22. Michelet wrote that the Commune decided to abide by the law and not fire the alarm cannon, and Chaumette ordered that the alarm bell in the Hôtel de Ville remain silent. This shows that the Commune was vacillating—because the Comité des Neuf was "maratiste," while the General Council was Jacobin, he concludes (*Histoire*, II, 362–363).
23. B & R, XXVII, 310; Jaurès, *Histoire*, VII, 450–462, passim. Jaurès writes that to symbolize the cooperation between the Evêché committee and the municipal authorities the tocsin in the belfry of the Hôtel de Ville was sounded at the same moment as the cannon of alarm was being fired.
24. B & R, XXVII, 317–318; Jaurès, *Histoire*, VII, 484–485; Tourneux, *Procès-Verbaux*, p. 148.
25. B & R, XXVII, 321. "The *procureur* of the Commune rises in indignation against this proposition mentioned for the third time. He says that if anyone dares to revive this [suggestion] again, he will denounce him to the same people, who applaud without realizing that they are applauding their own doom" (Tourneux, *Procès-Verbaux*, p. 148).
26. Schmidt, who is critical of Chaumette and Pache, admits that together with Dobsen they did all in their power to subdue the "fanatics" and succeeded only with great effort. *Tableaux*, I, 370.
27. Jaurès, *Histoire*, VII, 487, remarks, "It is not a glorious hour for the Commune: she is all defiance, false agitation, systematic faltering and hypocrisy. But who does not feel that she is about to boil over, to rise up?"
28. Mortimer-Ternaux, *Histoire*, VII, p. 391, n. 1, writes that of all the members of the Paris Commune during the three days of the insurrection, Chaumette alone did not want to act illegally. This means, of course, that he opposed the insurrection.
29. *Moniteur*, 16, no. 152 (1 June 1793), 518; B & R, XXVII, 326; Jaurès, *Histoire*, VII, 462–463.
30. The spokesman for Pont-Neuf informed the Convention of what had taken place in his section. According to him, Hanriot's order was undated. He then proceeded to the General Council and reported Hanriot's command. The Council decided *to ignore the order* [emphasis mine] under the motivation that only

the National Assembly (the Convention) could decree the firing of the alarm cannon (*Moniteur*, 16, no. 152, 1 June 1793, 523–524).

31. Tuetey, *Répertoire*, VIII, nos. 2712, 2713.

32. Ibid., VIII, nos. 2715, 2716.

33. Calvet, *Instrument*, p. 31. Calvet writes that although Pariset defined exactly the attitude of Molière et la Fontaine and of Pont-Neuf, he presented section Contrat-Social as sans-culotte and underestimated the "resistance" in Finistère, as also the anti-Girondin tendencies of Fraternité and of Butte-des-Moulins. It seems that the attitude of each section varied throughout the three days of the insurrection. Ibid., p. 31, n. 11.

34. Mortimer-Ternaux, *Histoire*, VII, 330, n. 1; *Moniteur*, 16, no. 153 (2 June 1793), 526.

35. *Moniteur*, 16, no. 153 (2 June 1793), 527.

36. Michelet, *Histoire*, II, 359–360.

37. Ibid., II, 360.

38. *Moniteur*, 16, no. 153 (2 June 1793), 536. The conflict in section Unité may be followed by examining the *procès-verbal* of its revolutionary committee from 19 April to 2 June. See Sée, *Le Procès Pache*, "Pièces provenant du Comité révolutionnaire de la Section de l'Unité du 19 avril au 2 juin 1793," pp. 111–132. "In most sections, much defiance, very little enthusiasm" (Mortimer-Ternaux, *Histoire*, VII, 329). But Mortimer-Ternaux admits that many Parisians attached to the moderate party were frightened by the words of Isnard threatening the destruction of Paris; they were equally discontented with the Commune because of its agitation (ibid., p. 330).

39. Mortimer-Ternaux, *Histoire*, VII.

40. Ibid.

41. AN F^{7*} 2497, pp. 28–29; Tuetey, *Répertoire*, IX, lxxvii.

42. *Moniteur*, 16, no. 154 (3 June 1793), 534; B & R, XXVIII, 55–59, quoting a letter from a grenadier named Brun-Lafont of the battalion of Butte-des-Moulins to a friend in the Gironde department recounting the incident and defending the insurrection. Among other arguments he refers to the government's practice of collecting forced levies when France was in danger and argues that Polish landlords had lost all in their country's partitions, which ought to be a warning to the wealthy of their own country. The letter is mistakenly dated 14 June 1792 instead of 1793.

43. Jaurès, *Histoire*, VII, 479–480. This incident is treated in Lamartine, *Histoire*, VI, 76–77; Michelet, *Histoire*, II, 367, 1070; Thiers, *Histoire*, IV, 47–48.

44. Louvet, *Mémoires*, pp. 89–90. Louvet wrote that had the section been disarmed, the Jacobins would have accused the Girondins of supporting the white cockade. It was the support of five other sections and their readiness to fight, he says, in addition to the obvious falsehood of the rumors, that led to the happy conclusion of this incident.

45. Jaurès, *Histoire*, VII, 480.

46. *Moniteur*, 16, no. 154 (3 June 1793), 533–534; Tourneux, *Procès-Verbaux*, p. 147. For Vergniaud's motion, see Mortimer-Ternaux, *Histoire*, VII, 338; AP,

LXV, 647; Tuetey, *Répertoire*, VIII, no. 2740; BVC, MS 120, fol. 144, 31 May 1793.

47. AN, BB³ 80, dos. 16, 31 May 1793: "Henriot est nommé provisoirement commandant général de l'armée Parisienne par le comité des neuf." See also Tuetey, *Répertoire*, VIII, nos. 2646, 2670. Hanriot was authorized to arrest the mayor, but this must have been a contingency plan in the event that Pache continued to oppose the insurrection (AN, BB³ 80, dos. 16, pc. 33, 31 May 1793).

48. AN, BB³ 80, dos. 16, pcs. 25, 28, 30, plus scattered documents for 31 May 1793; Tuetey, *Répertoire*, VIII, no. 2675. "Il est enjoint au comité[s] révolutionnaire[s] des quarante huit sections, pour ordre du Comité révolutionnaire central [sic] de prendre toutes les mesures les plus prompte[s] et les plus efficace[s], pour désarmer et mettre en état d'arrestation tous les hommes suspec[ts] de leurs sections" (ibid., pc. 30).

49. AN, BB³ 80, dos. 16, cited in Perroud, *Proscription*, p. 33.

50. AN, BB³ 80, dos. 16, pcs. 28, 30, 53, 31 May 1793; Tuetey, *Répertoire*, VIII, no. 2674, 31 May; AP, LXV, 656. Some documents contain orders that a reserve of fifty men be formed by each section in addition to the fifty available for guard duty, and that the armed men be paid forty sous per day during the insurrection. The original resolution was drafted and introduced by Loys of the Comité central (Tuetey, *Répertoire*, IX, lxxviii).

The *Chronique de Paris* reported, however, that since workers earned about double the amount provided them for bearing arms, few took the subsidy. Only those who could not earn a living accepted, and these were few (B & R, XXVII, 440).

51. Tuetey, *Répertoire*, VIII, nos. 2667, 2680, 2688–95. Leclerc wrote to the Comité central, "Friends, after having spent the whole night in sorting letters, we have put aside a portion which were found very suspicious and for different members of the Convention such as Buzot, etc., etc. Should we pass on all the letters to you that we suspect[?] Should we open them ourselves[?] It is on the above that we await a prompt and precise order." Signed, Leclerc.

The Comité central approved the operation of the Commission of Posts and authorized it to continue to examine all letters that appeared suspicious. AN, BB³ 80, dos. 16, pc. 162, 5 June 1793.

Tuetey was mistaken in thinking that it was Etienne Pierre Leclerc, member of the insurrectionary Commune of 10 August, who was the commissioner in the post office (*Répertoire*, IX, lxxviii). In AN, F⁷ 4774⁹, "Extraction, profession avant et depuis la Révolution, carrière politique et révolutionnaire, et état présente des affairs de Théophile Leclerc," the latter wrote, "On the night of 29 May I was elected a member of the Comité révolutionnaire of the Club central; on 31 May member of the Commission des postes." Undated, but probably 4 July 1794.

52. AN, BB³ 80, dos. 16, 1 June 1793. The Communique read, "The commission of the general council to the administration of Posts requests the general council to please replace it as promptly as possible . . . We have not budged since yesterday evening and we are dying of hunger." The commissioners asked that six others be appointed to relieve them so that they could have a bite to eat.

53. Ibid., 1 June 1793, signed by Leclerc.

54. AN, BB³ 80, dos. 16, pc. 51. This arrangement was to be in force until all danger to the Republic had passed.

55. AN, BB³ 80, dos. 16, pc. 49 (31 May 1793); Tuetey, *Répertoire,* VIII, no. 2735 (summarized); AP, LXV, 646. Despite the fact that Guadet had indicated that the delegates who asked to be heard were the same ones who had removed the duly constituted authorities, the Convention granted them permission to speak. The address was signed by Loys, president, and Gusman, secretary.

56. When a citizen asked that refractory priests, nobles, and signers of the so-called anti-civic petitions be arrested, the General Council referred his proposal to the "comité révolutionnaire, chargé essentiellement de toutes les mesures de sûreté" (Tourneux, *Procès-Verbaux,* p. 146).

57. Tuetey, *Répertoire,* IX, lxxx; VIII, no. 2668. The police commissioner was ordered to report to the Comité central every half hour "so that the people may not sacrifice them [deputies under attack] to their vengeance, and so that the Committee may, if necessary, give them help which is owed to the national representation" (AN, BB³ 80, dos. 16, 31 May 1793).

58. AN, F⁷* 2514, p. 15, 31 May 1793. This decree was communicated to the revolutionary committee of section Observatoire by a delegate from section Panthéon-Français.

59. Tuetey, *Répertoire,* IX, lxxii; VIII, nos. 2596, 2727, 2728. Réunion arrested a Jean-Joseph Compigny for tearing down placards claiming that the sections "ont bien mérité de la patrie" (ibid., no. 2917, 4 June—after the insurrection was over).

60. Louvet, *Mémoires,* pp. 88–89, 91. Rabaut kept shouting, "Illa suprema dies!"

61. Ibid., p. 95. In a footnote Louvet adds that Proly was an Austrian, Pereyra a Belgian, Pio a Florentine, Arthur an Englishman, Fournier an American, and Clootz a Prussian. It is hardly necessary to observe that "foreign agitators" has always been an accusation used by reaction against native revolutionaries. Fournier, for example, was about as American as Louvet was.

As for the uprising itself, Louvet declared that its purpose was to deliver Hébert, "convicted today" of having been a foreign agent, "and against a kind of raving lunatic by name of Varlet, a tireless agitator" (ibid., pp. 94–95). Louvet knew better than to blame the insurrection on the arrest of Hébert and Varlet, but an honest discussion of the real reasons for the *émeute* would have exposed the contradictions of his own principles and those of the party he defended.

62. *Moniteur,* 16, nos. 152, 153, 154 (1, 2, 3, June 1793), 522–524, 528–532, 535–538, respectively; B & R, XXVII, 323–341. The proceedings in the Convention have been summarized or analyzed by every historian who has written on the French Revolution, but few have added to the above sources. There is no need, therefore, to do more than indicate the main developments on that day. Tuetey observes that the text of the Convention's *procès-verbal* is mistaken in referring to the delegation as being from the General Council. The address had begun with the words, "L'Assemblée générale des sections nous envoie pour communiquer les mesures que nous avons prises." It was replaced in the Convention's minutes by, "Le Conseil général de la Commune nous envoie . . ." Fur-

thermore, it carries the signatures of Loys as president and Gusman as secretary of the insurrection committee (*Répertoire*, IX, lxxx).

In addition to the reports in the *Moniteur* and in Buchez and Roux, see the *procès-verbal* of the Convention reproduced by Meillan, *Mémoires*, pp. 208–225 (suppression of the Commission appears on p. 223). Mortimer-Ternaux states that the original *procès-verbaux* of the Convention's sessions of 27, 28, and 31 May were dishonestly revised after Marat's death. Objections were raised that since one of the secretaries, Penières, was a Girondin, the *procès-verbaux* reflected his prejudices (*Histoire*, VII, 353, n. 1).

Blanc cites Meillan's claim that no proper vote on suppressing the Commission had been taken but refutes this view by quoting from the observations of Hérault de Sechelles, Levasseur, and the Convention's *procès-verbal* (*Histoire*, VIII, 369–370). See also Thiers, *Histoire*, IV, 58–59; von Sybel, *Geschichte*, II, 289; Taine, *Origines*, II, 463; Michelet, *Histoire*, II, 364, 367.

63. Von Sybel cites sections 1792, Butte-des-Moulins, Mail, and Gardes-Françaises, in addition to Molière et la Fontaine, as defying the "patriots." Conservatives in section Contrat-Social were prepared to fire on their adversaries, he says (citing no sources). This gave Vergniaud the courage to move that "die pariser Sectionen hatten sich um das Vaterland wohl verdient gemacht" (that "the Parisian sections had merited well of the country").

64. Aulard, *Histoire politique*, p. 437.

65. Jaurès, *Histoire*, VII, 476–477. When Vergniaud's motion was reported to the General Council, the spokesman for the Commune began by saying, "This . . . will astonish you perhaps" (B & R, XXVII, 316).

66. Aulard, *Jacobins*, V, 216, 31 May 1793.

67. Tuetey reproduces the original address (*Répertoire*, IX, lxxxii–lxxxiv). The address presented in the Convention began, "Legislators, The men of 14 July, of 10 August, and of 31 May are in your midst. Delegates of the people who have never betrayed their cause, they have come to help you against the conspirators. One more effort and liberty will triumph." The spokesman then presented the demands of the delegation (AN, BB³ 80, dos. 8; AP, LXV, 651–652; Tuetey, *Répertoire*, VIII, no. 2840).

68. AP, LXV, 639, 31 May 1793. Lulier assured the Convention that persons and property were being scrupulously respected. Mortimer-Ternaux, *Histoire*, VII, 323, says that not a word of this appears in the *Moniteur*.

69. Walter, "Table Analytique, " in Michelet, *Histoire*, II, 1483.

70. Michelet wrote that as late as 29 May Robespierre still hesitated about supporting the proposal for the arrest of the Girondins because it would violate his principle of the "insurrection morale," but once the "insurrection brutale" had been unleashed by the Evêché assembly he lent his support to the proposition (*Histoire*, II, 360).

71. B & R, XXVII, 344–347, 349–350; Jaurès, *Histoire*, VII, 477–479. Every modern historian quotes the brief confrontation between Robespierre and Vergniaud.

72. B & R, XXVII, 350–351, article 3. The Convention also approved the order of the Commune assuring workingmen under arms the subsidy of two livres

per day. This decree was not to be carried out, however, until important concessions were made by the Comité central révolutionnaire to the Committee of Public Safety.

73. Aulard, *Jacobins*, V, 217. The society decided to ask Marat to explain by letter his proposal for a "chef" (B & R, XVIII, 402–403).

Aulard wrote that although Marat favored a republic it was to be under a dictator to whom power should be delegated for a time. It was to be a "plebiscitary dictatorship." This explanation is a bit ingenious. It is more likely that Marat was expressing his frustration of the moment rather than some theoretical formulation of a "dictatorship." He repudiated his own proposal later.

74. B & R, XXVII, 403, citing the *Journal de la Montagne*, n. 1 and v. "No . . . I demand a guide and not a master, and that's quite different."

Almost twenty years earlier, in 1774, Marat posed the idea of a dictatorship in his *Les Chaines de l'esclavage*, linking it to a distrust of the revolutionary spontaneity of the people. Masses of men and women were incapable of planning or of keeping a secret, thus giving their enemies time to stop them. For an uprising to succeed, therefore, it was essential to have a "chef," someone wise and courageous who would lead the masses against their oppressors. Cited in Albert Soboul, "Problèmes de l'Etat révolutionnaire," *Comprendre la Révolution*, p. 85.

75. Marat, *Le Publiciste*, no. 208 (5 June 1793). "Ainsi s'en alla en fumée et en vain bruit l'insurrection d'une ville immense: mais le feu couvoit sous la cendre."

76. Mortimer-Ternaux, *Histoire*, VII, 358, n. 1.

77. Cited in Michelet, *Histoire*, II, 381.

78. "Pache était très silencieux, enfin il se retourna avec vivacité, et leur [the municipal officials] dit: que toutes les fois qu'ils mettraient un Varlet à leur tête, il leur en arriverait autant." "Déclaration de Langlois," in Sée, *Le Procès Pache*, p. 177, 1 June 1793. The municipal officers cursed that "leur coup était manqué," according to Langlois's deposition. (Langlois was a member of section Bon-Conseil and had been arrested as a supporter of the Girondins. Vergniaud had him released.)

79. Tourneux, *Procès-Verbaux*, pp. 150–151; *Moniteur*, 16, no. 155 (4 June 1793), 542; B & R, XXVII, 355; Sainte-Claire Deville, *Commune*, p. 89.

80. AN, BB³ 80, dos. 16, 31 May 1793.

81. Ibid.

82. Jaurès, *Histoire*, VII, 462–463.

83. Ibid., pp. 495, 496. Jaurès maintains that this was why both Dobsen and Hébert replied "on the quiet" *(tout bas)* to Varlet's charge in which he denounced the inaction of the Convention.

84. Tourneux, *Procès-Verbaux*, pp. 151, 152 ("que toute proposition d'arrestation soit rejetée"); *Moniteur*, 16, no. 155 (4 June 1793), p. 542.

85. Tuetey, *Répertoire*, VIII, nos. 2783, 2784, 2785, 2787, 2789, 1 June 1793.

86. Ibid., no. 2772, 1 June 1793.

87. Ibid., no. 2757, 1 June 1793.

88. Tourneux, *Procès-Verbaux*, pp. 152, 153. A soldier in uniform told the Jacobins that if the Convention did not remove the forty corrupt deputies, the people themselves would do so (Aulard, *Jacobins*, V, 220).

89. Tuetey, *Répertoire*, VIII, nos. 2755, 2793.
90. Aulard, *Jacobins*, V, 220–223. Leclerc declared, "Le peuple se porte à la Convention; vous êtes peuple, vous devez y rendre" (ibid., p. 222).
91. B & R, XXVII, 360–366, passim; *Moniteur*, 16, no. 154 (3 June 1793), 539–540, and no. 155 (4 June 1793), 541; Sainte-Claire Deville, pp. 89–90; Tuetey, *Répertoire*, IX, lxxxv, and VIII, no. 2788. On Marat's proposal, six delegates had been elected from the General Council and six from the Evêché committee (*Moniteur*, 16, no. 155, 4 June 1793, 541–542; B & R, XXVII, 355).
92. AN, BB³ 80, dos. 16, *Gazette du Jour*, 4 June 1793; B & R, XXVII, 388; *Moniteur*, 16, no. 155 (4 June 1793), 548.

Perroud wrote that Hassenfratz played a moderating role in the Comité central and that he insisted on a decree of accusation rather than on one of arrest against the twenty-four (twenty-seven?) Girondins on his list (*Proscription*, pp. 33, 34, 35–36). See also Tuetey, *Répertoire*, VIII, nos. 2661, 2754. The General Council authorized and named a delegation of eleven individuals to present the address to the Convention. Among these were Hassenfratz "jeune" and Hassenfratz "aîné." The Hassenfratz in question was then thirty-eight years old, so he was probably the former.

Like Perroud, Jaurès embraced Hassenfratz as "a man of action" who was opposed to "the imprudence of the Enragés" as well as "the moderate policy" of the Commune (*Histoire*, VII, 430).

93. B & R, XXVII, 365–366. The address began, "Mandataires du peuple" and went on in this vein: The citizens of Paris demand that justice be rendered to the traitors. It is treasonable to allow the destiny of France to remain in the hands of counter-revolutionaries. Decree, and all will be in order. Decide between the Convention and those who would dishonor it by conspiracies, intrigues, and calumnies. Expel from your midst all that is not part of you, those who employ their talents against you, the gifts of nature against nature itself. Decree an act of accusation against them. And so on. AN, BB³ 80, dos. 16, pc. 45, n.d.; AP, LXV, 688.
94. Tuetey, *Répertoire*, VIII, no. 2771, citing the *procès-verbal* of section Molière et la Fontaine of 1 June 1793.
95. Marat, *Le Publiciste*, no. 208 (5 June 1793). Marat added, "on connoit ses [Barère's] principes de modérantisme et ses petits expédiens le moyen d'en être supris!"
96. This echoed the complaint of Chabot in the Jacobins that Danton had lost his "vigor" since the suppression of the Commission des Douze (Aulard, *Jacobins*, V, 219).
97. Marat wrote that a huge crowd followed him crying, "Marat, sauvez-nous!" and that he had reported what was transpiring to both the Committee of General Security and the Committee of Public Safety. He repeated that the measures taken by the Convention so far were insufficient and that only the arrest of the Commission des Douze and the denounced deputies would bring calm (*Le Publiciste*, no. 208, 5 June 1793).
98. B & R, XXVII, 368: "The National Convention decrees that the Committee of Public Safety undertake to present, within three days, measures necessary

to save public affairs: and that it will give a report on the petition presented by the constituted authorities of Paris. / The Department of Paris, the municipality and the citizens who may have documents against any of the members denounced, should hold them for presentation to the Committee of Public Safety."

99. *Moniteur,* 16, no. 155 (4 June 1793), 545. Marat's motion came after news of an uprising in the department of Lozère in which public functionaries had been massacred was reported to the Convention. (This chronology assumes that the proceedings in the Convention were reported in the *Moniteur* as they took place.)

100. Blanc, *Histoire,* VII, 452; AP, LXV (1 June 1793), 688–690.

101. "La majorité de la Convention a beau faire: elle sera subjuguée par la Commune, si elle ne terasse et si elle ne ferme, les clubs des Jacobins et des Cordeliers" (cited in Jaurès, *Histoire,* VII, 503).

102. Schmidt, *Tableaux,* I, 226, 14 May 1793.

103. Dutard reported the following exchange between an unnamed deputy of the Convention and a member of the Femmes révolutionnaires, who were blocking the door through which deputies entered the hall: " 'What are you doing here? Who gave you permission to be here?' Reply: 'Equality; aren't all of us equal? I have rights just like others.' The deputy: 'You've come here to trouble the assembly, and I'll soon find the means to have you leave.' Response: 'Go, Monsieur, this is not your place. Your place is in the hall, and despite all your efforts, we shall remain here, and we will place obstacles to your iniquities' " (ibid., I, 272, 22 May 1793). The women undoubtedly remained.

VII. The Insurrection Completed

1. *Moniteur,* 16, no. 155 (4 June 1793), 545, 547, 548; B & R, XXVII, 380–387, passim; du Maillane, *Histoire,* pp. 299–300. Every historian has reported this exchange between the two antagonists.

2. B & R, XXVII, 389; *Moniteur,* 16, no. 156 (5 June 1793), 550–551, reported that Richon cried out, "Save the people from themselves; save your colleagues, decree their provisional arrest."

The address carried the signatures of Marquet, president of the Comité central, and Marchand, its secretary, in addition to those of Louis Roux, president of the General Council, and Mettot, its secretary-registrar. It had been drafted by Marchand and had emanated from the Comité central (Tuetey, *Répertoire,* IX, xc–xci).

3. Tuetey, *Répertoire,* VIII, no. 2839; Meillan, *Mémoires,* pp. 228–229; du Maillane, *Histoire,* p. 122.

4. Jaurès, *Histoire,* VII, 430.

5. AN, BB³ 80, dos. 16, cited in Tuetey, *Répertoire,* IX, lxxxvii.

6. Tuetey, *Répertoire,* IX, lxxxvii–lxxxix. The decision of the Comité central to surround the Convention with an armed force was written in the hand of Génois on an undated document that read as follows: "In the name of the Comité central révolutionnaire, the commanding general of the Parisian armed force, will give the order to all the sections immediately to beat the general alarm, to place all the armed forces on a war footing, that the citizens of Paris had approved yesterday,

in expectation of resistance upon seeing their legitimate views unrecognized and slandered by the conspirators whom they denounce, pending which the people of Paris are quite determined this time not to lay down their arms until they have obtained the justice due to all the republicans of the departments." Signed, Génois (ibid., p. lxxxix).

7. Ibid., IX, xc.

8. AN, BB³ 80, dos. 6.

9. Meillan, *Mémoires,* p. 53.

10. Du Maillane, *Histoire,* p. 307. How long would it have taken one military man on horseback to distribute the *assignat* notes among soldiers without arousing the suspicion of their commanding officers?

11. Mortimer-Ternaux, *Histoire,* VII, 379–380. Moreover, he adds, the German soldiers of the Legion Rosenthal understood no French and were ready to carry out orders regardless of their nature.

12. Michelet, *Histoire,* II, 282.

13. Jaurès, *Histoire,* VII, 454–455, 456. Jaurès cites Beaulieu, who took notes every day (he published *Les souvenirs de l'histoire ou le Diurnal pour l'an de grace 1793*). He wrote "The whole city of Paris was under arms, without knowing toward what end." See also *Révolutions de Paris,* no. 203 (25 May–1 June 1793), pp. 426–427, 428.

14. Mortimer-Ternaux, *Histoire,* VII, 392, n. 1; Aulard, *Jacobins,* V, 223–224.

15. Mortimer-Ternaux, *Histoire,* VII, 406.

16. Michelet, *Histoire,* II, 386.

17. Ibid., p. 387, italicized in original.

18. Jaurès, *Histoire,* VII, 506. Garat quotes Cambon as he turned to Bouchotte: "Minister of War, we're not blind; I see very well that some employees of your office are among the heads and leaders of all this" (*Mémoires,* p. 141, italicized in original).

19. AN, BB³ 80, *Gazette du Jour,* 4 June 1793; Tuetey, *Répertoire,* VIII, no. 2847; B & R, XXVII, 393.

20. B & R, XXVII, 395–396; *Moniteur,* 16, no. 156 (5 June 1793), 552–553.

21. Marat, *Le Publiciste,* no. 208 (5 June 1793).

22. Michelet, *Histoire,* II, 391. Marat is sarcastic in describing this episode (*Le Publiciste,* no. 209, 6 June 1793).

23. Mortimer-Ternaux, *Histoire,* VII, 404.

24. *Moniteur,* 16, no. 156 (5 June 1793), 554; Jaurès, *Histoire,* VII, 509; Mortimer-Ternaux, *Histoire,* VII, 405, calls Hanriot's men "the rabble of 40 sous enrolees."

25. Mortimer-Ternaux, *Histoire,* VII, 406: "Dis à ton f—— président que je me f—— de lui et de son Assemblée, et que si, dans une heure, elle ne me livre pas les vingt-deux, je la ferai foudroyer."

26. AN, BB³ 80, *Gazette du Jour,* 4 June 1793; Aulard, *Jacobins,* V, 224; B & R, XVII, 399, which quotes him as saying, "One of the members of the rev-

olutionary committee, named Gusman, is known to me to be a Spaniard." Also in *Moniteur* issue cited in note 24 and in Jaurès, *Histoire,* VII, 509.

27. Jaurès, *Histoire,* VII, 510; Meillan, *Mémoires,* p. 57, italicized in original.

28. B & R, XXVII, 400, quote him saying, "Let us prove that we are free. I suggest that the Convention go and deliberate in the midst of the armed force, which undoubtedly will protect it." Also in *Gazette du Jour;* Meillan, *Mémoires,* pp. 57–58; du Maillane, *Histoire,* p. 127; *Moniteur* issue cited in note 24; Jaurès, *Histoire,* VII, 510. Jaurès compares Barère's gesture with that of Vergniaud on 31 May and says that it had no significance.

Michelet makes the strange statement that it was Robespierre who had ordered the Convention to be held prisoner (*Histoire,* II, 391–392), linking the captain of Bon-Conseil to Lulier and Lulier to Robespierre. "La foudre n'eut pas fait moins . . . Bonconseil, Lhuillier, Robespierre—trois mots synonymes." Thus, he concluded, the "Robespierristes" were pushed forward. *"The moral insurrection* being impossible, they unleashed what the Evêché wanted, *the brutal insurrection"* (ibid., pp. 388–389).

29. B. Barère, *Mémoires,* II, 92: "Que faites-vous la? vous faites un *beau gachis!"* Barère quotes Robespierre. To which the former supposedly replied loudly, "Eh bien! . . . le gachis n'est point à la tribune, il est au Carrousel; il est là." This reply ought to be accepted with some skepticism.

30. Sainte-Claire Deville, *Commune,* p. 92, n. 1. Robespierre did not join this move but remained in his seat.

31. B & R, XXVIII, 45–46, n. 1, citing "Compt rendu, et déclaration, par J. B. M. Saladin, député du département de la Somme, sur les journées des 27 et 31 mai, 1er et 2 juin 1793." Also in François-Nicolas Buzot, *Mémoires sur la Révolution française,* "Pièces justificatives," [Saladin's memoirs], (Paris, 1828), pp. 332–352.

32. Meillan, *Mémoires,* pp. 58–59, and Note D, p. 239; Mortimer-Ternaux, *Histoire,* VII, 410; Michelet, *Histoire,* II, 394–395; Lamartine, *Histoire,* VI, 105–106; Thiers, *Histoire,* IV, 72–74; Quinet, *Révolution,* II, 8; Mignet, *Histoire,* I, 396; Blanc, *Histoire,* VIII, 443; Taine, *Origines,* II, 468; Mathiez, *La Révolution,* II, 221; Sainte-Claire Deville, *Commune,* p. 93; Louvet, *Mémoires,* p. 96.

Michelet wrote that although the eighty thousand National Guardsmen favored the Convention, they were in no position to help the deputies, from whom they were cut off by the armed men under "a drunken general" (Hanriot). Gérard Walter adds that "Drunk or not, this 'drunken general' " was responsible for the perfect discipline of his troops and that it was owing to him that not one drop of blood was spilled on June 2 (*Histoire,* II, 393 and 1072, n. 2).

33. Meillan, *Mémoires,* p. 60; Michelet, *Histoire,* II, 394; *Moniteur,* XVI, no. 156, 5 June 1793, p. 554; B & R, XXVII, 401.

34. Mortimer-Ternaux, *Histoire,* VII, 411. Taine, *Origines,* II, 468 repeats these slogans.

35. Du Maillane, *Histoire,* p. 309.

36. Michelet, *Histoire,* II, 395.

37. Mathiez, *La Révolution,* II, 221: "Elle [the Convention] rentra humiliée

dans sa salle et se soumit." Michelet, II, 395, thought that had Herault and the deputies wanted to pierce the thin line of Hanriot's hesitant troops, they could have done so and would have found refuge among the mass of National Guardsmen. This is more than doubtful. Hanriot's men were stationed for the precise purpose of guarding against such a contingency. To believe otherwise is to doubt the control that Hanriot exercised over his troops.

38. Mortimer-Ternaux, *Histoire*, VII, 412, says that the Montagnards abandoned their colleagues, who followed them cowed and humiliated. Meillan writes that Marat arrived with about twenty boys in tatters ("d'enfans déguenillés") (*Mémoires*, p. 60). Jaurès cites Marat's report that to appease the people in the galleries he followed the deputies. To prevent violence to the deputies, sentries were stationed at their posts (*Histoire*, VII, 512). A good summary of events is given in the *procès-verbal* of section Molière et la Fontaine, AN, F⁷4432, cited in Tuetey, *Répertoire*, VIII, no. 2820. Marat gives his version of the events in "Détails de l'insurrection du juin," *Le Publiciste*, no. 209 (6 June 1793).

39. B & R, XXVII, 401; *Moniteur*, 16, no. 156 (5 June 1793), 554; Aulard, *Jacobins*, V, 224–225, quoting the reporter's statement that "le président était comme une statue" as the vote was taken.

40. There is a good bit of confusion as to the exact number placed under arrest. Mortimer-Ternaux gives it as thirty-one, but Perroud points out that both Boyer-Fonfrède and Rabaut-Saint-Etienne appeared on another list (Mortimer-Ternaux, *Histoire*, VII, 417–418; Perroud, *Proscription*, p. 38). Michelet gives the number as thirty-one (twenty of the twenty-two originally denounced in April, nine of the Commission des Douze, and the two ministers, Clavière and Lebrun). B & R give twenty-four names, plus those of all the members of the Commission except Fonfrède and Saint-Martin and the two ministers; then Ducos, Lanthenas, and Dussaulx were excepted (which would make a total of thirty-one). Those who remained on the list from 15 April to 2 June 1793 numbered fourteen in all. Of these only Lanjuinais survived (Perroud, *Proscription*, p. 39). Tuetey gives the list from AN, BB³ 80, d. 4, in *Répertoire*, VIII, no. 2851. The number arrested, says Tuetey, was twenty-nine (*Répertoire*, IX, 91). For the ultimate number of Girondins purged, see Sydenham, *Girondins*, pp. 40–42.

41. On 4 June Lebrun asked the Committee of Public Safety if he should continue to sign pressing documents dealing with foreign affairs despite his arrest; the committee replied that he should. He was not replaced until 21 June. Lebrun was condemned and was executed on 27 December 1793. Clavière stabbed himself the day he was to appear before the revolutionary tribunal (Mortimer-Ternaux, *Histoire*, VII, 539).

42. Jaurès, *Histoire*, VII, 514; Blanc, *Histoire*, VIII, 446: "Donnez un verre de sang à Couthon, il a soif." Taine's comment was, "Here is the final word of the comedy; it has no equal even in Molière" (*Origines*, II, 469).

43. Garat, *Mémoires*, p. 140.

44. Jaurès, *Histoire*, VII, 514; Tuetey, *Répertoire*, VIII, 2852.

45. Du Maillane, who was secretary of the session, wrote that numerous deputies protested to him that they were not free to vote their desire and even

signed a paper to that effect. Although he was asked to burn the paper after the Terror began to strike at the Girondins, he gave it to Lauze-Duparret, on whom it was found when he was arrested (*Histoire*, p. 128). Blanc admits that the "violence done to the Convention was so blatant" that its *procès-verbal* was rewritten by Thuriot (*Histoire*, VIII, 447).

46. Thiers, *Histoire*, IV, 75.

47. Meillan, *Mémoires*, p. 63. Among the unedited papers of Hanriot the following note appears in the margin of one document: "Citoyens de garde, laissez la principale entrée libre, afin que les députés sortent" (*Papiers inédits*, III, 303 [a facsimile], cited in Guérin, *Lutte*, I, 125).

48. Thiers, *Histoire*, IV, pp. 75–76.

49. Chaumette, *Papiers de Chaumette*, ed. F. Braesch (Paris, 1908), p. 183 (emphasis mine).

50. Ibid., pp. 183–184.

51. Pierre Caron, *Paris pendant la terreur* (Paris, 1910–1958), V, 247, 12 March 1794, report of Boucheseiche. "Tu voudrais bien [,] coquin, que l'on t'insultât, mais nous ne t'en donnerons pas le plaisir."

52. *Moniteur*, 16, no. 156 (5 June 1793), 550.

53. Calvet, *Instrument*, pp. 30–31, citing Pariset's *La Révolution* II, 95. Pariset summarizes the course of the insurrection and shows how several sections among the thirty-three that originally sent delegates to the Evêché assembly were uncertain on how to proceed.

In his "Compte Rendu," Marquet, president of the Comité des Neuf, praised the Parisians for not shedding a drop of blood during the "four" days of the Revolution (AN, BB³ 80, dos. 16, pc. 56, 3 June 1793). His address was presented to the Convention by Hébert. It began, "L'experience vient de vous démontrer d'une manière vraiment sublime que tôt ou tard la justice a son tour" (AP, LXVI, 20–21).

54. Tuetey, *Répertoire*, VIII, no. 2724, 31 May 1793.

55. Ibid., VIII, no. 2726, 31 May 1793.

56. AN, BB³ 80, dos. 16, pc. 58, 5 June 1793; Tuetey, *Répertoire*, VIII, no. 2919.

57. AN, BB³ 80, dos. 16, pc. 161, "Notes du 5 Juin"; also in Tuetey, *Répertoire*, VIII, no. 2919. When cannoneers of Butte-des-Moulins asked for the release of their sergeant-major, the Committee demanded proof of his civic conduct.

58. AN, BB³ 80, dos. 16, 1 June 1793.

59. AN, BB³ 80, dos. 16, pc. 225, 1 June 1793; Tuetey, *Répertoire*, VIII, no. 2765. The commissioners of Beaurepaire argued that they were merely assisting those of Cité and had no power to act.

60. AN, BB³ 80, dos. 16, pc. 149, 2 June 1793.

61. *Moniteur*, 16, no. 154 (3 June 1793), 535.

62. AN, BB³ 80, dos. 16, pc. 139, 31 May 1793. The order was signed by Destournelles, vice-president, and Dorat-Cubière, secretary-registrar (Tourneux, *Procès-Verbaux*, p. 150, 31 May 1793).

63. AN, BB³ 80, dos. 5, 1 June 1793.

64. AN, BB³ 80, dos. 5, pc. 205, 1 June 1793; Tuetey, *Répertoire*, VIII, no. 2770.

65. AN, BB³ 80, dos. 16, 1 June 1793.

66. AN, BB³ 80, dos. 16, pc. 28, n.d., signed by Marquet, president of the Comité central révolutionnaire. The revolutionary committee of section Amis-de-la-Patrie urged the disarming of suspects, probably in an independent dispatch (ibid., 31 May 1793).

67. Ibid., dos. 16, pc. 207, 1 June 1793.

68. Ibid., dos. 16, pc. 17, 31 May 1793, in a letter directed to the president of the Comité central révolutionnaire and signed by Rousillon.

69. Ibid., dos. 16, pc. 221, 3 June 1793. The original order given by the Comité central to the revolutionary committee of Unité was to seal the papers and effects of Prudhomme, as well as his press, but to allow him to remain at liberty if nothing suspicious were found among his papers. It stressed that the object of the revolution was "to protect, and not to oppress the citizens."

70. Tuetey, *Répertoire*, VIII, no. 2860, 3 June 1793.

71. Tuetey, *Répertoire*, VIII, no. 2859, citing the *procès-verbal* of section Unité's revolutionary committee, AN, F⁷* 2507, fol. 26.

Jaurès called Prudhomme "le pleutre Prudhomme" ("the contemptible Prudhomme"), clever at covering his machinations under "a false sentimentality . . . Prudhomme wants to drown the revolutionaries in an ocean of serenity." He berates him for his "perfidious article against the revolutionary committees" (*Histoire*, VII, 482).

72. Tuetey, *Répertoire*, VIII, no. 2496. Of the sixty-six *pièces* seized, Prudhomme was to be questioned on twenty-four. Thus he was arrested twice and released twice; not until 4 June did he definitively gain his freedom (Tuetey, *Répertoire*, IX, xcv). This statement of Tuetey's has to be modified in light of the determination of Unité's revolutionary committee to interrogate Prudhomme on 8 June.

73. AN, BB³ 80, dos. 5, pc. 288, n.d. Unité's revolutionary committee wrote to the Comité des Neuf, "Plusieurs sont partie[s] dans la nuit pour aller voir leurs femme[s]." Needless to say, most of these deputies escaped, many to launch the Federalist revolt in the departments. Théophile Leclerc charged that no serious effort was made to imprison them because they had too many friends in the Convention (*L'Ami du peuple*, no. 24, 15 September 1793).

74. Tuetey, *Répertoire*, IX, xcvii.

75. Tuetey, *Répertoire*, VIII, no. 2911, 4 June 1793; and no. 2949, 9 June 1793.

76. Tuetey, *Répertoire*, VIII, nos. 2952 and 2956. A sieur Gency was the leading oppositionist in the section. The revolutionary committee of the section did not want to arrest him because it desired "tranquility," it reported. A foreign merchant by the name of Mayer prevented the arrest of a suspect in Finistère (ibid., VIII, no. 2923, 5 June 1793).

77. Ibid., VIII, no. 2915, 4 June 1793.

78. Ibid., VIII, no. 2924, 5 June 1793; no. 2950, 9 June 1793. It reported, without explanation, that it could not arrest Lavigne, after all.

79. Ibid., VIII, no. 2495, 8 June 1793.
80. Ibid., VIII, nos. 2948 and 2943.
81. Several citizens of section Beaurepaire complained to the Committee of Public Safety (the former Comité central) of attacks on them in the general assembly for their politics "of yesterday" (Tuetey, VIII, no. 2944, 8 June 1793).
82. B & R, XXVII, vi–vii.
83. Michelet, *Histoire*, II, 398.
84. Lamartine, *Histoire*, VI, 108–112, passim.
85. Blanc, *Histoire*, VIII, 450, 453.
86. Quinet, *La Révolution*, I, 449, 464.
87. Carlyle, *The French Revolution*, p. 506.
88. Mignet, *Histoire*, I, 397, 398.
89. Aulard, *Histoire politique*, pp. 439–440, n. 1. The debate on the insurrection opened almost eighteen months after the expulsion of the Girondins, on 22 October 1794.
90. Mortimer-Ternaux, *Histoire*, VII, 426–427. Mortimer-Ternaux does not believe that the Girondins were less willing or less capable of repelling the Coalition than the Jacobins.
91. Pariset, *La Révolution*, II, 113. Pariset entitles the relevant chapter "Le coup d'état du 2 juin 1793."
92. Jaurès, *Histoire*, VII, 435–436. Jaurès rejects Barère's memoirs, noting that they omit the report of Garat on the Evêché assembly. If Barère had not wanted the insurrection to succeed, he could have warned the Convention to go into permanent session.
93. Ibid., VII, 514. Von Sybel wrote, "Die Gironde lag zu Boden; ihre politische Laufbahn war für immer zu Ende; für ihre Mitglieder was der Tag ganz so entscheidend, wie es der 10 August für das Königtum gewesen" (*Geschichte*, II, 369).
94. Mathiez, *La Révolution*, II, 221–222. The sans-culottes did not hesitate to mutilate the national representative body; the parliamentary fiction vanished as the time of dictatorship approached, he adds.
95. Lefebvre, *La Révolution*, p. 342.
96. Sydenham, *The Girondins*, p. 211.
97. Ibid.
98. François Furet and Denis Richet, *La Révolution: Des états généraux au 9—Thermidor*, Collection les grandes heures de l'histoire de France (Paris, 1965), I, 293.
99. Ibid. Although Furet and Richet believe that the Revolution continued in the general (bourgeois) direction given its impulse by the century, they explain its sans-culotte, democratic phase as a kind of deviation, a *"dérapage,"* meaning that it had accidentally run off the track. See Soboul's critique in *Comprendre la Révolution*, pp. 338–343.
100. Soubol, *Girondins et Montagnards*, pp. 16, 17.

VIII. The Enragés and the Insurrection

1. Albert Mathiez, "Les Enragés contre la constitution de 1793," *Annales révolutionnaires, Organe des études robespierristes*, XIII (1921), p. 303; "Le vote du premier maximum," *Annales révolutionnaires*, XI (1919), p. 304.

2. These remarks are based on Morris Slavin, *Left of the Mountain: The Enragés and the French Revolution*, an unpublished dissertation deposited in the library of Case Western Reserve University, 1961. See also the following: J. M. Zacher, *Dvezheneye "Beshenich"* [*The Revolutionary Movement of the Enragés*] (Moscow, 1961); Walter Markov, "Robespierristen und Jacqueroutins," in *Maximilien Robespierre 1758–1794, Beiträge zu seinem 200. Geburtstag* (Berlin, 1958), pp. 159–217; idem, *Jacques Roux oder vom Elend der Biographie* (Berlin, 1966); idem, *Die Freiheiten des Priesters Roux* (Berlin, 1967); idem, *Jacques Roux Scripta et Acta* (Berlin, 1969); idem, *Exkurse zu Jacques Roux* (Berlin, 1970); R. B. Rose, *The Enragés: Socialists of the French Revolution?* (London, 1965); Maurice Dommanget, *Jacques Roux le curé rouge* (Paris, n.d.).

3. Jaurès, *Histoire*, VII, 428–429 (emphasis mine). This is why they resolved to convoke the assembly in the Jacobins on 31 May. Jaurès concludes, "The General Council of the Department thus wanted to tilt the revolutionary movement towards the Jacobins. It was to put it, in a way, into the hands of Robespierre" (ibid., p. 429).

4. G. Lefebvre, *La Révolution*, p. 333. Most sans-culottes looked to the Montagnards and the Jacobins for leadership, but a few "impatients" like Varlet found them too moderate and prudent. They thought it necessary to take the initiative, and "they would not have hesitated to disperse the Convention and to take power themselves" (ibid., p. 332).

5. Rudé, *The Crowd*, p. 120.

6. BN, Lc² 227 and Lc² 227 bis, Jacques Roux, *Le Publiciste de la république française par l'ombre de Marat, l'ami du peuple* (Paris, 1793); BN, Lc² 704, Théophile Leclerc, *L'Ami du peuple* (Paris, 1793). See the bibliography for Varlet's publications.

7. AN, W 20, 1073, "Jacques Roux à Marat."

8. AN, F⁷ 3664, Turpin to the minister of the interior. For details of the riot see Louis Audiat, *Deux victimes des septembriseurs* (Lille and Paris, 1897), "Pièces justificatives," pc. 1, pp. 407–409.

9. BN, Lb³⁹ 8638, *Le Triomphe des braves parisiens sur les ennemis du bien public* (Paris, 1790). See p. 5, n. 1. See also BN, Lb³⁹ 5568, *L'Apotre martyr de la révolution* (Paris, 1790).

10. Walter Markov, *Maximilien Robespierre*, p. 173.

11. A fragment of an invitation to a Masonic banquet may be seen on the back of a sheet that Roux used for writing one of his orations (AN, W 20, 1073).

12. *Les Révolutions de Paris*, no. 80 (15–22 January 1791), p. 58. Roux was quoted as saying that he had accepted the Civil Constitution of the Clergy and was thus loyal to both the king and the law. The Revolution had made all men equal, just as they were before God.

13. Walter Markov, "Zu einem Manuskript von Jacques Roux," *Wissenschaf-*

tliche Zeitschrift der Karl-Marx Universität (Leipzig, 1958/1959), p. 279, n. 19a, says, "Without exaggerating the conclusiveness of modern graphological findings, their relationship to historical manuscripts is not without interest. Dr. Fritz Tögel . . . writes his opinions of 1/24/59 (abridged and summarized)" [I have translated the following passage from the German quoted by Markov].

14. Mathiez, *La Vie chère*, p. 364.

15. For a sketch of Varlet's revolutionary career, see Morris Slavin, "L'Autre enragé: Jean-François Varlet," in *Eine Jury für Jacques Roux* (Berlin, 1981), pp. 34–67; Rose, *The Enragés*, pp. 10–35. For a study of the milieu in which Varlet lived and worked, see Morris Slavin, *The French Revolution in Miniature: Section Droits de l'Homme, 1789–1795* (Princeton, 1984). See also Albert Mathiez, "Les enragés et la vie chère" in *La Vie chère*, Part II, especially chapters I and XI.

16. BN, Ln[27] 20067, *A ses chers concitoyens des tribunes et des Jacobins;* AN, F[7] 4775[40], from the report of the comité révolutionnaire of section Droits-de-l'Homme, 18 September 1793.

17. *A ses concitoyens*, pp. 3–7, passim.

18. Morris Slavin, "Jean Varlet as Defender of Direct Democracy," *Journal of Modern History*, 39 (December 1967), 387–404.

19. AN, F[7] 4775[40], *Le Panthéon François*, a brochure written in Plessis prison in 1795.

20. Tuetey, *Répertoire*, V, no. 3578.

21. BN, Lb[39] 10728, *Voeux formés par les français libres* (Paris, 1792); *Moniteur*, 16, no. 220 (7 August 1792), 340–341.

22. Schmidt, *Tableaux*, I, 149, 10 March 1793. See also *Journal de Paris*, III, no. 71 (12 March 1793), 283.

23. Tuetey, *Répertoire*, IX, no. 462, 11 and 13 March 1793; BHVP, MS 808, fol. 485, 15 March 1793; *Moniteur*, 15, no. 77 (18 March 1793), 718; Mortimer-Ternaux, *Histoire*, VI, 491–492, 493–494.

24. Garat makes the absurd statement that Varlet "was hardly twenty years old, and who for the past four years has appeared in all the seditious movements" (*Mémoires*, p. 101). This would mean that Varlet had begun his "seditions" at about sixteen years of age.

25. B & R, XXV, 62, Commune, 10 March 1793.

26. Aulard, *Jacobins*, V, 85–86. A delegation of sans-culottes from section Jardin-des-Plantes petitioned the Jacobins to hear him, and while the society was discussing the matter Varlet seized the tribune and shouted: "My heart is sore. I depart for the Vendée, I want to justify myself." This led to disorder, and while the comité du scrutin épuratoire (an admissions committee) was given the task of ruling on Varlet's request for readmission, the delegates left with Varlet. *Journal des Débats*, no. 413 (15 May 1793), for the session of 12 May.

27. Schmidt, *Tableaux*, I, 244–246. Dutard reported the session of 17 May, describing how the crowd was demanding "l'insurrection instantanée" and attacking the *noirs* of the Convention. A neighbor turned to Dutard and remarked that the people had to save themselves and not waste time on "niceties," and that the Cordeliers had already made certain preparations. Dutard does not distinguish between the Enragés, the Maratists, and the Cordeliers, but it can hardly be

doubted that the influence of the Enragés was high, as Jaurès admits (*Histoire*, VIII, 348, 350).

28. Jaurès, *Histoire*, VII, 375, quoting Dutard's report: "Eh bien! tant mieux, ils nous embètent; on fait fort bien des f—— dedans; si on les f—— tous, peut-être qu'ils nous laisseraient tranquilles et que les affairs en iraient mieux."

29. *Patriote Français*, no. 1375 (20 May 1793), 561, reporting on session of 19 May in Panthéon-Français.

30. Lefebvre, *Révolution*, p. 341.

31. Lamartine, *Girondins*, VI, 56.

32. Michelet, *Histoire*, II, 358–359. Braesch differs with Michelet, terming section Droits-de-l'Homme "moderately conservative" (*La Commune*, p. 166). This description is on the eve of Louis's fall, however, not some ten months later.

33. Michelet, *Histoire*, II, 359.

34. Ibid., p. 362 (italicized in original). Michelet cites B & R, XXVII, 308, for the above, but there is no mention of Varlet in this source, although there was an obvious spirit of rebellion in the General Council. Proposals were heard to give Pache an honor guard from all the forty-eight sections; others suggested that the mayor be taken under the safeguard of the sections.

35. Jaurès, *Histoire*, VII, 459.

36. *Moniteur*, 16, no. 163 (12 June 1793), 606.

37. BN, Lb⁴¹ 2979, Jean Varlet, *Déclaration solennelle des Droits de l'homme dans l'état social* (Paris, 1793), "Note historique," p. 23.

38. AN, F⁷ 4774⁹, 3 April 1794, written after his arrest.

39. Morris Slavin, "Théophile Leclerc: An Anti-Jacobin Terrorist," *The Historian: A Journal of History*, 39 (May 1971), 398–414.

40. AN, F⁷ 4774⁹.

41. B & R, XXVII, 17–19. Deputy Chassey quoted these remarks of Leclerc's after reading a petition from Lyons that revealed how the propertied of that city had succeeded in establishing a revolutionary tribunal against their rivals. The Convention decreed that the revolutionary tribunal of Lyons be prohibited from exercising any power.

42. *Moniteur*, 16, no. 139 (19 May 1793), 409; B & R, XXVII, 73, 16 May 1793 in Commune.

43. AN, F⁷ 4774⁹, "Extraction, profession avant et depuis la Révolution, carrière politique et révolutionnaire, et état présente des affaires de Théophile Leclerc," undated, but probably 4 July 1794.

44. *Moniteur*, 16, no. 158 (7 June 1793), 566.

45. B & R, XXVIII, 220; Aulard, *Jacobins*, V, 277–279.

46. AN, T 1001², a baptismal record in Spanish with an extract in French.

47. Ibid., 10 March 1794, revolutionary committee of section Pelletier and the Paris Commune.

48. Ibid. The contract spells the director's name "Danglas." The sum of "cinq mille livres de numeraire" was generous in that inflationary year.

49. Léopold Lacour, *Trois femmes de la révolution* (Paris, 1900), p. 327: "La

fille Lacombe . . . acquit, comme actrice, une assez grande reputation sur les thé-âtres de province," citing an observer by name of Proussinalle.

50. Lacour, *Femmes,* p. 357. The society's article XV reads as follows: "I swear to live for the Republic or to die for her; I promise to be faithful to the Regulations of the Society, so long as it will exist." The minimum age for membership was set at eighteen.

51. BN, Lc² 786, *Journal de la Montagne,* no. 22 (21 June 1793).

52. Buzot, *Mémoires,* p. 84. Buzot is no less flattering in describing the character of Marat, Robespierre, or Danton. "Marat, [whom] nature seemed to have formed in order to bring together in one individual all the vices of the human species . . . Robespierre, no less a coward and a paltroon, deliberately cruel . . . full of hatred, vindictive, jealous to an extreme . . . Danton, ambitious of glory . . . indifferent to crime as to virtue . . ." (ibid., pp. 92–93).

53. Aulard, *Jacobins,* V, 212.

54. AN, T 1001², "Les autorités constituées du département de Paris et les commissaires des sections aux Républicaines révolutionnaires." The officials compared them to the Spartans of old and praised them for having armed both their husbands and their children.

55. The resolution continued: "It is up to you, revolutionary Républicaines, to run to the squares, to enflame the youth, to promise it victory, and to guarantee it glory and civic crowns. You will do it; it is an insult to doubt it. You will do it, and the bewildered tyrants not able to support the gaze of virtue, will wither of rage and of shame." The resolution was signed by "L'homme libre, L. P. Dufourney, président" (ibid.).

56. AN, F⁷ 4774⁹, "Précis de la conduite révolutionnaire d'Anne Pauline Léon, femme Leclerc," 4 July 1794.

57. BN, 8⁰ Le³³ 3X (22), *Adresse individuelle à l'Assemblée nationale par des citoyennes de la capitale* (Paris, 1791). The quotation is from p. 3. Also in AP, XXXIX, 423–424. It is signed by "Léon, fille," and is followed by some three hundred other signatures.

58. BN, 8⁰ Le³³ 3x (22), *Adresse,* p. 4; AN, F⁷ 4774⁹, "Précis . . ."

59. AN, F⁷ 4774⁹, "Précis . . ."

60. Morris Slavin, "Jacques Roux: A Victim of Vilification," *French Historical Studies,* 3 (Fall 1964), 525–537.

61. AN, W 20, 1073. The original is difficult to read because much of it is corrected and recorrected, crossed out and rewritten—all in Roux's highly crabbed script.

Walter Markov has reproduced this address from Roux's dossier (cited above), which Zacher of Leningrad had published in part in his study of the Enragés. (The word *beshenich* in Russian means "extremists," or, in the more popular vernacular, "the crazies.")

Markov writes in his "Zu einem Manuskript" that limited though Roux was by the conditions of his time, he was able to go beyond them. He saw the Revolution surpassing the struggle of the Third Estate against feudalism. To him the end of the noble, financial, and priestly aristocracy was a unified act, as the three were closely tied together. Furthermore, he recognized the role of force and discerned the struggle between "the profiteers and oppressors" on the one hand and the industrious masses on the other. "Of course, the main enemy of yesterday, royalty, is still powerful; it approaches in alliance with Europe's dynasties, in order to put into effect the Restoration, and all patriots must stand together, in order to prevent it. Moreover, one must not deny that a popular revolution is not made to replace privileges of birth and status with those of property and power . . . The main blow must be directed against the rich, not from a desire to plunder or from envy, but rather, out of humanitarianism, out of love of the people" ("Zu einem Manuskript von Jacques Roux," in *Wissenschaftliche Zeitschrift der Karl-Marx-Universität* [Leipzig, 1958–1959], p. 286).

62. AN, W 20, 1073, "Discours sur les causes des malheurs."

63. Perrière, the police spy, wrote to Garat, "This dark hatred of the poor against the rich . . . manifests itself continually, and could explode in a terrible way" (Schmidt, *Tableaux,* I, 274, 22 May 1793).

64. AN, W 20, 1073, "Roux à Marat," p. 15.

65. *Moniteur,* 16, no. 153 (2 June 1793), 526. "Chenaux, Paris, Jacques Roux, and Faure are appointed commissioners to edit the history of the revolution unfolding at the moment."

66. AN, BB³ 80, dos. 16, pc. 140. It was signed by Destournelles, vice-president, and Coulombeau, *secrétaire-greffier.*

67. AN, F⁷ 2468, pp. 49–53, 31 May 1793; pp. 53–54, 1 June 1793; pp. 54–55, 2 June 1793. This reference contains the *procès-verbal* of section Gravilliers's revolutionary committee.

68. Henri Calvet, *L'Accaparement à Paris sous la terreur . . . Commission de Recherche . . .* (Paris, 1933), pp. 44–48. Anyone who concealed goods or refused to sell them daily and publicly was guilty of violating the law. Sections and municipalities were given the authority to verify the amount of merchandise held by wholesalers and retailers and to force them to sell at current prices. Violaters could be punished by death. Judgments rendered by the criminal courts in reference to this law were not subject to appeal.

In his report to the Convention, Collot d'Herbois made an interesting reference to the United States in 1778, which had also been forced to take measures against monopoly. The Congress "resolved, that it be earnestly recommended to the . . . states . . . to authorize and direct any civil magistrate . . . to issue his warrant . . . to seize . . . [any extraordinary quantity of grain or flour] . . . paying . . . such prices as may . . . appear proper, to prevent the practice of engrossing." *Journals of the Continental Congress,* ed. W. C. Ford (Washington, 1908), VII, 974–979.

69. Calvet, *L'Accaparement,* pp. 35–36: "The law of 26 July hardly solved the Terror. It did not destroy the monopolizers." It was abrogated on 1 April 1794 (ibid., p. 33).

70. Ibid., pp. 209–210, 23 October 1793, petition of sections to the Convention. "Vous avez frappé le petit marchand, et non pas l'homme riche," they concluded.

71. J. Roux, *Le Publiciste,* no. 249 (28 July 1793).

72. T. Leclerc, *L'Ami du peuple,* nos. 9, 10, 11, 13 (8, 10, 14, and 17 August

1793, respectively). In the issue of 14 August he called for a "scorched earth" policy against the foreign invaders.

73. Mathiez, *La vie chère*, p. 365.

IX. Anatomy of the Insurrection

1. Michelet, *Histoire*, II, 388–389. Jaurès, in a section entitled "L'illogisme de Michelet," criticizes him because, after holding the Girondins responsible for undermining the Revolution and even calling them supporters of the Vendée, he is scornful of Lulier and the revolutionaries of 31 May. This position constitutes wanting the Revolution without using the means to make it succeed, says Jaurès. Furthermore, he is convinced that the sectionnaires who invaded the Convention were respectful of and friendly to the deputies (*Histoire*, VII, 475–476). The last statement is not quite true, as will be seen.

2. Blanc, *Histoire*, p. 411. Blanc repeats Barère's charge that the Evêché committee included "foreigners" like Gusman, Pio, Dufourny, Proly, Pereira, and Arthur. As for the influence of "des violents," in light of the official violence of the Terror that lay on the horizon, it was obvious that the Evêché committee had no monopoly on this weapon.

3. Jaurès, *Histoire*, VII, 471.

4. Jaurès gives Lulier the credit for the impulse "which seemed both legal and revolutionary" of rallying the forces of the insurrection when the Evêché committee showed its weakness. He did this by reactivating the hostility to Isnard and the Gironde, says Jaurès. "Lullier rendered an immense service to the Mountain; he restored Paris to it," he concluded (ibid., 472–475, passim). This is not just an exaggeration; it misses the whole point of why the Jacobins convoked the delegates on 29 May, certainly before any "weakness"—or strength—of the Evêché committee had shown itself.

5. Cited in B & R, XVII, 409, issue of 31 May 1793 (emphasis mine).

6. Gustave Laurent, MS on Dobsen.

7. AN, BB³ 80, dos. 16, pc. 21; Tuetey, *Répertoire*, VIII, no. 2673. Tuetey's citation on p. 2 of the chapter entitled "The Insurrection of May 31" speaks of a Comité des Dix, not one of Neuf.

8. Guérin, *Lutte*, I, 121. See Guérin's analysis of this development, ibid., pp. 120–121. "The official powers absorbed the extra-legal power. The insurrection was channeled."

9. BN, Lb⁴¹ 4090, *L'Explosion* (Paris, 1 October 1794); and another brochure written shortly thereafter, with no noticeable changes, BN, Lb⁴¹ 1330, *Gare l'explosion!* (Paris, 5 October 1794). The quotation is from the first brochure, p. 6 (emphasis mine).

10. Mortimer-Ternaux, *Histoire*, VII, 407, n. 1; Tuetey, *Répertoire*, VIII, no. 2916, 4–5 June 1793. Gusman allegedly told Sebastien Mercier long after the insurrection that they should have removed the leading Jacobins, Robespierre and Marat, as well as the Girondins (cited in Sainte-Claire Deville, *Commune*, p. 118).

11. Cited in Guérin, *Lutte*, I, 112; and in Henri Wallon, *Les Représentants du*

peuple en mission et la justice révolutionnaire dans les départements (Paris, 1889), III, 209. Lacroix (1764–1794) came from a well-to-do bourgeois family and studied law. When the Revolution broke out, he became a journalist and a strong supporter of Robespierre. After the overthrow of Louis he was sent as a *commissaire* to the department of the Marne and then to Marseilles under the Terror. Upon returning to Paris he became politically active in his section, Unité. He was framed with Hébert and the others and was guillotined on 10 April 1794 (Walter, "Table Analytique," in Michelet, *Histoire*, II, 1458). Jean Dautry, "Sebastien Lacroix," *Annales historiques*, XII (1933), 49–60 and 516–533, reviews his revolutionary career and his shady dealings with various individuals. He calls him a "libeler" and finds him "one of the most interesting and most dubious among the Parisian revolutionaries." Although Dautry discusses Lacroix's role in the arrest of Prud-homme, he says nothing of consequence on his activities during the insurrection of 31 May–2 June.

12. Guérin, *Lutte*, I, 122.

13. Aulard, *Jacobins*, V, 368. The secretary wrote his name as "Héloyse."

14. Caron, *Paris pendant la terreur*, V, 246–247, report of Boucheseiche, 12 March 1794. Mathiez in a footnote gives the name of the reporter as Mamin, and Jaurès gives the date of the session as 13 March 1794 (*Histoire*, VII, 440).

15. Garat quotes Barère, "We shall yet see if it is the Commune of Paris that represents the French Republic, or if it is the Convention" (*Mémoires*, p. 141, italicized in original).

16. B & R, XXVII, 99; Aulard, *Jacobins*, V, 194–195. Legendre concluded, "Je déclare, moi, que je commençerais à suspecter cette société, s'il y avait un Comité secret."

17. Fillon, *Autographes*, no. 547, p. 66; Charavay, *Catalogue* (1862), no. 98, p. 61, and item 15, p. 63. Item 12 of Fillon's no. 547 and Charavay's reference cite four individuals who were sent to the Committee of Public Safety.

18. B & R, XXXII, 209. Gérard Walter points out that Dufourny was one of the organizers of the 31 May *journée* but has been insufficiently studied, and that we know little of his role as president of the Paris department (Michelet, *Histoire*, II, "Table Analytique," p. 1372). Dufourny had antagonized Hébert and Vincent and was expelled from the Cordeliers. He strongly criticized the trial of Danton and therefore was denounced by Robespierre as "an intriguer." He was arrested and remained in prison until Robespierre's fall, after which he was released and appointed to a commission of Jacobins to track down the Robespierrists in hiding. Accused by Cambon of being a "Septembriseur," he was arrested and not released until the amnesty of 26 October 1795. He died soon thereafter (ibid., pp. 1372–74).

19. Calvet, *Instrument*, pp. 45–46. Calvet cites the *Journal des Débats et de la correspondance des Jacobins*, no. 428.

20. BN, Lb⁴¹ 4136, L. P. Dufourny, *Justice Sévérité Vélocité Sentinelle, prends garde à toi* (Paris, 31 October 1794). The quotation is from pp. 6–7 (italicized in original). Among Dufourny's proposals was to continue to celebrate the insurrection of 31 May because it was the greatest event of the Revolution, "après le 10 Août" (p. 15). Throughout his brochure he attacks the Girondins as "Federalists."

21. Charavay, *Catalogue* (1862), no. 98, pc. 19, cited in Calvet, *Instrument*, p. 46, n. 38. Calvet questions whether it was Dufourny who called for the new assembly or whether that was done on the initiative of the department (ibid., p. 46).

22. Mortimer-Ternaux, *Histoire*, VII, 331, n. 1.

23. Ibid.

24. B & R, XXVII, 372; *Moniteur*, 16, no. 156 (5 June 1793), 550; Blanc, *Histoire*, VIII, 438.

25. AN, BB³ 80, dos. 1, 2 June 1793; Tuetey, *Répertoire*, VIII, no. 2803.

26. Alphonse Aulard, *Recueil des actes du Comité de salut public* (Paris, 1889–1951), IV, 431, 3 June 1793.

27. Calvet, *Instrument*, p. 32.

28. Ibid. Calvet cites Perroud's reference to Hassenfratz's role in instigating the extinction of the Committee (in *La Proscription*, pp. 35–36).

29. Calvet states that this offer eased considerably the Commune's concern (*Instrument*, p. 33). Tuetey points out, however, that the General Council did not act on the offer. Furthermore, the Comité continued to exercise its powers for some days thereafter (*Répertoire*, IX, xciii).

30. This address bore the signature of Marquet and was carried to the Convention by Hébert, Fournerot, Clémence, Simon, Marchand, and Courtois (Tuetey, *Répertoire*, IX, xciii).

31. AN, BB³ 80, dos. 3, pc. 164, 5 June 1793; Tuetey, *Répertoire*, VIII, no. 2494, 4 June 1793, and no. 2918, 5 June 1793.

32. Tuetey, *Répertoire*, VIII, no. 2901. Four members of the Comité central, together with Pache, visited the Committee (Aulard, *Actes*, IV, 441, 4 June 1793). "The mayor of Paris, summoned by letter on this day, proceeded to the Committee with four members of the Comité révolutionnaire [Comité central]. The latter were informed of the necessity to deposit their powers and proposed to do so at the Assembly convoked by the department for Thursday or even earlier if they were satisfied with the promise of the subsidy for the National Guards and citizens who had taken up arms on 31 May, 1st and 2nd of this month."

33. Tuetey, *Répertoire*, VIII, no. 2903, 4 June 1793.

34. Ibid., no. 2854, 2°. The undated note found among the papers of the Evêché committee reads as follows: "A member reported on the follow-up of his mission before the committee of public safety for obtaining the necessary sums to subsidize the revolutionary army. The result is that the committee would not have the sums until the comité révolutionnaire central will have surrendered its powers." AN, BB³ 80, cited in Calvet, *Instrument*, p. 45.

Mortimer-Ternaux, *Histoire*, VIII, "Notes et éclaircissements," quotes a *pièce* of the Comité central dated 4 June that cites Loys as reporting to the General Council on the conference with the Committee of Public Safety regarding the payment of forty sous per day. It is signed Marchand, president per interim (ibid., p. 45, n. 35).

35. Calvet thinks that the Committee of Public Safety hoped to range the troops called out by the Comité central against their leaders by withholding the funds due them (*Instrument*, p. 45).

36. Tuetey, *Répertoire*, VIII, no. 2800, 4 June 1793.

37. AN, BB³ 80, dos. 4; Tuetey, *Répertoire*, VIII, no. 2902.

38. *Adresse présentée à la Convention nationale* (Paris, 1793), cited in R. B. Rose, *Les Enragés and the French Revolution, 1789–1794. An Early Attempt at Practical Socialism.* Ph.D. dissertation, Victoria University of Manchester, 1952, II, 270.

39. Calvet, *Instrument*, p. 33.

40. B & R, XXVIII, 157.

41. Tuetey, *Répertoire*, VIII, no. 2932, 6 June 1793. "This report, so impatiently awaited, condemned the *journée* of June in terms as clear as prudence then would allow. Everything concerning the Girondins was presented in a vague and dubious manner" (B & R, XXVIII, 167).

42. Quoted in Calvet, *Instrument*, p. 29. This is when he charged that "this tyranny is in the committee of the Commune."

43. Rapport inédit de l'observateur Mengaud, Archives du Ministre des Affairs étrangères, *France-Mémoires et documents*, 323, fol. 138, cited in Calvet, *Instrument*, p. 30.

44. Robespierre, *Oeuvres*, ed. Laponneraye, III, 606; Calvet, *Instrument*, p. 29.

45. Calvet, *Instrument*, pp. 39–42, passim; B & R, XVIII, 169–170, 172.

46. Perroud, *Proscription*, p. 42, n. 1, points out that it became only an office of denunciation, *not having any power over the constituted authorities* (emphasis mine). After 25 September 1793 it took the name of Comité de surveillance because a decree of this date forbade the use of the words *public safety* by any constituted body except the Convention. It was finally suppressed in June 1794.

Guérin writes that the Evêché committee settled for subsidizing the sans-culottes under arms for the three days and established posts for themselves as political police paid by the Committee of Public Safety. "Le 'second pouvoir' se vendit pour un plat de lentilles" (*La Lutte*, I, 128).

47. Tuetey, *Répertoire*, IX, civ–cv; Calvet, *Instrument*, p. 10. Biographical sketches of the men who composed the new committee are given in Calvet, pp. 52–77.

48. Tuetey, *Répertoire*, IX, 94, 98–99.

49. AN, BB³ 80 dos. 16, pc. 56, 3 June 1793; Tuetey, *Répertoire*, VIII, no. 2861, 3 June 1793.

50. AN, BB³ 80, dos. 16, pc. 52, n.d.; Tuetey, *Répertoire*, VIII, 2794, 2 June 1793.

51. This resolution was introduced by Couthon and supported by Robespierre after news arrived that Buzot was trying to organize the departments against Paris and that Félix Wimpfen, the general appointed by the Girondins, had informed the Convention of the arrest of Romme and Prieur, its representatives-on-mission in Calvados (B & R, XXVIII, 202).

52. Tuetey, *Répertoire*, IX, c–ci, lists eleven resolutions. Among these were its agreement to a request by Mail to arrest certain members of that section, particularly Tranchelahausse; it also heard Varlet recite several preliminary articles

against the "liberticide faction." The previous day it heard appeals from several sections on various matters (ibid., pp. xcviii–c).

53. Ibid., p. cii.

54. Ibid., pp. ciii, civ.

55. Ibid., pp. cv, cvi, cvii. See the resolutions of various sections in Tuetey, *Répertoire*, VIII, nos. 2968–2988.

56. APP, A A/266, pièces diverses, fol. 324, cited in Calvet, *Instrument*, p. 47, n. 40.

57. Calvet, *Instrument*, p. 48.

58. Ibid., pp. 48–49.

59. Ibid., p. 49, citing AN, BB³ 80, letter of the *procureur-général-syndic* of the department to the Comité central.

60. B. Barère, *Mémoires*, II, 91, 93. Barère says flatly that "the events of 31 May, organized by Danton and Lacroix and by the Commune of Paris" proved Gensonné right (ibid., p. 78).

61. Ibid., pp. 94–95, 99.

62. Ibid., p. 348. It hardly needs to be added that Barère's memoirs are self-serving and filled with rancour against Robespierre, Danton, Marat, and others. Barère admits that "Des rédacteurs de pétitions et d'adresses extravagantes semblaient les maîtres de l'esprit public, et portaient les législateurs à une effrayante sévérité."

63. "Les 31 mai, 1er et 2 juin 1793. Fragment par M. Le Comte Lanjuinais, avec Un de ses Discourses," in du Maillane, *Histoire*, pp. 296–297.

64. Louvet, *Mémoires*, p. 88.

65. Meillan, *Mémoires*, pp. 55–56.

66. Cited in Aulard, *Histoire politique*, p. 439.

67. Levasseur, *Mémoires*, I, 242, 247–248, 252, 266, 269. A kind of "pall" settled over the Convention after 2 June, writes Levasseur.

Bibliography

Archival Sources

ARCHIVES NATIONALES

The following "C" documents were especially valuable: C 256, pl. 488 and 489; C 355, pl. 1859–1871; C 156, pl. 304. These include letters and petitions of popular societies and individual sections, reports of the Commission des Douze, police observations, and events and proceedings on the eve of the insurrection.

BB³ 80 contains the resolutions, decrees, and notes of the Comité central révolutionnaire, plus important communications to and from the sections during the insurrection.

Série F⁷ (Individuals): Appert, Nicolas (4580); Arfelière, Gérard-Jean (4581); Canaple, Jean-François-Esprit (4632); Caudel, Jean-Louis (4635); Chazot, Claude-François (4644); Clément (clockmaker) (4649); Collin (4651); Dubois, Jean-Pierre-Marie-Cattin (4635); Dumoulin, Jean-Noel (4687); Duval, Louis-Nicolas (4699); Fielval, Pierre-Rémi (4707); Flicourt, Jean-Baptiste-Firmin (4768); Grappin [sic], Laurent (4732); Grillot, Pierre Alexandre (4733); Gurnot, Nicolas (4737); Lacombe, Claire (4756); Langlois, Isidore (4764); Leclerc, Théophile, and Pauline Léon (4774⁹); Leroux (4580); Maillet, François (4774³⁰); Pagès, Raymond, fils (4774⁶¹); Paris, François-Marie (4774⁶³); Ravette, Hardoin-Thomas-Hus-Clément (4774⁸⁷); Roland, Augustin-Pierre (4774⁹⁷); Roman, Louis (4774⁹⁸); Rossignol, Eustache-François (4774⁹⁹); Ruffier, Alexandre-Guillaume (4775⁴); Saguier (4774⁶¹); Tassin, David (4775²⁵); Taveau, Louis (4775²⁵); Tranchelahausse, Jean-François (4775³³); Varlet, Jean-François (4775⁴⁰).

F⁷ (Miscellaneous): Section Molière et la Fontaine (4432); Revolutionary committee of Observatoire (*2514); Revolutionary committee of Gravilliers (2648); Turpin's letter to minister of interior (3664).

Published documents: Resolution of section Molière et la Fontaine, 31 May 1793, to help Convention maintain public order (AD XVI, 70, p. 56); "Mémoires de Chaumette, sur la révolution du 31 mai, premier récit" (T 604², liasse 9e, b).

BIBLIOTHÈQUE NATIONALE

A tous les Républicains de France, sur la société des Jacobins de Paris. Paris: Imprimerie du Cercle Social, 29 October 1792. 47 pp.

Adresse lue à la Convention nationale . . . By section Gardes-Françaises. Paris: Imprimerie Vezard & Le Normant, 31 May 1793. 3 pp.

Adresse présentée par le Citoyen Burgburu à la section [Gardes-Françaises], & lue à la Convention nationale. Paris: Imprimerie Vezard & Le Normant, 31 May 1793. 3 pp. (Similar to Lb[40] 1849.)

Affair Chazot and section Gardes-Françaises. Paris: 19 September 2e [1793–1794].

Arrêté de la section du Contrat-Social portant que les membres du comité révolutionnaire de la section, ayant abusé des pouvoirs . . . Paris: Imprimerie de la Section, 23 November 1794. 42 pp.

Bergoeing: Député de département de la Gironde, & membre de la Commission des Douze . . . Caen: Le Roy, 1793. 44 pp.

Discours, Imprimé par ordre de la société fraternelle de patriotes, de l'un et de l'autre sexe . . . séant aux Jacobins. Paris, November 1790, 14 pp.

Dufourny, L. P. *Justice Sévérité Velocité Sentinelle, prends garde à toi.* Paris: Imprimerie de Ballard, 1 November 1795. 15 pp.

Extrait du procès-verbal de l'assemblée générale & permanente de la section de Molière et la Fontaine. Paris: Imprimerie Nationale, 31 May 1793. 2 pp.

Guerre aux intrigans. Réponse de la société fraternelle du Panthéon. Paris: 2e [1793–1794]. 8 pp.

Léon, Pauline. *Adresse individuelle à l'Assemblée nationale par des citoyennes de la capitale.* Paris, 1791. 4 pp.

Lettre de Jérome Pétion aux parisiens. Paris: Imprimerie d'Antoine-Joseph Gorsas, 1793. 16 pp.

Opinion du Citoyen Saint-Just, sur les subsistences. Paris: Imprimée par ordre de la Convention nationale, 1792. 14 pp.

Rapport fait à l'assemblée générale de la section de l'Unité. Paris: Imprimerie C. F. Perlet, 28 February 1795. 25 pp.

Roux, Jacques. *L'Apôtre martyr de la Révolution.* Paris: Imprimerie de Henri IV, 1790. 24 pp.

———— *Le Triomphe des braves parisiens sur les ennemis du bien public.* Paris, 1790. 32 pp.

Varlet, Jean. *A ses chers concitoyens des tribunes et des Jacobins.* Paris: Imprimerie de la Société Typographique, 1792. 7 pp.

———— *Voeux formés par des français libres.* Paris, 1792. 8 pp.

———— *Déclaration solennelle des droits de l'homme dans l'état social.* Paris: Imprimerie de Didot, 1793. 24 pp.

———— *Le Panthéon français.* Paris: Imprimerie Laurens, 1794. 5 pp.

Important documents may also be found in the Archives de Paris, the Archives de la Préfecture de Police, the Bibliothèque Victor Cousin (especially MS 120), and the Bibliothèque historique de la ville de Paris.

Other Primary Sources

Aulard, Alphonse. *Recueil des actes du Comité de salut public avec la correspondance officielle des représentants en mission et le registre du conseil exécutive provisoire.* 28 vols. Paris: Imprimerie Nationale, 1889–1951.

————— *La Société des Jacobins. Recueil de documents pour l'histoire du Club des Jacobins de Paris.* 6 vols. Paris: Librairie Léopold Cerf and Librairie Noblet, 1889–1897.

Barère, Bertrand. *Mémoires de B. Barère.* 4 vols. Publiés par MM Hippolyte Carnot et David [d'Angers]. Paris: Jules Labitte, 1842–1844.

Braesch, Frédéric, ed. *Papiers de Chaumette.* Paris: Au siège de la société, 1908.

Buzot, François Nicolas Léonard. *Mémoires sur la Révolution française.* Paris: Pichon et Didier, 1828.

Calvet, Henri. *L'Accaparement à Paris sous la Terreur: essai sur l'application de la loi du 26 juillet 1793.* Paris: Imprimerie Nationale, 1933.

Caron, Pierre. *Paris pendant la Terreur: Rapports des agents secrets du ministre de l'intérieur.* 6 vols. Paris: Librairie Alphonse Picard et Fils, 1910–1964.

Charavay, Jacques, ed. *Catalogue d'une importante collection de documents autographes et historiques sur la Révolution française depuis le 13 juillet 1789 jusqu'au 18 brumaire an VIII.* Paris: Charavay Librairie, 1862.

Deprez, Eugène, Georges Lefebvre, Marc Bouloiseau, and Albert Soboul, eds. *Oeuvres complètes de Robespierre.* 10 vols. Paris and Nancy: Imprimerie Georges Thomas, 1910–1967.

Fillon, Benjamin. *Inventaire des autographes et des documents historiques composant la collection de M. Benjamin Fillon.* Series I and II. Ed. Etienne Charavay and Frédéric Naylor. Paris, 1877.

Garat, Dominique Joseph. *Mémoires sur la Révolution, ou exposé de ma conduite dans les affaires et dans les fonctions publiques.* Paris: Imprimerie de J. J. Smits & Co., 1795.

Laponneraye, Albert. *Oeuvres de Maximilien Robespierre.* 3 vols. New York: Lenox Hill, 1970. (Originally published 1840.)

Levasseur, René. *Mémoires de R. Levasseur (de la Sarthe) ex-conventionnel.* 2 vols. Paris: Rapilly, 1829.

Louvet de Couvrai, Jean Baptiste. *Mémoires de Louvet de Couvray, député à la Convention nationale.* Paris: Baudouin Frères, 1823. Saint-Albin Berville and Jean François Barrière, eds., Collection des mémoires relatifs à la Révolution française . . . 56 vols., vol 34.

Maillane, Durand du (Pierre Toussaint). *Histoire de la convention nationale par Durand du Maillane: suivie d'un fragment historique sur le 31 mai par le Comte Lanjuinais.* Paris: Baudouin Frères, 1825. Berville and Barrière, eds., Collection des mémoires . . . , vol. 23.

Markov, Walter. *Scripta et Acta.* Berlin: Akademie Verlag, 1969. (Writings and speeches of Roux, plus reports on his activities.)

Mavidal, M. J., M. E. Laurent, et al., eds. *Archives parlementaires de 1787 à 1860;*

recueil complet des débats législatifs et politiques des chambres françaises. Imprimés par ordre du sénat et de la chambre des députés. Series I, 90 vols. Paris: Librairie Administrative de Paul du Pont, 1879–.

Meillan, Armand Jean. *Mémoires de Meillan, député, par le département des Basses-Pyranées, à la Convention nationale avec des notes et des éclaircissemens historiques.* Paris: Baudouin Frères, 1823. Berville and Barrière, eds., Collection des mémoires . . . , vol. 35.

Schmidt, Wilhelm Adolf. *Tableaux de la Révolution française.* 3 vols. Leipzig: Veit & Co., 1867.

Sée, Adrien. *Le Procès Pache.* Paris: Société de l'Histoire de la Révolution française, 1911.

Tourneux, Maurice. *Procès-verbaux de la Commune de Paris (10 août 1792–1er juin 1793).* Paris: Société de l'Histoire de la Révolution française, 1894.

Tuetey, Alexandre. *Répertoire général des sources manuscrits de l'histoire de Paris pendant la Révolution française.* 11 vols. Paris: Imprimerie Nouvelle, 1890–1914.

Secondary Sources

Audiat, Louis. *Deux victimes des septembriseurs: Pierre Louis de la Rochefoucauld dernier évêque de Saintes et son frère, évêque de Beauvais.* Lille and Paris: Desclée, de Brouwer & Co., 1897.

Aulard, Alphonse. *Histoire politique de la Révolution française: Origines et développement de la démocratie et de la république, 1789–1804.* Paris: Armand Colin, 1901.

Blanc, Louis. *Histoire de la Révolution française.* 12 vols. 2d ed. Paris: Pagnere/Furne & Co., 1866.

Bourdin, Isabelle. *Les Sociétés populaires à Paris pendant la Révolution française.* Paris: Recueil Sirey, 1937.

Boursier, A. M. "L'émeute parisienne du 10 mars 1793." *Annales Historiques,* 208 (April–June 1972), 204–230.

Braesch, Frédéric. *La Commune du dix août 1792.* Paris: Librairie Hachette, 1911.

Calvet, Henri. "Les Origines du comité de l'évêché." *Annales Historiques,* 7 (1930), 12–23.

————— *Un Instrument de la Terreur à Paris: le Comité de salut public ou de surveillance du département de Paris (8 juin 1793–21 messidor an II).* Paris: Librairie Nizet et Bastard, 1941.

Carlyle, Thomas. *The French Revolution: A History.* New York: Heritage Press, 1956.

Dautry, Jean. "Sebastien Lacroix." *Annales Historiques,* 12 (1933), 49–60, 516–533.

Dommanget, Maurice. *Jacques Roux, le curé rouge, et le manifeste des "Enragés."* Paris: Spartacus, n.d.

Dressler, J. "Un magistrat révolutionnaire: Claude-Emmanuel Dobsen, l'homme de 31 mai." *Annales Historiques,* 145 (1956), 395–399.

Furet, François, and Denis Richet. *La Révolution: Des états généraux au 9–Thermidor.* 2 vols. Collection les grandes heures de l'histoire de France. Paris: Réalités Hachette, 1965.

Gaumont, Jean. *Précurseurs et prémices.* Histoire générale de la coopération en France, vol. 1. Paris: Fédération Nationale des Coopératives de Consommation, 1924.

Gendron, François. *Le Jeunesse dorée épisode de la Révolution française.* Québec: Les Presses de l'Université du Québec, 1979.

Godechot, Jacques. *Les Institutions de la France sous la Révolution et l'Empire.* Paris: Presses Universitaires de France, 1951.

Guérin, Daniel. *La Lutte de classes sous la première république Bourgeois et bras nus.* 2 vols. Paris: Gallimard, 1946.

Hatin, Eugène. *Histoire politique et littéraire de la presse en France.* 8 vols. Geneva: Slatkine Reprints, 1967.

Jacob, Louis. *Hébert Le Père Duchesne: Chef des sans-culottes.* Paris: Gallimard, 1960.

Jaurès, Jean. *Histoire de la Révolution française.* 8 vols. A. Mathiez, ed. Paris: Editions de la Librairie de l'Humanité, 1924. New York: AMS Press, 1973.

Kuscinski, A. *Dictionnaire des conventionnels.* Brueil-en-Vexin, Yvelines: Editions du Vexin Français, 1973.

Lacour, Léopold. *Trois femmes de la Révolution: Olympe de Gouges, Théroigne de Mericourt, Rose Lacombe.* Paris: Librairie Plon, 1900.

Lamartine, Alphonse de. *Histoire des Girondins.* 8 vols. in 4. Brussels: Société Typographique Belge, 1847.

Laurent, Gustave. [Biography of Claude-Emmanuel Dobsen.] Reims: Bibliothèque Municipale de Reims, n.d. (manuscript).

———— "Un magistrat révolutionnaire: Claude-Emmanuel Dobsen, l'homme du 31 mai." *Annales Historiques,* 15 (1938), 2–11.

Lefebvre, Georges. *La Révolution française.* Louis Halphen and Philippe Sagnac, eds. *Peuples et civilisations.* Paris: Presses Universitaires de France, 1951.

Markov, Walter. "Robespierristen und jacqueroutins." In *Maximilien Robespierre 1758–1794, Beitrage zu seinem 200. Geburtstag,* pp. 159–217. Berlin: Rütten & Loening, 1958.

———— "Zu einem Manuskript von Jacques Roux," *Wissenschaftliche Zeitschrift der Karl-Marx-Universität.* Leipzig: der Rektor der Karl-Marx-Universität, 1958–1959.

————*Jacques Roux oder vom Elend der Biographie.* Berlin: Akademie Verlag, 1966.

———— *Die Freiheiten des Priesters Roux.* Berlin: Akademie Verlag, 1967.

———— *Exkurse zu Jacques Roux.* Berlin: Akademie Verlag, 1970.

Mathiez, Albert. *La Vie chère et le mouvement social sous la Terreur.* Paris: Payot, 1927.

———— *Girondins et Montagnards.* Paris: Firmin-Didot & Co., 1930.

————*La Révolution française*. 3 vols. 10th ed. Paris: Armand Colin, 1951.

Michelet, Jules. *Histoire de la Révolution française*. Ed. Gérard Walter. 2 vols. Paris: Gallimard, 1961.

Mignet, Auguste. *Histoire de la Révolution française depuis 1789 jusqu'en 1814*. 2 vols. 16th ed. Paris: Firmin-Didot & Co., 1886.

Mitchell, C. J. "Political Divisions within the Legislative Assembly of 1791." *French Historical Studies*, 13 (Spring 1984), 356–389.

Mortimer-Ternaux, Louis. *Histoire de la Terreur, 1792–1794*. 7 vols. Paris: Michel Lévy Frères, 1868–1881.

Pariset, Georges. *La Révolution, 1792–1799*. Histoire de France contemporaine, vol. 2, ed. Ernest Lavisse. Paris: Hachette, 1920.

Patrick, Alison. *The Men of the First French Republic: Political Alignments in the National Convention of 1792*. Baltimore and London: Johns Hopkins University Press, 1972.

Perroud, Claude M. *La Proscription des Girondins (1793–1795)*. Toulouse and Paris: Edouard Privat and Félix Alcan, 1917.

Quinet, Edgar. *La Révolution*. 2 vols. 6th ed. Paris: Librairie Internationale, 1869.

Reinhard, Marcel. *Nouvelle histoire de Paris: La Révolution, 1789–1799*. Paris: Diffusion Hachette, 1971.

Riffaterre, C. *Le Mouvement antijacobin et antiparisien à Lyon dans le Rhône-et-Loire en 1793 (29 mai–15 août)*. 2 vols. Lyon and Paris; Librairie Picard Fils, 1912.

Rose, R. B. "Les Enragés and the French Revolution, 1789–1794: An Early Attempt at Practical Socialism." Ph.D. dissertation, Victoria University of Manchester, 1952.

Rudé, George. *The Crowd in the French Revolution*. Oxford: Clarendon Press, 1959.

Sainte-Claire Deville, Paul. *La Commune de l'an II: Vie et mort d'une assemblée révolutionnaire*. Paris: Librairie Plon, 1946.

Slavin, Morris. *Left of the Mountain: The Enragés and the French Revolution*. Cleveland: Freiburger Library of Case Western Reserve University, 1961.

———— "Jacques Roux: A Victim of Vilification." *French Historical Studies*, 3 (Fall 1964), 525–537.

———— "Jean Varlet as Defender of Direct Democracy." *Journal of Modern History*, 39 (December 1967), 387–404.

———— "Théophile Leclerc: An Anti-Jacobin Terrorist." *The Historian: A Journal of History*, 33 (May 1971), 398–414.

———— "L'Autre enragé: Jean-François Varlet." In *Eine Jury für Jacques Roux*, pp. 34–67. Berlin: Akademie Verlag, 1981.

————*The French Revolution in Miniature: Section Droits-de-l'Homme, 1789–1795*. Princeton: Princeton University Press, 1984.

Soboul, Albert. *Les Sans-culottes parisiens en l'an II*. Paris: Librairie Clavreuil, 1958.

———— *Girondins et Montagnards*. Paris: Société des Études Robespierristes, 1980.

————*Comprendre la Révolution: Problèmes politiques de la Révolution française*

(1789–1797). Paris: François Maspero, 1981.

Sybel, Heinrich von. *Geschichte der Revolutionszeit von 1789 bis 1795*. 5 vols. Düsseldorf: Verlagshandlung von Julius Buddeus, 1877.

Sydenham, M.J. *The Girondins*. London: University of London, Athlone Press, 1961.

Taine, Hippolyte. *Les Origines de la France contemporaine*. 6 vols. 12th ed. Vol. 2, *La Révolution*. Paris: Hachette & Co., 1879–1894.

Thiers, Louis Adolphe. *Histoire de la Révolution française*. 8 vols. 14th ed. Paris: Furne & Co., 1846–1866.

Tønnesson, Karen D. *La Défaite des sans-culottes*. Oslo and Paris: Presses Universitaires and Clavrreuil, 1959.

Wallon, Henri. *Histoire du tribunal révolutionnaire de Paris*. 6 vols. Paris: Librairie Hachette, 1880–1882.

_____*La Révolution du 31 mai et le fédéralisme en 1793, ou la France vaincue par la commune de Paris*. 2 vols. Paris: Librairie Hachette, 1886.

Journals

Affiches de la commune
L'Ami du peuple (Leclerc)
Journal des débats et des décrets
Journal de Paris
Mercure universel
Réimpression de l'ancien Moniteur
Le Patriote français
Le Père Duchesne (Hébert)
Le Publiciste de la République française (Marat)
Les Révolutions de Paris (Prudhomme)
Journal de la Montagne

Index